BEES
OF THE
WORLD

BEES
OF THE
WORLD

Christopher O'Toole
& Anthony Raw

☑
Facts On File
New York • Oxford

Bees of the World *latest ed 10/01*

Copyright © 1991 Blandford Publishing, an imprint of Cassell plc, London, UK

Text copyright © 1991 Christopher O'Toole and Anthony Raw

Photographs copyright © 1991 Premaphotos Wildlife, except where stated otherwise

Facts on File, Inc.
460 Park Avenue South
New York NY 10016
USA

Library of Congress Cataloging-in-Publication Data

O'Toole, Christopher.
  Bees of the world / Christopher O'Toole and Anthony Raw:
  photographs by Premaphotos Wildlife.
  p.   cm.
  Includes bibliographical references and index.
  ISBN 0–8160–1992–4
  1. Bees.   I. Raw. Anthony.   II. Title.
  QL563.087 1992
  595.79′9—dc20   90–49023
                                                                  CIP

Facts on File are available at special discounts when purchased in bulk
quantities for business, associations, institutions or sales promotions.
Please contact the Special Sales Department of our New York Office at
212/683–2244 (dial 800/322–8755 except in NY, AK or HI).

Typeset by August Filmsetting, Haydock, St Helens, UK
Printed and bound in Yugoslavia by Papirografika

10 9 8 7 6 5 4 3 2 1

Contents

This book is for our parents,
the late Christopher Ernest O'Toole
Margaret O'Toole
and
the late John Frank Raw
Sarah Maud Raw

The chiefest cause, to read good bookes,
That moves each studious minde
Is hope, some pleasure sweet therein,
Or profit good to find.
Now what delight can greater be
Than secrets for to knowe
Of Sacred Bees, the Muses' Birds,
All which this booke doth showe.

Charles Butler, *The Feminine monarchie*

Preface

We are fortunate as adults to be able to indulge our boyhood passions for natural history in general and for bees in particular and to earn our livings from them; we hope that, through this book, our readers will be able to share some of the pleasure we have had in studying bees.

In recent years, high-quality television programmes on natural history have increased public awareness of the diversity of life on this planet. More people than ever before are alive to the complex, life-sustaining interrelationships between animals, plants and their environments. Our book is therefore ecological and evolutionary in outlook.

There has been no popular book on bees which adequately reflects the astonishing diversity of life style in these industrious little animals. Although in the last thirty years there has been a great deal of exciting research on them, most of the results are scattered in scientific journals and are unavailable to the general reader. We hope, therefore, that our book will fill an important gap in the popular literature of natural history.

The association between bees and humans is a long and close one. Bees are important not only as providers of useful substances such as honey and wax, but also as pollinators of crops. And mythology and folk medicine are rich in bee lore.

Evolution through natural selection has shaped the bodies of bees and their behaviour, the kinds of nests they build and the places, some of them bizarre, where they build them. The relationships between bees and flowering plants are highly specialized and some bees collect pollen from only one plant species or a group of closely related ones. The evolutionary history of bees is closely interwoven with that of flowering plants; each has contributed to the making of the other. So let us declare at the outset that, in writing about bees and their ways, we write about the products of natural selection, which has wrought, over millions of years, the many beautiful adaptations we see, not only in the exuberant tropics but also in our own back gardens.

Christopher O'Toole
Oxford

Anthony Raw
Brasilia

7

Acknowledgements

We thank our wives, Linda Losito and Omowume Ogundele-Raw, for their cheerful and patient tolerance of the eternal triangle of O'Toole, Raw and bee. Their support and encouragement were major contributions to this book.

We are grateful to Drs Steve Simpson and George McGavin of Oxford University for their critical reading of several chapters of this book. Dr Donald Baker read much of the text and we have benefited enormously from his unsurpassed knowledge of bees. We are also grateful to Drs Paul Williams and Graham Stone for access to some of their unpublished information on bees. We also thank Professor Dan Gerling of Tel-Aviv University for the opportunity to publish one of his X-ray photographs of the interior of a nest of the carpenter bee, *Xylocopa pubescens*.

In a work of this kind, formal literature citations are out of place. We take this opportunity of acknowledging the published work of researchers too numerous to mention and on whose labours we have drawn, though in some important cases we mention the discoverer of particular information in the appropriate place in the text. Unless otherwise stated, information given for bees from Israel and Britain is the result of fieldwork by Christopher O'Toole, while that for Jamaica and Brazil results from work by Anthony Raw.

Finally, we acknowledge the fine corpus of research on bees by Charles D. Michener, Emeritus Professor of Entomology at the University of Kansas at Lawrence. The tradition of bee research at Lawrence, established by Professor Michener more than forty years ago and maintained by him and many generations of his research students, is an inspiration to all who work with bees.

Stuart Booth, our Blandford editor at Cassell, showed patience and forbearance above and beyond the call of duty and we thank him.

All photographs are by Premaphotos Wildlife except those on pages 31, 38, 62, 94 (© Christopher O'Toole); pages 39, 64, 65, 77 (© Anthony Raw); pages 106, 107 (© Peter O'Toole); page 113 (top) (© Nichola Bradbear); pages 118, 126, 151 (© Oxford Scientific Films). All line drawings are by Rosemary Wise except where otherwise credited.

INDIVIDUAL ACKNOWLEDGEMENTS –
CHRISTOPHER O'TOOLE

I thank Professor David Spencer Smith, Hope Professor of Entomology at Oxford University, for his encouragement and support of my work on bees.

Much of the information in this book which deals with the natural history of bees in Israel could not have been gleaned without the friendship of many Israelis. I thank Dr Amots Dafni of the Institute for Evolution, Haifa University, and his wife, Irit, for endless hospitality and for introducing me to the bee fauna of Israel. Other Israeli friends and colleagues have made it possible for me to travel widely throughout Israel and to study bees in many different habitats. I thank Dr Amnon Freidberg, Ms Fini Kaplan and Professors Dan

Gerling, Abraham Hefetz and Joshua Kugler, of the Department of Zoology, Tel-Aviv University, all of whom have shown me great kindness.

I thank Dr Avi Shmida and Professor Dan Cohen of The Hebrew University, Jerusalem, for having me as their guest and for facilities at the laboratory of the Israeli Plant Information Centre (ROTEM), Har Gilo. I thank Avi Shmida particularly for teaching me much about the flora of Israel.

For many kindnesses and hospitality, I also thank Professor Dini Eisikowitch and Dr Azaria Lupo of the Department of Botany, Tel-Aviv University, together with Ran Gil, Rani Kasher, Hagar Leschner, and Ilan and Minna Yarom.

Finally, I thank Drs Terry Griswold, Phil Torchio and Vince Tepedino of the USDA Bee Biology and Systematics Laboratory, Logan, Utah and their former director, Dr Frank Parker, for hospitality and the opportunity to discuss and observe bees in North America.

INDIVIDUAL ACKNOWLEDGEMENTS – ANTHONY RAW

It is impossible to thank individually all of the people who have helped me with my studies of bees over the past twenty-five years. These range from the relative strangers who kindly provided an apparently eccentric entomologist with lifts to otherwise inaccessible places and whom they never saw again to the following friends whose hospitality enabled me to study bees in a variety of places in Brazil: the McGregor family of Goias Velho, the Walker family in Brasilia, Donald Smith and his family in Salvador and Michael Turner in Rio de Janeiro.

I also thank the following colleagues who have supported and encouraged me over the years: Drs Ivone Rezende Rocha of the University of Brasilia, Donald H. Smith of the Federal University of Bahia, Salvador, north eastern Brazil, Victor O. Becker of the Brazilian Ministry of Agriculture and Ronald J. McGinley of the Smithsonian Institution, Washington, DC.

I am grateful to the following institutions which have supported and/or sponsored my research on bees: The Ford Foundation, University of the West Indies, Jamaican Ministry of Agriculture, Universidade de Brasilia, Brazilian Science Research Council, The Royal Society, the Hope Entomological Collections of the University Museum, Oxford and the Smithsonian Institution, Washington, DC.

NOTE

Measurements are given in metric units. For those over 10 cm, an Imperial units conversion is given.

Chapter 1
What Are Bees?

The murmuring hum of bees on a warm afternoon is surely part of everyone's mental picture of a perfect summer's day. But that relentless hum, soporific, perhaps, to the idling human, is in reality the product of a machine-like urge to work – to work against the clock of the seasons, to gather enough pollen and nectar before the weather breaks, before the blooms fade.

The industry of bees is proverbial. It takes honeybee workers 10 million

A female leaf-cutter bee, *Megachile willughbiella*, forages at a flower of Spear thistle, *Cirsium vulgare*. Soon, she will transfer the pollen grains trapped among her body hairs to the pollen scopa, just visible here, on the underside of her abdomen (Family: Megachilidae).

With her pollen scopae already packed with pollen, this female solitary mining bee, *Agapostemon* sp. forages on a daisy in the Rocky Mountains of Colorado, USA (Family: Halictidae).

Dusted with pollen, a nesting female of a common Eurasian mining bee, *Andrena haemorrhoa*, forages at dandelion, *Taraxacum officinale* (Family: Andrenidae).

The beautiful blue markings on this African female cuckoo bee are typical of the genus *Thyreus*. The markings are made up of very short, dense, flattened hairs. Species of *Thyreus* are cuckoos in the nests of mining bees of the genus *Amegilla* (Family: Anthophoridae).

foraging trips to gather enough nectar to make 0.5 kg (1 lb) of honey. In pre-war Germany, it was estimated that honeybees visited 10 trillion flowers per day. The members of a single hive may make four and a half million visits to flowers in the course of one day's work and more than one thousand workers will die every day in the summer. Cause of death? Sheer exhaustion. Life expectancy? At the height of the nectar-gathering season, a mere six weeks.

11

The honeybee, *Apis mellifera*, is the best known of all bees simply because we have been robbing it of honey and wax for thousands of years. Moreover, it is now, together with the fruit fly and laboratory rat, one of the most intensively studied of animals.

Honeybees, like stingless or meliponine bees of the tropics and bumblebees (*Bombus* spp.), are social insects and live in colonies. Each colony is a family unit, comprising a single, egg-laying female or queen and her many sterile daughters called workers. The workers cooperate in food-gathering, nest-building and rearing the offspring. Males are reared only at the times of year when their presence is required.

The great majority of bee species, however, are non-social or solitary. These bees have no worker caste and the individuals do not cooperate with one another. Instead, each female works alone to construct her own nest. She provisions the cells with pollen and nectar and lays an egg in each one.

Between the two extremes of the solitary and highly social bees, there are intermediate levels of social organization. Some social species never achieved the cohesion and complexity of the honeybee colony; these stragglers along the evolutionary road provide insights into the primitive social states which may have preceded the highly organized, permanent sociality of the honeybee. We emphasize, however, that there are many ways of being a bee and the solitary and semi-social species are not disadvantaged because they do not live in large, highly organized colonies. They employ different strategies to survive and rear their offspring. Indeed, the vast numbers of species and individuals that are solitary demonstrate the success of their life styles.

But before unfolding this evolutionary story, we shall try to answer two questions: what are bees and where did they come from?

Bees range in size from the tiny, 1.5 mm-long workers of some tropical stingless bees, to those giants of the bee world, the carpenter bees, some of which can be 30 or 40 mm long. They range in colour from sober, archdeacon black, through thousands of nondescript 'little grey and brown jobs', to the gaudy exuberance of some of the tropical species, which are bright metallic green, blue or bronze.

Bees are a group of specialized insects that evolved from wasps, but, unlike wasps, they provide pollen as a protein-rich food for their larvae rather than insect prey. In order to do this the adult females possess specially modified structures on their legs and bodies to trap and carry the pollen grains.

All the different kinds of wasps, together with the ants and bees, form the great insect order Hymenoptera, which has more than 100,000 described species. The name Hymenoptera literally means 'membrane wing' (Gk: *hymen* = membrane; *pteron* = wing). They possess two pairs of membranous wings, the forewings being larger than the hind pair. In flight, the wings are linked together by a row of tiny hooklets or hamuli. These lie along the leading edge of the hindwing and engage a fold in the trailing edge of the forewing. At rest, the wasp or bee disengages the two pairs of wings and folds them over the abdomen.

ORIGINS

Bees belong to the suborder of Hymenoptera called the Apocrita, character-ized by the possession of a 'wasp waist', which is a constriction between the first

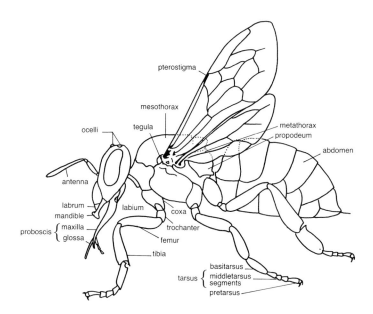

Fig. 1   Side view of a generalized bee's body to show the main structures.

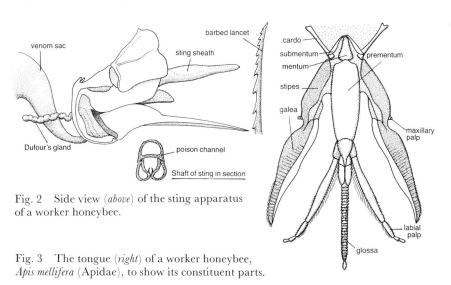

Fig. 2   Side view (*above*) of the sting apparatus of a worker honeybee.

Fig. 3   The tongue (*right*) of a worker honeybee, *Apis mellifera* (Apidae), to show its constituent parts.

and second segments of the adult abdomen (Fig. 1). The first abdominal segment is incorporated into the back of the thorax and is called the propodeum. This means that the apparent first segment of the abdomen is really the second. The 'wasp waist' allows great flexibility of abdominal movement and, without it, the female bee would be unable to bend her abdomen sufficiently to lay an egg at the bottom of a narrow cell.

13

The Aculeata is a subgroup of the Apocrita and includes the ants, bees and hunting wasps. The name 'Aculeata' is derived from the Latin *aculeus*, meaning 'sword' and refers to the sting (Fig. 2), which the bee uses to defend herself and her nest. The sting is a modified egg-laying tube or ovipositor; in aculeates, the ovipositor has lost its egg-laying function and the egg issues directly from the body at the base of the ovipositor.

Hymenoptera also possess both sucking and biting mouthparts. This was a prerequisite for the evolution of 'beeness' because bees suck liquid nectar and use their jaws in nest construction (Fig. 3).

The particular sort of wasps which gave rise to the bees belonged to the family Sphecidae, whose modern members are usually called hunting wasps. The essential differences between sphecid wasps and bees are behavioural. Female sphecids hunt insect prey which they paralyse by injecting venom with their stings, and the larval wasp is therefore a carnivore. Female bees use their stings solely for defence. They collect pollen and nectar and their larvae are vegetarians. Although bees have evolved structural modifications for the gathering of nectar and pollen (see Chapter 11), these do not obscure their sphecid origins. Bees have a number of morphological characters in common with sphecid wasps, the most obvious of which is the structure of the thorax or mid-part of the body. The pronotum extends backwards along the sides of the mesonotum and does not touch the tegula, a small plate which overlies the base of the forewing (Fig. 4). These characters arose only once in the Hyme-

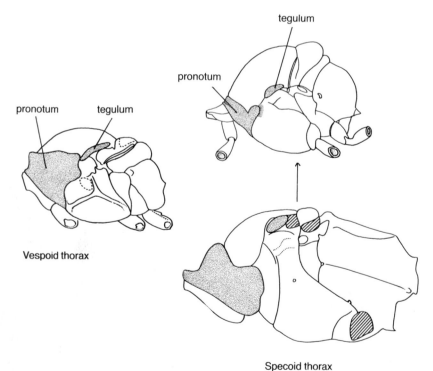

Fig. 4   The thorax in vespoid and sphecoid wasps and bees, showing the uniquely derived features which unite sphecoids and bees.

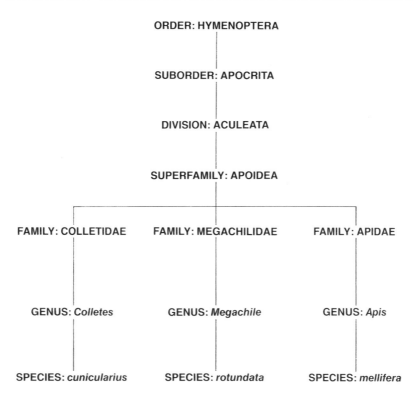

ORDER: HYMENOPTERA

SUBORDER: APOCRITA

DIVISION: ACULEATA

SUPERFAMILY: APOIDEA

FAMILY: COLLETIDAE   FAMILY: MEGACHILIDAE   FAMILY: APIDAE

GENUS: *Colletes*   GENUS: *Megachile*   GENUS: *Apis*

SPECIES: *cunicularius*   SPECIES: *rotundata*   SPECIES: *mellifera*

Fig. 5   The classification of three species of bee.

Many flies are excellent mimics of bees and wasps and temporarily fool even entomologists, as well as the intended dupes: insectivorous lizards and birds. This hoverfly, *Eristalis taeniops*, is a superb mimic of *Apis mellifera syriaca*, the subspecies of honeybee found, with the fly, in the Middle East (Families: Syrphidae and Apidae).

noptera and are good evidence for believing that modern sphecid wasps and modern bees share a common ancestor unique to themselves. Bees can be distinguished from sphecids by their branched body hairs and the expanded basal segment of the hind tarsus.

We can now see where the bees fit into the classification and how they relate to other Hymenoptera. Bees have a wasp waist and therefore qualify for membership of the suborder Apocrita; the ovipositor has lost its egg-laying function and is used as a sting and bees are thus members of the Aculeata. The detailed structure of the thorax of bees allies them very strongly with the sphecoid wasps. Finally, the bees are bees because they feed pollen and nectar to their young rather than insect prey. A full classification of three bee species is given in Figure 5.

THE WASP HERITAGE

Bees inherited two important traits from sphecoid wasps, the nesting habit and their mode of development. There is a wide diversity of nest types found among bees (Chapters 3–8); sphecoid wasps, too, have the same range of nesting habits. These include burrows excavated in the ground or solid wood, the use of existing cavities and the active construction of exposed nests, using collected building materials such as mud or resin. Nest type, therefore, is no help in trying to unravel the evolution of nest-building behaviour in wasps and bees.

However, we can be sure of one thing: in maintaining the nesting habit evolved by their wasp ancestors, bees also inherited the obvious but vital ability to find their way back to the nest after each foraging trip.

ORIENTATION TO THE NEST

Wasps and bees find their way back to their nests with unerring accuracy. They do this in much the same way as we would ourselves: they memorize both near and distant landmarks, building up a mental map of the position of the nest relative to objects and features of the landscape. Nearby landmarks might include stones or grass tussocks close to the nest, while more distant landmarks might be a hillock near the nest site or a tree or building on the horizon. During the course of nest construction, the female makes regular orientation flights. A typical flight takes the form of a looping pattern around the nest entrance, and this increases in range and height, as the female distances herself from the nest. All the time, she memorizes the landmarks she will need to find on her return flights. She will make such orientation flights regularly throughout the foraging period, enabling her to update her mental map. This is essential because small objects around the nest may be displaced by wind or the activities of animals.

Nesting bees and wasps have an additional way of finding their way back to the nest. It is called sun–compass orientation and this is an ability we do not share with them. A female bee memorizes the position of the sun relative to the nest entrance each time she leaves the nest. She has a built-in clock which takes into account the movement of the sun, so she can follow its changing position. Her internal clock is accurate to about four minutes which allows her to detect a change of about 3 degrees in the sun's position.

A female *Halictus rubicundus*, a primitively social species of mining bee, rests at her nest entrance in the Cotswold Hills of England. This species is common throughout Eurasia and North America (Family: Halictidae).

If the sun is obscured by cloud, tall trees or a mountain peak, she has another skill, one which is found only in insects and related arthropods: she can detect the direction of polarized light and use this to find her way home. It works something like this: light rays from the sun travel in straight lines and each ray vibrates in a wave which is roughly at right angles to the direction of travel. Normally, such wave vibrations are in all transverse directions. However, in blue sky, the light is partially polarized. That is, the majority of the wave vibrations are in one plane, at right angles to an imaginary line between the observer and the sun. This pattern of polarization follows the sun across the sky, but is destroyed by the interruption of a thick cloud or a range of hills. So long as there is some blue sky, however, the bee can use the direction of polarization of the light to give her a 'fix' on the position of the sun. Presumably, this is bound up with her time sense of the sun's movement.

Armed with this formidable array of directional skills and a spatial memory, the female bee can locate not only her nest on return journeys, but also the position and site of productive food sources on her outward journeys.

The intricate and elegantly designed experiments which led to our understanding of the bee's homing abilities were largely carried out by the Austrian behaviourist, Karl von Frisch and his associates, using the western honeybee, *Apis mellifera*, as their subject. This work was summarized in 1967 in a classic book, *The Dance Language and Orientation of Bees*. There is no doubt that the solitary bees share the homing skills of the honeybee. As we shall see in Chapter 11, large euglossine and carpenter bees in South America make round trips of 25–40 km when foraging at widely separated flowering forest trees.

DEVELOPMENT OF THE YOUNG

All Hymenoptera have four very distinct stages in their development: egg, larva, pupa and adult. This is called a complete metamorphosis. In most insects with this kind of development the larval diet is different from that of the adult, but bees are an exception to this general rule.

The eggs of bees are pearly white, sausage-shaped and usually slightly curved. In highly social bees, where the queen lays enormous numbers per

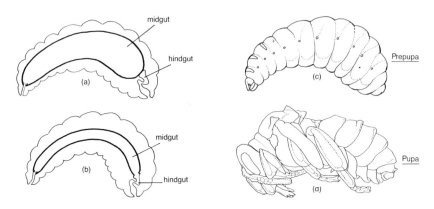

Fig. 6 Sections through the body of a bee larva to show: ((a) the midgut and hindgut unjoined in an early instar; (b) the union of midgut and hindgut in the last instar, when defecation takes place; (c) the post-defecating larva or prepupa; (d) pupa of a solitary bee, *Andrena viburnella* (Andrenidae). ((a) and (b) redrawn after Michener, C.D., 1974 and (c) and (d) redrawn from Stephen, W.P., Bohart, G.E. & Torchio, P.F., 1969.)

day, the eggs are rather small, being no more than 1.5–2.0 mm long. In contrast, the females of solitary bees produce relatively few, large eggs in their lifetime. Females of some carpenter bees, *Xylocopa* spp., lay the largest of insect eggs. A bee with a total body length 30 mm or less lays eggs 15 mm long.

The egg usually hatches a few days after being laid. Its shell is soft and disintegrates on hatching to expose the young larva. The larva is a white, legless grub, with very limited powers of movement. It has thirteen body segments and the sensory organs are much reduced. The antennae, for example, are no more than a pair of small tubercles on the front of the head and there are no eyes. The larval stage is one of active feeding and rapid growth and corresponds to the caterpillar stage of moths and butterflies. Typically, the larva moults its skin four or five times as it increases in size. The stage between each moult is called an instar.

When we consider its life style, living in an enclosed space and surrounded by all the food required for growth, it is easy to see why the larva is so simple in structure. Nevertheless, it is a life style that has its own problems and these larvae are well adapted to it. In most species, the midgut is not connected with the hindgut until the final instar (Fig. 6). The larva postpones defecation until the end of larval life, when it has finished feeding, and thus avoids fouling its food. Bee larvae extrude faeces as dry, elongated pellets. In some genera, defecation is not postponed until the end of larval growth but begins in one of the earlier instars, the faeces being deposited at the opposite end of the cell from the food. The larvae of many species spin a cocoon immediately after defecation, although there is often an overlap between these two activities, so that faecal pellets are incorporated into the structure of the cocoon.

Cocoons are made from silk produced in a gland opening on to the labium just below the mouth. The larva produces silk as glistening, colourless threads, which quickly harden on contact with the air. After a few hours, the silk becomes pink and then dark, reddish-brown. The cocoon usually consists of two layers: an outer one of coarser, darker fibres is built first and then an inner one of fine, pale-coloured fibres forms a lining where the insect lies.

After defecation and cocoon formation, particular changes take place in the larva. The body straightens from the curved shape of the feeding instars and the cuticle becomes more opaque and wrinkled in appearance. This final, non-feeding stage of larval life is often called the *prepupa* (Fig. 6). There is no moult of cuticle to mark the onset of the prepupal stage. The cuticle of the last larval instar persists until the pupa forms.

The prepupa is an inactive stage and those species of bee which do not overwinter as adults do so in this stage. In the tropics, bees often spend the dry season as prepupae. It follows that the prepupal stage is often longer than the larval, pupal and adult stages combined.

Towards the end of the prepupal period, the cuticle of the pupa becomes differentiated from that of the last larval instar and the pupal phase proper begins when the larval cuticle is shed. The wings, legs and antennae of the pupa are attached freely to the surface of the body (Fig. 6d).

The pupa is also a non-feeding stage. It is sometimes referred to as a resting stage, but this is inaccurate. Despite the external appearance of quiescence, drastic changes take place in the body of a pupa. In ways which are still poorly understood, most larval organs and tissues are broken down and reassembled to form adult structures. The pupa then has the basic body shape of the adult, and the adult cuticle forms and hardens; the eyes darken and eventually become black. The rest of the body changes from the waxy white of larval and early pupal life to the darker colours of the adult.

The colourless pupal skin, which looks like a mummified version of the adult, is shed when the adult cuticle has hardened. The wings are then expanded by the pumping of blood into their veins before they also harden. The bee is now ready for adult life.

Most of the organs of the adult insect cannot grow because the body is enclosed in an outer skeleton or exoskeleton of chitin and sclerotin – horny substances which combine lightness with great strength.

The adult stage in all insects is adapted for two vital functions: dispersal and reproduction. All adult behaviour is geared to achieving these ends and in bees it has become an elaborate and complex process.

THE ROAD TO BEEHOOD

There is strong circumstantial evidence that the first bees appeared during the 70 million years which were the Cretaceous period (146 million to 76 million years ago). At that time the continents had barely started to separate, but two evolutionary adventures of great significance to humankind had their origins in this period. The first true mammals appeared and would go on to replace the reptiles, especially the dinosaurs, which had ruled the Cretaceous land, sea and sky; and the first true flowering plants appeared, pre-requisites for the evolution of 'beeness'. The fossil record for bees is disappointing but there are Cretaceous fossils of sphecid wasps which are generalized enough to be ancestral to the bees.

We will never know precisely when it was that some of the sphecid wasps first began to abandon their predatory way of life in favour of gathering pollen and nectar. Nevertheless, it is tempting to speculate on the evolutionary events which took place in the un-observable past, and some realistic assumptions can be made about the origins of bees.

The late Russian entomologist, Professor S.I. Malyshev, suggested that bees evolved from wasps related to the modern sphecid genus *Psenulus*, whose species, like many wasps and bees, feed on honeydew, a sugary exudation excreted by sap-sucking aphids and plant lice. *Psenulus* females also prey on aphids, killing them with their jaws rather than using their stings. It is inevitable that the wasps would taste and eat the sweet body fluids of the aphids. Thus, the adult wasps would have eaten some of the animal food destined for their larvae, which would have tasted the same as honeydew, which was part of the normal adult diet. Here, we have a situation which is identical to that of the bees, but unlike that of all other sphecids, in that the food of the adult is similar in kind to that provided for the larvae.

Malyshev argued that it was a small step from collecting sweet-tasting aphids to collecting a sweet mixture of nectar and pollen and that wasps ancestral to modern *Psenulus* may well have given rise to the bees. *Psenulus* wasps also anticipate some of the bees in that females line their nest cells with a transparent membrane secreted by special glands. The adults of modern sphecid wasps feed on fluids exuding from the bodies of their stung and paralysed prey and also on the energy-rich nectar of flowers.

Whether or not Malyshev was right, we can be sure that, with the diversification of flowering plants, an ever-increasing new food source was available for adult sphecid wasps. As nectar and pollen became more important in the diets of adult wasps, it is possible that the females used these new foods to augment the larval diet of insect prey. Some species of wasps will have been more adept than others at gathering nectar and pollen and would therefore find these activities less costly in time and energy than searching for elusive prey.

Evolution is an opportunistic process and natural selection, acting over long periods, led to the development of modified tongues and pollen-collecting and transporting structures. This enabled the wasps to exploit the new food resources more efficiently. Full 'beehood' was achieved when the sphecid wasps became totally committed to pollen and nectar as food for themselves and their larvae.

Although this book is about those bees which have descended from sphecid wasps, 'beeness' has evolved independently in another family of wasps, the Masaridae. This is a small family of little-known, solitary vespoid wasps, related to the yellow-jackets; they have developed the bee-like habit of collecting pollen and nectar rather than insect prey and parallel some of the structural adaptations for this way of life.

Thus, we have the confusing situation in which some vespoid wasps became bees in the same behavioural sense that some sphecid wasps became bees. Malyshev took note of the behavioural definition of beeness when he coined the term 'vespoid bees' for the Masaridae and 'sphecoid bees' for what most of us would call 'true bees'.

The vespoid bees need not concern us further. They never developed the complexities of social behaviour which make the more advanced true bees such a source of wonder, nor have they any place in the evolutionary history of the sphecoid bees. From here onwards, we use the word 'bee' to refer to sphecoid bees.

At the same time that some sphecid wasps were becoming bees by virtue of their growing dependence on flowering plants, the plants themselves became increasingly dependent on bees. Some plants had flowers which were slightly more attractive to bees than others and therefore stood a better chance of reproduction through cross-pollination. The stage was thus set for the evolution of closer adaptations between bees and flowering plants. We discuss this in greater detail in Chapter 11.

The oldest known fossil bee was described as recently as 1988. It is a stingless bee, given the name *Trigona prisca* by the American entomologists, Charles Michener and David Grimaldi. The fossil is well preserved in amber from the Upper Cretaceous of New Jersey, from 96–74 million years ago. Fifty million years separate the beginning of the Cretaceous, when flowering plants appeared, and the time that individual of *T. prisca* was trapped in the resin oozing from a tree. The specimen is indistinguishable from modern *Trigona* and, what is more, is clearly a worker.

Thus, bees, even highly social forms, of modern appearance, appeared quite early. This leads one to suppose that either the evolution of bees was extremely rapid or flowering plants evolved earlier than is commonly thought and were present in the upper Jurassic.

Fifty million years is not such a long time for the evolution of bees. After all, *Trigona* is near the top of the evolutionary tree although the genus was present at least seventy million years ago. Of one thing, though, we can be sure: the increasing diversification of flowering plants in the Cretaceous is our best evidence that the bees originated during that period, for it is clear from the present-day mutual dependence of bees and flowering plants that their evolutionary histories are closely intertwined; each contributed to the making of the other.

Chapter 2

The Families of Bees and Where They Live

This chapter is an outline of the eleven families of bees. It is intended as a point of reference to enable the reader to gain his or her bearings among the many different bees mentioned in this book. All the genera of bees discussed in later chapters are listed here in their families, under 'included genera'. The supposed evolutionary relationships between the families and subfamilies of bees

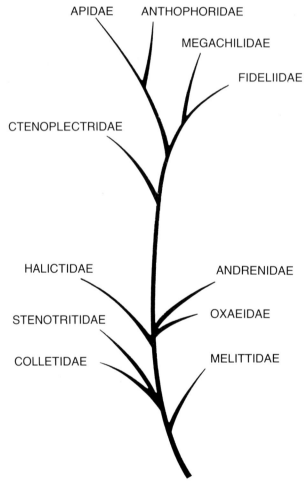

APIDAE   ANTHOPHORIDAE

MEGACHILIDAE

FIDELIIDAE

CTENOPLECTRIDAE

HALICTIDAE   ANDRENIDAE

STENOTRITIDAE   OXAEIDAE

COLLETIDAE   MELITTIDAE

Fig. 7   A family tree of the bees, showing the presumed relationships between the families.

are shown in Figure 7. The grades of sociality mentioned in this chapter are explained in Chapters 9 and 10 and are cited in the glossary.

Recently, some bee specialists have suggested that all the bees be lumped into one family, the Apidae, reducing all the other families to subfamily status. This approach may ultimately prove to be correct, but until a detailed modern study of the higher classification has been completed, we feel this action is premature.

All family names end in '–idae'. The names form the root of adjectives used in the text, for example, andrenid and megachilid, for Andrenidae and Megachilidae. Subfamily names end in '–inae' and these, too, form the root of adjectives, e.g. andrenine and megachiline.

Five families (Stenotritidae, Oxaeidae, Melittidae, Ctenoplectridae and Fideliidae) contain only species with solitary life styles. The majority of species in the following five (Colletidae, Andrenidae, Halictidae, Anthophoridae and Megachilidae) are also solitary, but all have some species which are, in the broadest sense, social. The last family, the Apidae, consists primarily of social species and embraces those with the most highly developed social behaviour.

The first seven families in the outline that follows are the so-called short-tongued bees and, with a few exceptions, they do have short tongues. They are regarded as more primitive than the remaining four families, which constitute the long-tongued bees.

The females of nesting species employ four methods of transporting pollen to their nests. Members of the Subfamily Hylaeinae of the Colletidae have no external structure to transport pollen so they swallow it and carry it in their crops. The females of nesting species of Megachilidae and Fideliidae lodge the pollen among the hairs of the brush-like scopa on the underside of the abdomen. The non-parasitic members of the Apidae differ from all other bees in the way that they transport pollen. These bees have a pollen basket or corbiculum on the tibia of each hind leg. The pollen basket comprises the flattened or concave outer face of the tibia, the margins of which are fringed with stiff, erect bristles. In all the other nesting bees the female bears a scopa of hairs on each hind leg. In some groups the scopae are more developed on the hind tibiae, while in others the hairs are stronger on the hind femora. Sometimes the scopal hairs extend to the sides of the propodeum and the underside of the abdomen.

STENOTRITIDAE

Robust, fast-flying, solitary bees, 14–20 mm long, restricted entirely to Australia. Abdomen with conspicuous hair bands. Until recently, these bees were regarded as a subfamily of the Colletidae, but the blunt rather than bilobed glossa of the tongue distinguishes them from other groups. There are two genera. All known species nest in the ground, sometimes in aggregations; brood cells are lined with a varnish-like secretion. *Stenotritus* has many species, some of which excavate nests up to 33 cm (13 ins) deep. There are nine species of *Ctenocolletes*. *Ct. albomarginatus* and *Ct. nicholsoni* dig nests as deep as 3 metres.

COLLETIDAE

All members of this family have a short, bilobed tongue and members of the subfamily Hylaeinae lack any pollen-carrying structure. In particular, hylaeines strongly resemble sphecid wasps and the Colletidae has long been regarded as the most primitive family of bees. This view has recently been challenged because the bilobed tongue of colletids may be a derived (=advanced) feature; the females use it as a kind of paint brush to apply a glandular secretion to the walls of the brood cells.

Female colletids line their brood cells with a liquid mixture of chemicals called macrocyclic lactones. These dry to form a clear, transparent, cellophane-like membrane which is waterproof and resistant to fungal attack. The lactone mixture is secreted by a large gland in the abdomen called the Dufour's gland.

The family occurs worldwide, with two cosmopolitan genera, *Hylaeus* and *Colletes*, but the greatest diversification of genera has taken place in Australia. There are two subfamilies:

HYLAEINAE

Relatively hairless bees, lacking a pollen scopa; females swallow pollen and transport it in their crops. Most species are black, with conspicuous yellow or white markings, especially on the face; a few are red- or orange-marked. Some species of this group were originally described as sphecid wasps. The subfamily is greatly diversified in Australia, where more genera occur than anywhere else in the world. Almost all species are totally solitary. Many species nest in plant stems, some nest in plant galls, in old beetle borings and disused cells of other bees and wasps, while some nest in the ground. Genera include *Hylaeus*, *Euryglossa*, *Xanthesma*.

COLLETINAE

More or less robust, hairy bees, often with conspicuous bands of appressed hairs fringing the abdomen. *Colletes* is found in all parts of the world except Australia. Many species of this genus are oligolectic, specializing in collecting pollen from one or a few closely related species of plants. All species are solitary and most nest in soil. *Caupolicana* and the nocturnal *Ptiloglossa* are South American.

HALICTIDAE

This enormous family of small to middle-sized bees is found in all parts of the world. Many species are metallic in coloration and, apart from the honeybee, they are among the most common bees at flowers. This one family includes virtually the whole range of social behaviour to be found in bees. Within one genus, *Lasioglossum*, there are strictly solitary, communal, semisocial and primitively eusocial species. Most species excavate nests in the soil, but a few do so in rotten wood. The nests of some species are very complex structures (Chapter 9). The females of Nomiinae and Halictinae line their brood cells with a mixture of lactones. Unlike that of the colletids, the cell lining is not in the form of a transparent membrane easily detachable from the soil. Instead, it has a shiny, varnish-like finish, which impregnates the soil.

The Halictidae comprises three subfamilies:

DUFOUREINAE

Species of this subfamily live in Eurasia, Africa and North America with one known South American species. Some included genera are *Dufourea* and *Systropha*. Females line their brood cells with mainly aliphatic esters, which sets this subfamily apart from the rest of the Halictidae, and there are growing doubts as to whether dufoureines are correctly placed in the Halictidae.

NOMIINAE

A large group found in the Old World tropics and the Mediterranean region, with a few species in North America. The males are noted for the greatly modified hind legs, the femora and, occasionally, the tibiae being massively swollen and usually armed with stout spines. Most species are solitary, some are communal, and others are quasisocial or semisocial. Some included genera are *Nomia* and *Pseudapis*.

HALICTINAE

Members of this world-wide group are often called sweat bees because in hot weather they are attracted to human perspiration, which they lap up, probably for the salts it contains. The small, bright green bees of South and Central America that insistently come to sweat belong to this subfamily. Social behaviour has arisen independently several times in this subfamily.

The many genera include *Agapostemon*, *Augochlorella*, *Augochloropsis*, *Pseudaugochloropsis*, *Augochlora*, *Halictus*, *Lasioglossum*, *Nomioides*, *Sphecodes* and *Paralictus*. The first five genera are restricted to the New World, *Halictus* and *Lasioglossum* are common to the Old and New Worlds. *Sphecodes* and *Paralictus* are cuckoos in the nests of other halictids.

OXAEIDAE

The two genera of this family, *Oxaea* and *Protoxaea*, are large, fast-flying bees, often with metallic marking on the abdomen. They are restricted to drier parts of the tropics and subtropics of the Americas. The females excavate deep burrows in the soil and males are often aggressively territorial. None of the Oxaeidae is social, but more than one female of *O. flavescens* may share parts of a nest. Until recently, the family was regarded as a subfamily of the Andrenidae, but studies on larval and pupal structure suggest they have no close relatives among modern bees and so they are now placed in a family of their own.

As in the Colletidae, the females line their brood cells with a mixture of macrocyclic lactones, secreted by the Dufour's gland.

ANDRENIDAE

Members of this family live in all continents except Australia. All species nest in the soil and the great majority are strictly solitary, although the females of many species nest in dense aggregations. A few species are communal, with two or more females using parts of a nest. There are two subfamilies:

ANDRENINAE

The majority of species belong to the genus *Andrena*, of which there are several hundred in both Eurasia and North America and where they are often among the commonest bees in spring. Many species are oligolectic. Females line their brood cells with two classes of chemicals, terpenes and farnesyl esters, secreted by the Dufour's gland and which impregnate the cell walls with a waxy finish.

The genera include: *Andrena* and *Melittoides*, the latter restricted to Turkey and the Levant.

PANURGINAE

Many species in this group are relatively hairless and have conspicuous yellow or cream markings. Nests are often in pure sand and there may be more than one entrance per nest. Brood cells are often unlined.

Some included genera in Eurasia are: *Camptopoeum*, *Melitturga*, *Panurgus* and *Panurginus*. *Panurginus* is also found in North America, where panurgines are well-represented by genera such as *Calliopsis*, *Nomadopsis* and *Perdita*. The last genus is restricted to the New World where there are very many species.

MELITTIDAE

This small family is represented in Eurasia, Africa and North America. There is one Australian species and none in South America. A few species nest in wood, but most excavate nests in the ground. Where brood cells are lined with a Dufour's gland secretion, the lining is composed of a class of chemicals called alkyl butanoates. The scopae on the hind legs are massively developed in species of the Old World genus *Dasypoda*. All known species are solitary, except for one *Dasypoda*, in which two or more females may share a nest. Some other included genera are *Melitta* and *Macropis*, found in both Eurasia and North America, and *Hesperapis* found in North America and South Africa. *Rediviva* is found in Zaire and South Africa, where it has an unusual relationship with flowers of *Diascia* species, members of the figwort family, Scrophulariaceae (Chapter 11).

CTENOPLECTRIDAE

This small family comprises two genera, the mainly tropical *Ctenoplectra*, which ranges from Africa to China and Australia and the oriental *Ctenoplectrina*, which is thought to be a cuckoo in the nests of *Ctenoplectra*. All known species of *Ctenoplectra* are solitary ground-nesters and some, at least, are specialized for collecting plant oils. The bees are small to medium-sized, relatively hairless except for the well-developed scopa of the female. Some species are metallic dark blue.

Formerly included in the Melittidae, the family has more affinities with the long-tongued bees than with short-tongued families.

FIDELIIDAE

This small family comprises three genera of fast-flying, densely hairy bees. The family has a curious distribution. *Neofidelia* occurs in Chile and *Fidelia* and

Parafidelia are from arid regions of Namibia and North Africa. The bees secrete no linings to their cells.

This is an intriguing group of bees. Both sexes share some primitive features with Colletidae and Andrenidae. However, they resemble the Megachilidae in possessing a pollen scopa on the underside of the abdomen rather than on the hind legs. Their larvae are also undistinguishable from those of the Megachilidae. Because these bees have restricted distributions, the group must have evolved before Africa and South America began to separate in the Cretaceous, some 136 million years ago. They must, therefore, be one of the oldest groups of bees.

The evidence suggests that the Fideliidae gave rise to the Megachilidae and probably never had any direct evolutionary connection with the other primitive bee families, the Colletidae, Andrenidae and Melittidae.

MEGACHILIDAE

This very large family is found on all continents. Many species are important pollinators of crop plants. There are two subfamilies:

LITHURGINAE

There are two included genera, *Lithurgus*, which is known from North America, Eurasia and Australia and *Trichothurgus*, which is restricted to South America. All species of *Lithurgus* are solitary and they excavate nests in both sound and rotten timber. The cells are unlined. Nothing is known about the biology of *Trichothurgus*.

MEGACHILINAE

This is an enormous subfamily with thousands of species commonly called leaf-cutter and mason bees. Many species have conspicuous abdominal bands or tufts of dense, pale hairs. Species of *Anthidium* and related genera have bright yellow markings. The majority of species make nests in existing cavities such as beetle tunnels in dead wood; others build exposed nests on the surfaces of rocks or buildings and some nest in snail shells or in the ground. None secrete linings for their brood cells. Instead, females collect materials for cell walls, or at least cell partitions, from outside the nest. Nest materials vary according to the species and include leaves, petals, a mastic of chewed leaves or petals, plant or animal hairs, plant resin, mud and small pebbles. Species of mud-building *Chalicodoma* mix Dufour's gland secretion with the mud to make it water-resistant. A few species are communal, most are strictly solitary.

Some included genera are *Trachusa*, *Anthidium*, *Rhodanthidium*, *Dianthidium*, *Micranthidium*, *Serapista*, *Prochelostoma*, *Chelostoma*, *Heriades*, *Osmia*, *Hoplitis*, *Anthocopa*, *Ashmeadiella*, *Chalicodoma*, *Megachile* and *Creightonella*. Cuckoo genera include *Stelis*, *Dioxys*, *Ensliniana*, *Coelioxys*, *Torridapis* and *Liothyrapis*.

ANTHOPHORIDAE

This very large family is found in all parts of the world. Many are robust and resemble bumblebees.

27

Their nests are diverse in structure. Species nest in the ground, in plant stems or solid wood. Most pollen-collecting species have a rapid, darting flight and a very long tongue, sometimes as long as or longer than the body. Ground-nesting species line their brood cells with a secretion of the Dufour's gland which comprises a mixture of fatty compounds called triglycerides. In *Anthophora* and perhaps other genera, the triglycerides are also mixed in with the larval food store. The family is notable for the large numbers of species which have adopted the life style of cuckoo or social parasite, losing their pollen scopae in the process; one subfamily consists entirely of cuckoo bees. Many are often brightly coloured with wasp-like liveries of yellow and black. Some are red, others have conspicuous tufts of brilliant white hairs on legs and body contrasting sharply with dense, blue-black hairs. There are three subfamilies and it is convenient to divide these into tribes:

ANTHOPHORINAE

Most species nest in the ground, while a few excavate in dead wood. The many genera are grouped into nine tribes, many of which are restricted to the Americas or have the greatest numbers of species there. All members of the first six tribes construct their own nests, while all species of the last three are cuckoo bees.

Tribe Exomalopsini   These are small bees found mainly in the New World and in warm temperate and tropical climates. The pollen scopae are usually thick, with dense, feathery hairs. All known species of the New World genus, *Exomalopsis* are at least communal and possibly semisocial. The Neotropical genera *Paratetrapedia* and *Monoeca* collect oils of Malphigiaceae flowers and *Ancyloscelis* specialize in pollen of the Malvaceae. Old World genera include *Tarsalia* and *Ancyla*.

Tribe Emphorini   These are robust bees restricted to the Americas. Their abdominal segments are densely covered with short, appressed hairs. Members of *Melitoma* are largely restricted to flowers of Malvaceae. Other genera are *Diadasia* and *Ptilothrix*.

Tribe Tetrapediini   A single genus, *Tetrapedia*, is restricted to the Neotropics; the females collect floral oils from flowers of Malphigiaceae.

Tribe Eucerini   This is a large group of robust, often fast-flying, ground-nesting bees, found in all continents except Australia. The males of nearly all species have very long antennae and are colloquially known as 'longhorn bees'. The tribe is most diverse in the Americas, with many genera. *Synhalonia* and *Tetralonia* are common to North America and Eurasia, the latter extending also to much of Africa. Some included New World genera are *Peponapis*, *Melissoptila*, *Melissodes* and *Svastra*, the last two genera containing species which live in communal nests. *Eucera* is a large genus, widespread in Eurasia, and often occurring in very large numbers. A few species are communal.

Tribe Anthophorini   World-wide in distribution, this group contains many species in relatively few genera. Anthophorini comprises medium-sized, to large, fast-flying, hairy bees, some of which resemble bumblebees. Many species have extremely long tongues. No species are known to be social. Included genera are *Anthophora*, found in North America and Eurasia and the entirely Old World *Habropoda*.

A related genus, *Amegilla*, has many species in southern Europe, Africa, Asia and Australia, while *Paramegilla* is restricted to south-west and central Eurasia.

Tribe Centridini   Fast-flying, medium-sized to very large bees. The two genera, *Centris* and *Epicharis*, are entirely restricted to the tropical and warm temperate parts of the Americas. All known species are solitary. *Epicharis* nests in the ground, several in dense aggregations. Most *Centris* species nest in the ground, but some use beetle tunnels in wood and others nest in the sides of termite mounds.

Tribe Melectini   All species of Melectini are cuckoos in the nests of other anthophorine bees. Many species are strikingly patterned with distinct patches of dense, silvery, metallic blue-green or white hairs, against a blue-black background. *Melecta* occurs in North America and Eurasia and North Africa, while *Eupavlovskia* and *Thyreus* are restricted to the Old World. North American genera include *Zacosmia*, *Xeromelecta* and *Brachymelecta*.

Tribe Rhathymini   The single genus, *Rathymus*, comprises long, slender, red, or red and black bees, found only in South America, where they are cuckoos in the nests of species of *Epicharis*.

Tribe Ericrocini   Restricted to South America, all are cuckoos in the nests of other anthophorids, especially *Centris*. Genera include *Acanthopus*, *Mesonychium*, *Mesocheira* and *Mesoplia*, all of which are dark metallic blue and green.

NOMADINAE

All species of this subfamily are cuckoos in the nests of other bees. Many are strikingly wasp-like in appearance. Species of *Nomada* occur world-wide, *Epeolus* is common to Eurasia and North America, while *Triepeolus* and *Odyneropsis* are restricted to the New World. *Oreopasites* is North American and *Ammobates* and *Pasites* are from the Old World.

XYLOCOPINAE

These are the carpenter bees, so-called because of their habit of excavating nests in solid wood or the pith of plant stems. There are three tribes:

Tribe Ceratinini   This and the following tribe together form the so-called 'dwarf carpenter bees'. The Ceratinini are a world-wide group of small, relatively hairless bees. Many species are black, with patterns of yellow or cream markings, especially on the face. Some are brilliant metallic green or blue. They usually nest in pithy stems or the rotten centres of vines. *Ceratina* is common in the Old and New World and contains both solitary and primitively social species. *Pithitis* is restricted to the Old World tropics and, so far as is known, all the species are solitary.

Tribe Allodapini   *Allodape* and its relatives form a group in the tropics and subtropics of the Old World called the 'allodapine' bees. Many of the species are subsocial or primitively eusocial. Other Old World genera are *Allodapula*, *Braunsapis*, *Exoneurella* and *Halterapis*. Species of *Eucondylops*, *Inquilina* and *Nasutapis* are cuckoos in the nests of other allodapine bees.

Tribe Xylocopini   There are three included genera, the Eurasian *Proxylocopa*, which nests in the ground, *Lestis*, restricted to Australia and which nests in the leaf stems of cycads, and *Xylocopa*, which is found in warm temperate and tropical areas in both Old and New Worlds. The last genus includes some of the largest of all bees, the so-called 'giant carpenter bees', which excavate their nests in solid wood. Some species are temporarily social.

APIDAE

This group, comprising three subfamilies, includes all the highly social (eusocial) bees. Sociality is thought to have arisen independently in two of the subfamilies, Meliponinae and Apinae.

BOMBINAE

Members of this subfamily are robust-bodied bees found in Eurasia and North and South America. There are two tribes:

Tribe Euglossini   Restricted to the American tropics, this group contains some of the most colourful and gaudy bees, many of which are metallic green, blue, bronze or purple. Some species are hairy and resemble the bumblebees in colour pattern. Almost all have very long tongues, hence the tribal name. All are extremely fast flyers. The males are associated with orchid flowers, for which they are often the sole pollinators (Chapter 12). The bees nest in a variety of places, either underground or on exposed surfaces. The nests are made of mud, resin, or, occasionally, mixtures of these substances with dung and bark chippings. Some species are solitary, others are communal and some may be quasisocial. The genera are *Euglossa*, *Eulaema* and *Eufriesea* and two cuckoo genera, *Exaerete* (in nests of *Eulaema* and *Eufriesea*) and *Aglae* (in nests of *Eulaema*). Euglossines probably share a common ancestry with the bumblebees.

Tribe Bombini   These are the true bumblebees, which live in temporarily eusocial colonies. They occur in most parts of the world, but are absent from Africa south of the Sahara and Australia. Species are most numerous in temperate regions and are found throughout Eurasia and North and South America. Nest cells are made of wax secreted initially by the colony-founding queen and later by the workers. The bees often mix pollen with the wax. The two genera are *Bombus* and *Psithyrus*, the latter being cuckoos in nests of the former.

MELIPONINAE

This subfamily comprises the stingless bees which are cosmopolitan in the

Bees are particularly diverse in warm, dry areas, such as this typical
Mediterranean scrub, Mount Carmel, Israel.

Wadi Lotz in the highlands of the Negev Desert, Israel: even deserts have rich and
specialized bee faunas. Dried water courses or *wadis* provide forage and also nest
sites in the cliff faces.

tropics, being especially diverse in South America. The bees nest underground, in hollow logs and tree trunks and in termite nests. They make cells of wax or a mixture of wax with resin and pollen. Meliponines are highly social and live in perennial colonies. Some included genera are the pantropical *Trigona*, the South American *Melipona* and the African *Dactylurina* and *Meliponula*. There are two genera of robber bees, *Lestrimelitta* in the American tropics and *Cleptotrigona* in Africa, which steal stored food and wax from the nests of other stingless bees.

APINAE

These are the true honeybees and, like the stingless bees, they live in highly social, perennial colonies. Nests are in the form of double-sided, vertical wax combs of hexagonal cells, which, according to species, are built in hollow trees, rock clefts, or exposed, suspended from tree limbs. There are seven species in a single genus, *Apis*. These are: *A. mellifera*, the western honeybee and the largely oriental *A. cerana*, *A. dorsata*, *A. laboriosa*, *A. florea*, *A. andreniformis* and *A. koschevnikovi*.

BIOGEOGRAPHY OF BEES

With a world fauna of at least 25,000 described species, bees easily outstrip amphibians and reptiles (5,500 species), birds (8,600 species) and mammals (3,500 species). There are about 4000 species of bees in North America and a similar number in Eurasia. There are more than 7,000 species in South America, about 4,000 in Africa and an estimated 3,000 in Australia. To add to this, many new species are found every year in Central and South America, Africa, Southeast Asia and Australia.

Bees have invaded almost all parts of the world where there is vegetation on the ground. Some species brave the rigours of life in the arctic tundra and make the best of the few, long days during the very short summers. Others cope with similarly demanding climates in the high Andes and Himalayas, where bees have been found at altitudes over 4,500 m (more than 14,500 ft). Most bees, however, are warmth-loving creatures and the greatest diversity of species is to be found in warm, temperate areas: the semi-deserts and scrublands of the south western United States, northern Argentina, southern Africa, parts of Australia, the Mediterranean, Middle East and the dry steppes of southern Central Asia.

As one might imagine, social species with permanent colonies are more common in the humid tropics where the climate is warm and flowers are available throughout the year. Almost all the members of the family Apidae are tropical in origin. Solitary species are particularly common in seasonal climates where flowers are abundant only at some times of the year.

Like other groups of animals, the Australian bee fauna includes many primitive forms. More than 40 per cent of its bee species belong to the family Colletidae. Less than 5 per cent of the North American bee fauna are of this family.

The geographical areas which species inhabit vary enormously in size. Several species are found throughout the Holarctic (the region of Eurasia and North America). These include *Megachile centuncularis*, *Andrena clarkella* and *A.*

wilkella, Halictus rubicundus, Bombus pratorum and *Anthophora furcata*. The last mentioned species is represented by several subspecies in North America where some populations have distinctive colours. Some species are also widespread in the Palaeotropics (occurring in the tropical parts of Africa and Asia). In contrast, some species have very limited distributions. One such is a carpenter bee *Xylocopa grossa* which is confined to an area of about 80–100 sq km (30–39 sq miles) in south-eastern Jamaica.

As a general rule, diversity is lower on islands. France has more than 800 species, while Britain has 260 and Ireland has only 85. Likewise there are 3,000 species in Australia and only 23 in New Zealand.

Parts of the Neotropics (South and Central America) have high bee diversities: Brazil has more than 4,000 species; Panama has 352; while Trinidad, with an area of 4,821 sq km (1,864 sq miles) is smaller than the English county of Norfolk, but nevertheless has more than 200 species. Israel, a small country about the size of Wales, with an area of 20,770 sq km (8,020 sq miles), has a bee fauna estimated at 1500–2000 species. This is remarkable when one remembers that 70 per cent of the country is desert.

Oceanic islands have a special type of bee fauna. Some groups are adept at being transported for long distances over water. Species which nest in tunnels in wood are especially common on islands. Presumably logs containing their nests were washed up on islands and the bees emerged to colonize a new place. Carpenter bees, leaf-cutter bees and some mason bees are typical denizens of oceanic islands. An extreme example is the Galapagos Islands. The carpenter bee, *Xylocopa darwini*, is the only species of bee found there. Another carpenter bee, *X. sonorina*, is the only large bee species in the Hawaiian archipelago. The closest relatives of both species are found only in the Americas.

Several species have been accidentally transported over long distances within historical times, presumably in cargoes and the timbers of ships. *Megachile gentilis*, a species of the western United States, arrived in Hawaii this century. Several European species have been taken to North America. These include *Hoplitis anthocopoides, Chelostoma campanulorum, Ch. fuliginosum* and *Anthidium manicatum*. The latter species is also well established in southern Brazil. However, the best known accidental introduction is an east European leaf-cutter bee, *Megachile rotundata*, which is now a major pollinator of alfalfa in North America.

Some of the more notable introductions are of Old World bees which were carried to the Caribbean, probably via the slave trade. These species are now established on many West Indian islands. Of the African leaf-cutter bees, *M. concinna* is common in Jamaica and Hispaniola and *Chalicodoma disjunctum* is found on Barbados. Two mason bees also occur there. The Indian species, *Ch. lanata*, is commonly encountered on many of the islands and the widespread African species, *Ch. rufipennis*, is locally common in Jamaica.

Chapter 3

Background to the Solitary Life

There are at least 20,000 described species of bee and the vast majority of these are solitary. That is, each nest is the work of a single female working alone. There is no caste of cooperating workers and each female constructs her nest and provisions it with pollen and honey without the help of others.

Solitary bees can be divided into two groups on the basis of their nesting habits: one in which females line their nest cells with their own glandular secretions and one in which females line their nests with other materials, for example, mud, leaves or resin, which they collect outside the nest. As a general rule, the first group nest in the ground and are called burrowing or mining bees. They are the subject of Chapter 4. The females of the second group nest in existing cavities such as old beetle borings in dead wood, in the hollow stems of plants, or even exposed on the surface of rocks and buildings. They are the mason, leaf-cutter and carder bees and we deal with them in Chapters 5, 6 and 8. However, despite their very different nesting habits, the two groups of solitary bees have several important features in common. For example, all solitary bees have a very similar cycle of nesting behaviour, going through the same sequence of activities. We can summarize it thus:

Emergence→mating→search for nest-site→construction/preparation of nest tunnel→construction/preparation of first brood cell→provisioning of cell→egg-laying→closure of cell→construction of second brood cell, and so on.

After completion of the first cell, the female goes on to excavate (or construct) and provision further cells, laying a single egg in each one. The number of cells per nest depends on the species involved; the females of some species make one-celled nests. After completion of the nest, the female usually makes one or two more nests, but never lives long enough to see her offspring.

The female provisions each cell with all the pollen and nectar necessary for growth and development of her larvae. This is called 'mass provisioning'. By contrast, the highly social bees, such as the honeybees and some bumblebees, practise 'progressive feeding': the larva lives in an open cell and worker bees feed it throughout its development.

EGG PRODUCTION

A typical female bee, such as a species of *Andrena* or *Osmia*, starts life with a complement of about thirty eggs. If she makes only six to twelve cells, then rather more than one half to two-thirds of her eggs are never laid.

Some of this apparent wastage comes about because under some circumstances a female bee will resorb some of her eggs. During the nesting period, it is quite usual for there to be periods of up to five or six consecutive days when bad weather prevents foraging and feeding. During these periods, the bee resorbs one or more mature eggs, using them as a standby food.

In bees, fecundity is very low by comparison with other insects. This is because of the particular reproductive strategy evolved by solitary bees. Many insects produce vast numbers of eggs. A butterfly may lay five hundred eggs in a day, but most of them will fall victim to predators and very few will survive to become adults. Such insects produce large numbers of eggs to increase the chance that some of their offspring will successfully run the gauntlet of natural enemies.

An alternative strategy is to lay fewer eggs and to invest time and energy in taking care of the offspring to ensure that a high proportion of them survive. Bees do this by creating a protected environment for their young (the nest) and stocking it with food. In this respect bees resemble birds and mammals. In almost all bees, the mother alone bears the responsibility of caring for the offspring. It is normally called 'maternal' or 'parental investment'.

A female solitary bee may live for only three to four weeks, though some species are much longer-lived. Females of the Eurasian mining bees, *Anthophora plumipes*, *A. libyphaenica* and *A. dispar* live for about ten weeks, while those of the neotropical euglossine bees may live for several months. However, very few female solitary bees live to see their offspring, despite having invested so much time and energy in them.

SEASONALITY

Most solitary bees are highly seasonal, have only one generation a year and time their emergence to coincide with the peak of flowering in their particular habitats. Thus, in north-west Europe, and temperate North America, the greatest numbers of solitary bees are active in late spring and early summer, say, from mid-May to the end of June. In Israel, the association of high bee diversity with spring is particularly marked and perhaps 75 per cent of all solitary bee species are found between February and the end of April. However, some species do emerge and are active in summer; Israel also boasts a specialized bee fauna which appears in early winter, timed to exploit the blooming of bulbous plants such as *Crocus* and *Sternbergia* species, which flower after the first winter rains.

In the tropics, often erroneously regarded as non-seasonal, many bee species emerge at the end of the rainy season and take advantage of the flush of flowering which takes place immediately after the rains. In one neotropical genus of solitary mining bees, *Centris*, there are some species which are strictly seasonal and have only one generation a year, while other *Centris* species are found throughout the year and pass through several generations.

The timing of nesting and provisioning behaviour dictates which is the developmental stage which passes through the winter or dry season. Thus, the progeny of solitary bees which are active in spring overwinter as adults in their natal cells and emerge in the following spring or at the end of the dry season. Species which are active in summer overwinter as prepupae and complete their development the following spring or after the first rains which herald the end of the dry season.

We do not yet understand just how it is that seasonally active bees are able to time their emergence so that they appear at just the right time. It is likely that they detect appropriate cues such as increases in soil temperature and/or moisture.

In North America, Dr K.V. Krombein found that in the mason bee, *Proche-lostoma philadelphi*, the developing individuals in some nests remained as pre-pupae for two seasons before pupation. Overwintering for a second time is widespread in solitary bees. It has been suggested that, in populations where the numbers of bees fluctuate wildly from year to year because of unpredict-able climatic extremes, it may be advantageous for part of the population each year to remain in the nests as immatures. In other words, 'dropping out' for a year is a strategy that ensures that at least some members of a local population can survive the occasionally disastrous season.

More recently, Drs P.F. Torchio and V.J. Tepedino have described a simi-lar phenomenon in three species of mason bee, *Osmia montana*, *O. californica* and *O. iridis*, from the western United States. They found that those bees which delayed their emergence for two years spent the first winter as prepupae and the second winter as adults. They coined the term 'parsivoltinism' to refer to this phenomenon, drawing upon the Latin *pars* for part or partial and the Italian *volta* for season or cycle. In entomological literature, 'voltinism' is used to refer to the number of generations per year, as in 'univoltine' (1 per year) or 'multivoltine' (many per year).

Torchio and Tepedino noted that in a ten-year study period, the popula-tions of *O. montana* and *O. californica* did not fluctuate very much and that *O. iridis* was rarely abundant. They concluded, therefore, that factors more com-plex than a response to environmental unpredictability were important in the evolution of 'dropping out' strategies.

BEE VILLAGES

Many species of solitary bee nest in dense aggregations. Hundreds or even thousands of females may nest in a limited area. We like to use the term 'village' for such aggregations. Like the human version, a bee village may have several or very many individual dwellings, the occupants of which are more (or less) tolerant of each other.

Most commonly it is mining bees which nest in villages, but surface-nesting mason bees often nest in dense aggregations too. Thus, the mud nests of *Chalico-doma parietinum* often form villages on rock outcrops or buildings in central and eastern Europe. The same is true for *Ch. siculum* in the Mediterranean region.

The Eurasian mining bee, *Andrena armata*, often forms conspicuous villages in town gardens and parks. The same is true of *Colletes thoracicus* in North America. In the west coast dunelands of Britain, villages of *C. cunicularius* can be as dense as 30 nests/sq m. A population of *C. succinctus* along the banks of Sleddale Beck in North Yorkshire, has a nesting density greater than this. In a good year, a 100 m length of the river bank has an estimated population of 60 to 80 thousand females. But some species have even higher nest densities: in his book, *The social behaviour of bees: a comparative study*, Dr C.D. Michener published a photograph of a village of the anthophorid *Paratetrapedia oligotricha* which he found in a vertical clay cliff in Brazil. Using the scale bar in the photograph, we estimate that, at its densest, there were 5,000 nests/sq m.

The largest ever aggregation of ground nesting bees was recorded from one bank of the River Barysh in Russia by Dr N.N. Blagoveshchenskaya. She noted that it varied in width from 10 to 150 m and extended for 7 km. This was a huge metropolis rather than a village. It was formed by two species of *Halictus* and the melittid *Dasypoda altercator* (given as *D. hirtipes*). The density of the *Halictus* species averaged 13 nests per sq m, while that of *D. altercator* averaged 21 nests per sq m. These densities were not as high as that of *Paratetrapedia oligotricha* in Brazil, but over the entire nesting area of 36 hectares (89 acres), Blagoveshchenskaya estimated that there were just under $12\frac{1}{4}$ million nests.

Why is it that some species nest in huge densities and others do not? There are several possible explanations. It seems that in some species, at least, there is a strong tendency for females to initiate nests close to the place where they were born. This makes sense because if a particular nest site has proved suitable for one generation then it is likely to prove so again. It may also explain why one often finds large nesting villages restricted to a relatively small part of what seems, to the human eye at least, to be a much larger and uniform area of bare ground.

In some localities mining bees may be forced into high nesting densities because of a limited availability of suitable soil textures and/or factors such as aspect, slope and exposure to sunlight. Our own observations on several British populations of *Colletes succinctus* suggest that soil texture may play some part.

In the heathlands of southern Britain, *C. succinctus* rarely if ever nests in large, dense villages. Nests in the New Forest are scattered among patches of bare, flinty soil between clumps of heather. In this area the only dense aggregation we found was in a woodland clearing, about 0.4 km (0.25 miles) from the nearest heather, which is the principal food plant of this species. The 34 nests were excavated in the light soil attached to the roots of an uprooted tree. This suggests that patches of bare, light soil are at a premium and, if necessary, the bees will nest at some distance from their foraging areas. In the huge Sleddale population of *C. succinctus*, already mentioned, bees nested in the light alluvial soil forming the banks of a stream side. This site is the only area in the valley with any extensive exposure of light, friable soil and has the additional advantage of being within a hundred metres of large tracts of heather.

The village-forming habits of some bees may be of importance to other species. In the Negev Desert of southern Israel, the bee community nests in the continually eroding vertical clay cliffs of seasonal water courses or *wadis*. There seems to be a definite succession of bee species.

The pioneers are *Anthophora fulvitarsis* and *Proxylocopa rufa*. They are the first to colonize a new exposure. Both species nest in villages, with *Anthophora fulvitarsis* having the higher density of nests, with up to 75/sq m. Often the two species nest in mixed villages and the cliff face becomes riddled with their nest holes, each of which is about 1–1.5 cm in diameter. After several seasons, the cliff face erodes to expose old cells and sections of nest burrow. Females of two smaller anthophorids, *Amegilla quadrifasciata* and *A. pipiens*, begin to use the newly exposed cells of the *Anthophora* and *Proxylocopa*, applying their own cell linings to reduce the size of the cells. The females of *Amegilla* also extend the nest tunnels of the larger bees, so that the cliff eventually becomes even more riddled with tunnels and cells.

The large cells of *Proxylocopa* and *Anthophora fulvitarsis* may also be used by a large and as yet undescribed species of mason bee, a *Chalicodoma* species. The females of this bee nest mainly in partially exposed cells, which they repair and modify for their own use by applying mud to the original structures. The old nest cells of this *Chalicodoma* are used in turn by a smaller mason bee, *Osmia latreilli*, the females of which use a mastic of chewed leaves to partition and

Solitary mining bees often nest in dense aggregations or 'villages'. Here, a village of *Colletes succinctus* nests in the banks of a moorland stream in Yorkshire, N. England (Family: Colletidae).

reduce the size of the cells they commandeer. Meanwhile, the founding pioneers, *Anthophora fulvitarsis* and *Proxylocopa rufa*, have moved on, to initiate new villages elsewhere. Thus, the *wadi* systems in the Negev are home to shifting populations of village-nesting bees.

Nesting in large, dense villages may not be without its disadvantages. A dense population increases the likelihood of the spread of disease and makes it easier for parasitic flies and cuckoo bees to find the nests of their hosts.

The pressure from cuckoo bees may in fact exert some influence on the nesting densities of bees and may provide another possible reason for the scattered nests of southern populations of *Colletes succinctus*. Of the 34 nests in the New Forest community excavated in the soil attached to the roots of an upturned tree, 15 contained larvae of the cuckoo bee, *Epeolus variegatus* (See Chapter 14). By nesting sparsely, southern populations may reduce their losses to cuckoo bees. By contrast, *E. variegatus* is unknown in the Sleddale area of Yorkshire, so a dense village in that area is not exposed to the same risk.

Another potential problem for a bee which nests in a dense village is finding its own nest amongst a plethora of entrance holes. The returning forager will find her way back to the general area of the village by means of her mental map of memorized distant and near landmarks, which we discussed in Chap-

Part of the river bank excavated to expose the cellophane-like brood cells of *Colletes succinctus*. At this site, the cells were at a density of 350 per cubic metre (Family: Colletidae).

ter 1. Scent almost certainly plays a part too, especially in species of *Colletes*.

A dense village of *C. cunicularius* is detectable by even the relatively insensitive human antenna, especially if one sits downwind of the nest site. The heady scent is linalool, which these bees produce in their mandibular glands and which functions as a fungicide and bacteriocide. We are certain that the bees orientate to this too and that the scent also attracts females which are looking for a new nest site. Linalool is also implicated in the mating behaviour of *Colletes*, which we discuss in Chapter 13.

Having got as far as the village, our homeward-bound female uses close landmarks to get to the immediate area of her nest entrance. A female often inspects several nest holes with her antennae before deciding which is her own. This makes it a near certainty that scent plays a role here. A female *Colletes* often drags her abdomen around on the sand at the entrance and we have circumstantial evidence that females mark their nest entrances with a scent from glands lying between the segmental plates (sternites) of the underside of the abdomen.

In a study of British populations of *C. cunicularius*, the contents of sternal glands were analysed, together with samples of sand taken from the nest entrance. The glands contained the same mixture of macrocyclic lactones which the Dufour's gland secretes, and which polymerize to form the membranous brood cell lining (See Chapter 4). They also contained a mixture of hydrocarbons. The sand samples were impregnated with the same profile of hydrocarbons as in the glands, but no lactones were detected. The absence of lactones in the sand is almost certainly because the sand samples were collected (as an afterthought) several days after the bees had finished nesting; the lactones had evaporated. Lactones, in their liquid form, have a pungent smell. In fact, they are chemically related to such heavy scents as muscone, from musk deer and civetone, from civet cats, which are used in the perfume industry.

The females of *C. cunicularius* have up to six lactones in the glands and it is likely that the relative proportions of them vary between individual bees. This is certainly the case in the primitively social halictid, *Lasioglossum malachurum*. This was demonstrated by Dr Abraham Hefetz of Tel-Aviv University. In this species, the blend of lactones unique to each individual forms the basis of chemical recognition between nestmates (See Chapter 9).

A nesting village of solitary bees may persist for many years. Christopher O'Toole helped make a television film which featured a large village of *Anthophora plumipes* in crumbling mortar in the walls of Worcester College, Oxford. While filming, an elderly local resident told us that this nesting aggregation had persisted for at least the fifty years he had lived there. We marvelled at how oblivious of the bees were the many passers-by on their way to and from Oxford's railway station.

Shortly after the film was televised, the authorities at Worcester College had the wall re-pointed and the old village of *A. plumipes* was destroyed. But Oxford has many crumbling walls . . .

It is clear that the factors leading to the establishment and maintenance of nesting villages are complex and diverse. Much more research needs to be done before we can claim to understand the doings of these fascinating little animals.

Fig. 8 (*opposite*) (a) A vertical section through the nest of a solitary mining bee, *Andrena armata* (Andrenidae); Eurasia. Each cell is closed with a plug of soil. In North America, *A. erythronii* has a similar nest architecture; (b) In *A. viburnella*, nests are constructed differently and the cells are positioned vertically. Cells are closed by soil pellets arranged in a spiral. (Redrawn by C. O'Toole from Stephen, W.P., Bohart, G.E. & Torchio, P.F., 1969.)

Chapter 4
Miners

Every Spring, the natural history museums of Europe and North America receive enquiries from the public about little mounds of earth which appear in lawns. These mounds are not worm casts but tumuli of excavated earth; they betray the presence of mining bees. Each tumulus is the work of a single female bee and it grows larger as she digs her nest.

There are many species of mining bees throughout the world, in several families. All known species of Andrenidae, Melittidae, Oxaeidae and Fideli-idae nest in the ground and many members of the Colletidae and Anthophor-

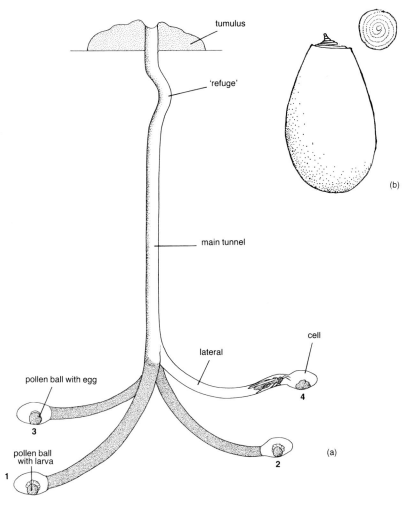

tumulus

'refuge'

main tunnel

cell

lateral

pollen ball with egg

3

4

pollen ball with larva

1

2

(a)

(b)

idae do likewise. Most of the species of Halictidae burrow in the ground, but a few in North America use rotten wood.

The commonest solitary mining bees in Europe and North America belong to the genus *Andrena*, with about 360 species in Europe and the near East and more than 500 from North America. Several species appear as early as March and April and are, together with willow catkins and Yellow Coltsfoot, the true harbingers of Spring in Europe and North America. The vast majority of *Andrena* species are solitary, but a few make communal nests (See Chapter 9). Other commonly seen solitary mining bees include the many species of *Colletes*.

Two solitary mining bees, *Andrena armata* (sometimes called *A. fulva*) and *A. erythronii*, have very similar life histories. The tawny-red females of *A. armata* are some of the most conspicuous spring bees in Britain and Europe. They often attract attention by their habit of nesting in large numbers in paths and well-mown lawns. The males are altogether more drab, being a dull brown, with a tuft of white hairs on the lower part of the face. The North American species, *A. erythronii*, commonly nests in open woodland, before the trees are in leaf.

Females of both species are active for about a month in spring. They mate as soon as they emerge from the ground and begin nesting soon afterwards. The female burrows into the ground by loosening soil with her mandibles and then scrapes it backwards with her front two pairs of legs. She uses her hind legs to brace herself against the side of the burrow. Later, when she has burrowed a distance greater than her own body length, she uses her hind legs and abdomen to push soil to the surface. On warm days, when the bee works rapidly, she resembles a terrier digging into a rabbit burrow, flinging soil out of the entrance.

The nests of the two species are similar in structure (Fig. 8a) though there are minor differences. In the nest of *A. armata*, just below the entrance there is a slight kink in the burrow called the refuge. During bad weather, when the female cannot fly, or when she rests from digging and foraging, she sits in the

A female of one of the commonest Eurasian mining bees, *Andrena armata*, forages at dandelion, *Taraxacum officinale* (Family: Andrenidae).

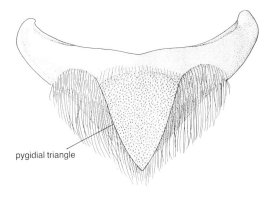

pygidial triangle

Fig. 9   The pygidial plate of a female mining bee, a modification of the last visible dorsal abdominal segment, used as a kind of trowel to apply cell-lining secretion from the abdominal Dufour's gland. This is found in families such as the Andrenidae, Melittidae and Anthophoridae.

In the Rocky Mountains of Colorado, USA, this female mining bee, a species of *Andrena*, forages on a dandelion flower. Her pollen scopa, a dense brush of specialized hairs, is clearly visible on the hind leg (Family: Andrenidae).

refuge, out of sight of the entrance. Sometimes, she will sit at the entrance sunning herself, with her head exposed, but will retreat to the refuge when a cloud obscures the sun or if a shadow falls across her. The nest of *A. erythronii* lacks a refuge and there is a sharper angle between the lateral branches and the main tunnel than in the nest of *A. armata*.

When the bee has excavated a lateral branch 10–15 cm (4–6 in) long, she excavates the first cell. Each cell is a specially prepared space where she stores food and lays a single egg. The cell is elliptical in section, with a remarkably smooth inner surface. The cell lining consists of two layers. The female constructs the outer layer by compacting particles of soil using a special structure at the tip of her abdomen called the pygidium; this is a raised, triangular plate (Fig. 9) which she uses rather like a brick-layer's trowel. She secretes the inner, waterproof lining of the cell from the Dufour's gland in her abdomen and uses the pygidium to apply it to the cell wall. She takes about a day and a half to excavate the main tunnel of the nest and construct the first cell, probably working during the night.

With the completion of the first cell, the bee faces the second strenuous task of her life, for she now has to provision it with pollen on which her first offspring will feed. The females of *A. armata* collect pollen and nectar from a wide range of spring-flowering plants. *A. erythronii* is more specialized, with a preference for the flowers of dogtooth violet, *Erythronium mesochoreum*.

The bee returns to her nest with her hind legs fully laden with pollen, which she scrapes into the cell. She adds a little honey and fashions the mixture into a smooth ball. The honey of *Andrena* and other solitary bees is much more watery than that of honeybees because it is not 'ripened' for so long (See Chapter 10). The female adds pollen to the ball after each subsequent trip.

A female of *A. armata* makes between eight and ten foraging trips to collect all the pollen for one cell. Foraging trips vary in duration from fifteen to a hundred minutes. On warm days, foraging begins at about 8.00 am and continues until 4 or 5.00 pm. During this time the female will make up to five foraging trips.

The completed pollen ball of *A. armata* is about 6 mm in diameter, and that of *A. erythronii* is about 5 mm. When the pollen ball is complete, the female lays an egg on it. The eggs of both species are about 2.5 mm long and 0.7 mm wide and, like those of most bees, are pearly white and slightly curved. Next, the bee

A female of the large South American solitary mining bee, *Centris* sp., uses her long tongue to drink water oozing from damp sand, where she is joined by four worker stingless honeybees, a species of *Trigona*. Bees replace body salts in this way. The massive pollen scopa, typical of female *Centris*, is clearly visible on the hind legs (Families: Anthophoridae and Apidae).

closes the cell with a plug of soil. *A. viburnella* closes the cell with a spiral of soil pellets (Fig. 8b).

After closure of the first cell, the female of *A. armata* excavates another lateral at about the same depth as the first one, pushing the loose soil from this operation into the first lateral. In this way she avoids having to take the soil all the way up to the nest entrance.

The females of *A. armata* and *A. erythronii* make four or five cells per nest, each one at the end of a lateral tunnel. Both species make two or three nests.

NEST ARCHITECTURE: DESIGNS FOR LIVING

The nest architecture of solitary mining bees is of great interest. It is often characteristic for a given species and can tell us much about the bees' biology. The shapes of food stores in the brood cells are also interesting and for the same

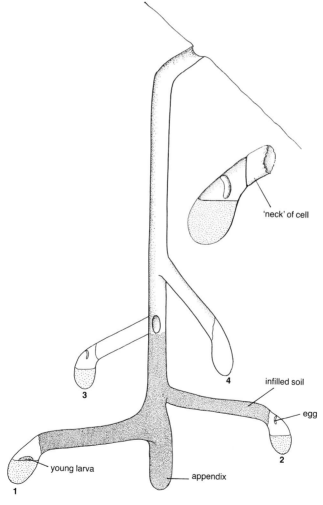

Fig. 10   Vertical sections through the nest of *Colletes cunicularius* (Colletidae).

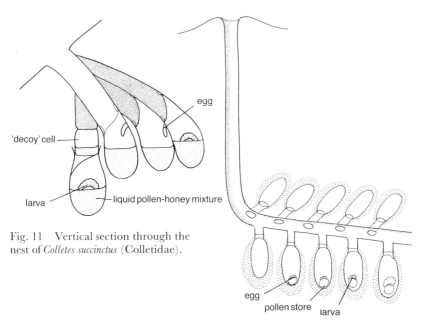

Fig. 11 Vertical section through the nest of *Colletes succinctus* (Colletidae).

Fig. 12 Vertical section through the nest of *Eucera longicornis* and *E. difficilis* (Anthophoridae). (Redrawn from Friese, H., 1923, *Die Europaischen Bienen.*)

reason. Nevertheless, there is a wide range of architectural types to be found among the nests within, say, the genus *Colletes*. Species such as *C. cunicularius* (Fig. 10) have a branched nest not unlike that found in many species of *Andrena*. This species is widespread in Europe and extends eastward as far as the shores of Lake Baikal in Soviet Central Asia, nesting in almost pure sand. *C. succinctus* (Fig. 11) has a cluster of cells at the end of a short tunnel.

Nest architecture in the Halictidae is very varied, and especially so among the social species (Chapter 9).

In Anthophoridae, there is a wide range of architectural styles in nest building. Among the more distinctive are the nests of the subfamily tribe Eucerini. In Europe, *Eucera longicornis* and *E. dificilis* construct cells at the end of short vertical branches from a near horizontal or slightly sloping main burrow (Fig. 12). Vertically orientated branch tunnels and cells are also characteristic of *Melissodes foxi*, a eucerine found only in Jamaica.

All female solitary bees which nest in the ground have the same problem: how to provide a safe nest for the storage of food and the development of their young, especially in the face of the ever-present danger of excessive dampness and fungal infections. This is important, because the females will not be around to protect their young once the cells and nest are completed. The wide range of nest architecture found in solitary mining bees emphasizes that natural selection can arrive at many different solutions to a shared set of problems.

THE NEST ENTRANCE
Nest entrances of mining bees are surprisingly varied. The simplest consist of a

Fig. 13   Vertical section through a nest of *Anthophora parietinum*, (Anthophoridae), excavated in a vertical clay cliff, showing the nest entrance turret characteristic of this species; Eurasia.

Fig. 14   Sections through the nest of the solitary mining bee, *Panurgus banksianus* (Andrenidae), showing the successive stages in its construction and the false entrance; Europe (Redrawn after Munster-Svendsen, 1970, *Ent. Scand.*, **1**: 93–101.)

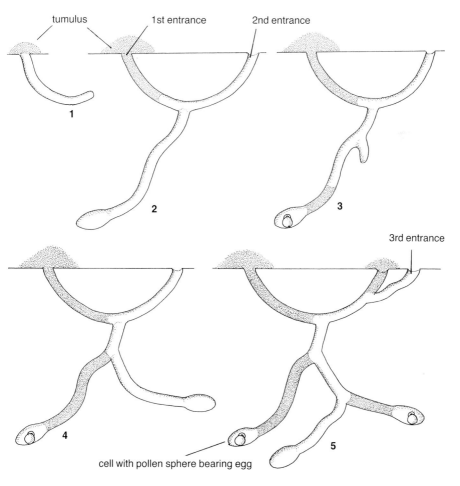

turret

tumulus   1st entrance   2nd entrance

1

2

3

3rd entrance

4

5

cell with pollen sphere bearing egg

heap of soil surrounding the entrance. Others, however, are more elaborate. *Anthophora parietina* is found in much of central Europe, where it nests in vertical banks. The entrance is unusual in that the female extends the main burrow beyond the entrance in the form of a down-curved turret (Fig. 13). She makes this out of small pellets of earth stuck together with some sort of secretion. A North American species, *A. occidentalis*, also makes turrets in this way and, like that of *A. parietina*, the turret always has a slit on its upper side. In North America, species of the mining bee genus *Diadasia* construct turreted nest entrances, the form of which is often characteristic of the species.

Turrets of this kind are also found in some solitary wasps. Their function is unknown. It has been suggested that they may deter cuckoo bees and parasites from entering the nest, but turret-making species are not notably freer from such unwelcome visitors than those which omit turrets. Another possible function is to prevent wind-blown sand and dirt from entering the nests. Whatever their purpose, turrets do not seem to be vital to the species which make them because they are often washed away in the first heavy rain after their construction. Moreover, when turrets are destroyed experimentally, the bees make no effort to repair them.

The European species, *Panurgus banksianus*, has more than one entrance to a nest. Before digging the main tunnel, the female makes a short side tunnel which curves downwards and then up to the soil surface (Fig. 14). The excavated soil accumulates as a tumulus at the first entrance. A female sometimes makes a third entrance after she has completed four or five cells.

DEPTH OF THE NEST

Most species of mining bee have nests in which the cells are within 60 cm (2 ft) of the soil surface. Occasionally, however, an individual female will build an unusually deep nest for no apparent reason. Normally nests of *Andrena nigroaenea* are not more than 40 cm (16 in) deep, but we discovered one with an unusually long main tunnel and a single cell more than a metre deep.

One species of solitary bee in Britain and Europe excavates deep nests as a matter of course. The nest of *Dasypoda altercator* in light, sandy soil may exceed one metre in depth.

In nests of species of Halictidae, the main burrow is always excavated to a depth which is much greater than that at which any cells are built. In their book *The Nest Architecture of the Sweat Bees*, the Japanese entomologist Dr S.F. Sakagami and Dr C.D. Michener suggested that the extra tunnel length may function as a sort of storm drain to allow excess water to run off. If this is true, then one may well wonder why it has not evolved in other families of mining bees.

The deepest nest recorded for a solitary bee was discovered in Colombia by an American entomologist, Dr Radclyffe Roberts. The nest of *Oxaea flavescens* was at least 2.5 m (8 ft 4 in) deep. Unpublished reports from Brazil give depths of up to 5 m (16 ft) for this species. Roberts and his helpers spent two days digging out one side of the nest. He found the first cell at a depth of 2.1 m (7 ft); it was only partially provisioned and clearly the female bee had been interrupted by the excavation.

It has been suggested that the presence of an individual female in such a deep nest indicates that the nest is the work of a number of generations of bees.

A female hairy-legged mining bee, *Dasypoda altercator*, excavates her nest in the sandy soil of a heath in southern England. Females of this widespread Eurasian species often nest in huge, dense aggregations and are noted for the massively developed pollen scopae on their hind legs (Family: Melittidae).

Fig. 15 The left hindleg of a South American mining bee, *Centris plumipes* (Anthophoridae), to show the basitibial plate, used by the bee to gain purchase on the sides of the nest burrow and the dense pollen scopa of plumose hairs. (Original drawing by C. O'Toole.)

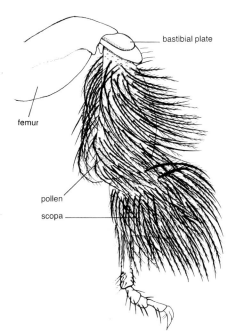

Presumably the first daughter to emerge each season takes over the maternal nest and then evicts her sisters which leave the nest to found their own nests, elsewhere.

Many other solitary bees excavate long, vertical tunnels deep underground.

A female has no difficulty in running up and down the tunnel and does so at a surprising speed. She accomplishes this by using special structures on her hind legs. At the base of each hind tibia there is a basitibial plate, which is often pointed (Fig. 15). The plates dig into the wall of the nest tunnel as the female bee runs up and down, enabling her to gain purchase on the very smooth surface. In some groups, the plate is a well-developed, two-tiered structure. Moreover, in the large neotropical genus *Centris*, the mining species which excavate vertical tunnels into the ground have well-developed basitibial plates, while these structures are vestigial in species which nest in short, horizontal tunnels and in existing cavities.

THE NUMBER OF CELLS IN A NEST

The great majority of mining bees make several cells per nest. The nests of *Panurgus* contain as many as ten cells. The females are rapid workers and the first cell may be completed on the same day the nest was started. The nest of *Anthophora plumipes* comprises a cluster of three or four cells at the end of a short tunnel of perhaps no more than 5 cm in length (Fig. 16). There are five or six cells in a completed nest of *Colletes cunicularius* (Fig. 10), *C. succinctus* and *C. halophilus* (Fig. 11) in Europe and *C. bicolor* in North America.

Females of the European *C. daviesanus* and North American *C. michenerianus* nest in the vertical faces of sandy cliffs. Each nest contains up to ten cells arranged end-to-end, so that the convex rear of each cell lining fits snugly into the concave cap of the cell behind it.

Some species, like the North American *Perdita maculigera*, make a single cell at the end of a short burrow. This species nests in almost pure sand, a mobile, unstable and apparently unsuitable substrate. Other species are more flexible.

Fig. 16   A section through a nest of *Anthophora plumipes* (Anthophoridae), excavated in soft mortar in the walls of Worcester College, Oxford.

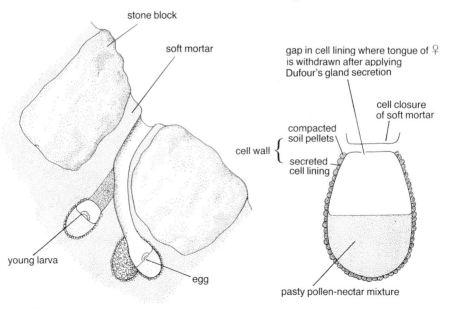

stone block

soft mortar

gap in cell lining where tongue of ♀ is withdrawn after applying Dufour's gland secretion

cell closure of soft mortar

compacted soil pellets

cell wall {

secreted cell lining

young larva

egg

pasty pollen-nectar mixture

Returning with a full pollen load, a female primitively social species of mining bee, *Halictus rubicundus*, alights at her nest entrance in the ground. This species is common throughout Eurasia and North America (Family: Halictidae).

The nests of *Anthophora plumipes* usually have a cluster of several cells, but in very hard soils, nests may comprise only one cell. Single-celled nests, however, are the rule in the North American species *A. edwardsii*.

The habit of making only one cell per nest is connected with the likelihood that a complex, multi-celled nest would be liable to collapse in sand. Moreover, as Drs C.D. Michener and E. Ordway have pointed out, bees nesting in sand are much more likely to make one-celled nests than those nesting in harder soil because, in such easily worked material, the economy of labour in making multi-celled nests is relatively unimportant.

LENGTH OF LATERAL TUNNELS
The cells of Halictidae are attached only by a short neck to the main or a lateral burrow. That is, they are built without an individual lateral tunnel leading to each cell. Presumably this is a labour-saving adaptation.

The solitary halictid species, *Halictus tumulorum*, is a common Eurasian bee. In the nest the brood cells are clustered about the main burrow (Fig. 17), an arrangement which is more common in the social species. In many species of Halictidae, the cell cluster is built at the side of the burrow and often with a chamber excavated around it. In other species, females build the chamber first and construct the cells within it. In either case, the end products are indistinguishable from each other.

CELL CONSTRUCTION
Although there is some variation in nest architecture among mining bees, there is a uniformity in the shape of brood cells throughout the families Andre-

51

nidae (Fig. 8), Halictidae (Fig. 17) and Melittidae. The cell is usually arranged with its long axis horizontal or at a slight angle from the horizontal. Rarely, its long axis is vertical, as in the North American *Andrena viburnella* (Fig. 8b) and the halictid, *Nomia melanderi*, (Fig. 18a). Before applying the cell lining, the female packs a layer of fine soil particles about 1–2 mm thick around the cell walls.

There is also a strong uniformity of shapes in nest cells of *Colletes* species. However, unlike *Andrena* and members of the Halictidae, a female *Colletes* spends little time in preparing the surface of the cell wall. Instead, she merely removes the larger surface irregularities and then applies the lining secretion from her Dufour's gland.

Andrena fulva and *A. erythronii* seal their cells by blocking the entrance with a plug of compacted soil (Fig. 8a), but females of the European *A. vaga* and North American *A. viburnella* close the cell with a cap of little soil pellets arranged in a spiral (Fig. 8b).

CELL LINING

The majority of mining bees line their cells with a secretion from a gland in the abdomen, the Dufour's gland, which is named after the French biologist and historian of the nineteenth century, who first discovered it. It is the source of brood cell linings in the families Andrenidae, Melittidae, Halictidae, Colletidae, Oxaeidae, and Anthophoridae. The gland is reduced or absent in species which do not secrete cell linings, like *Dasypoda* (Melittidae) and members of the family Megachilidae.

In andrenid bees, the secretion is a mixture of chemicals called terpenes and their derivatives; in melittids, the secretion is a mixture of alkanyl butanoates. After application, the secretion dries to form a highly polished layer with a waxy appearance.

In the Halictidae, Oxaeidae and Colletidae, the glandular secretion is a mixture of chemicals called macrocyclic lactones. The lactones of halictid bees seep into the soil to a depth of about 0.5 mm. They are dark brown or grey and give the cell wall a waxy or varnished finish.

The cell lining of *Colletes* is different. It does not impregnate the soil, but forms a transparent, cellophane-like membrane, which is easy to separate intact from the surrounding soil. Christopher O'Toole and a team from the University of Oxford investigated the origin and nature of the cell linings of two European species, *Colletes cunicularius* and *C. succinctus*.

To line the cell wall, the female of *Colletes succinctus* folds her body so that her mouthparts are close to the tip of her abdomen. She releases a droplet of a clear, oily liquid from the Dufour's gland which oozes from the base of the exposed sting. Then, with forward movements of her head, she brushes the fluid with her tongue over the cell wall. The bilobed tip of the tongue, typical of colletid bees (Fig. 19) is well suited for the task. The liquid dries quickly to form a continuous membrane, covering abut 5 sq mm. Because the female uses her tongue to apply the secretion, she does not have the raised pygidium used by female andrenids, halictids and anthophorids.

The cell lining of *Colletes* is a polymer, that is, a substance consisting of a series of identical molecular units, that are linked to each other by other molecules. The cell linings of *Colletes* species are polymerized macrocyclic

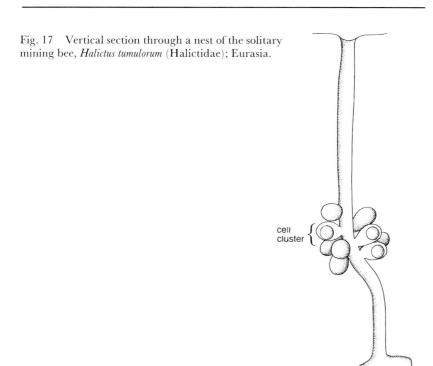

Fig. 17 Vertical section through a nest of the solitary mining bee, *Halictus tumulorum* (Halictidae); Eurasia.

cell cluster {

Fig. 18 (a) section through a nest of the Alkali bee, *Nomia melanderi* (Halictidae); (b) section of a cell of *N. melanderi*, showing pollen sphere and egg. (c)–(e) specially sculpted pollen stores in three species of *Nomia*; all from North America. (Redrawn after Stephen, Bohart and Torchio, 1969.)

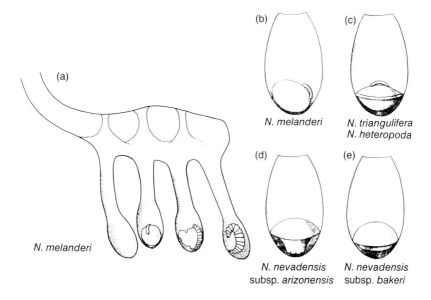

(a)

N. melanderi

(b)

N. melanderi

(c)

N. triangulifera
N. heteropoda

(d)

N. nevadensis
subsp. *arizonensis*

(e)

N. nevadensis
subsp. *bakeri*

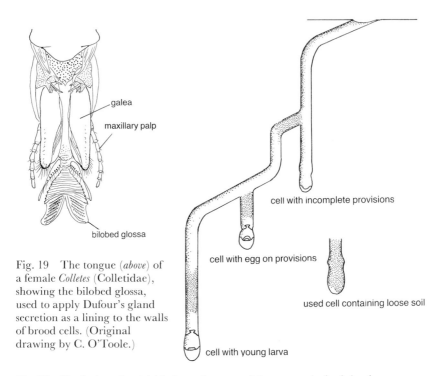

Fig. 19   The tongue (*above*) of a female *Colletes* (Colletidae), showing the bilobed glossa, used to apply Dufour's gland secretion as a lining to the walls of brood cells. (Original drawing by C. O'Toole.)

Fig. 20   Vertical section (*right*) through a nest of the neotropical mining bee, *Centris fasciata* (Anthophoridae).

lactones cross-linked with amino acids. They are very resistant to decay and old cells may persist in the soil for years.

The cell linings of three American species, *C. inaequalis*, *C. thoracicus* and *C. validus*, are very similar. These polymerized lactones secreted by the Dufour's gland of *Colletes* have been called 'laminesters' by Dr Abraham Hefetz and his colleagues.

The cell lining of *Anthophora* and, probably, other Anthophoridae, is yet another type of material, a mixture of oily triglycerides. Malyshev noted that a female *Anthophora* squirts a liquid from the tip of her abdomen into the cell. This, again, is a secretion of the well developed Dufour's gland and it dries to form a brittle, greyish layer, with an egg-shell finish.

Before applying the cell linings, the female of the South American anthophorid, *Centris fasciata*, carries light sandy soil into the nest on her pollen scopae. She compacts this around the walls of the cell. In bringing in material to form part of the cell lining, this species anticipates the cavity-nesters which are discussed in the next two chapters. *C. fasciata* closes each cell with an extension of the cell lining, which is moulded into a wide, hollow papilla (Fig. 20).

The wide variety of substances used by female mining bees to line their brood cells all have two things in common: they are waterproof and resistant to fungal attack. And herein lies the reason why a female mining bee invests so much energy in converting pollen and nectar into complex chemicals. Stored food and growing larvae are liable to infestation by moulds if the humidity within brood cells rises because of soil water seepage. At the same time, it is important that some level of humidity is maintained within a cell or the developing larva may become dehydrated and die. Clearly, there is a fine balance between the levels of humidity required to keep the stored food in a suitable state for the developing larvae and the level at which infection with moulds becomes a problem.

Although the cells of Andrenidae and Halictidae are lined with a wax-like, waterproof layer, the cells are not completely waterproof because the female bee cannot line the whole of the inner surface of the cell closure. Moreover, the amount of moisture required to bring about the germination of mould spores is not great. If the soil plugging the neck of the cell becomes slightly damp, this alone may be sufficient to stimulate the growth of any spores lying in the cell.

There is no doubt that a high proportion of mortality among the larvae of mining bees is a result of mouldy food. We found up to 20 per cent of cells infected with mould in one Oxfordshire population of *Andrena clarkella* and also in a Jamaican population of *Paratetrapedia swainsonae*. Mould is not the only danger from too much moisture in the cell. There is also the possibility that the honey fraction of the food store will liquefy and drown the larvae.

Because each individual bee spends the greater part of its life in its natal cell, the ability of a female to construct completely waterproof cells is of great survival value to her offspring. Some species can line the whole of the cell closure and this enables them to nest successfully in very moist and even flooded conditions. Unlike the brood cells of most bees, those of *Colletes* are completely lined and are wholly waterproof. The female makes a perfect seal when she closes her cell. The method was described by S.I. Malyshev, who studied a Russian population of *C. cunicularius*. The bee extends a section of the cell lining beyond the entrance of the cell by a distance roughly equal to the diameter of the entrance (Fig. 10). Malyshev called this extension the 'threshold' and the bee uses it to close the cell by bending it inwards after she has completed her provisions and laid her egg. She then glues the threshold into position by applying more gland secretion, to form a perfect seal.

We have described in Chapter 3 a population of *Colletes succinctus* at Sleddale, in north Yorkshire, where the bees have nested for many years in a dense aggregation in the banks of a moorland beck. In winter, the nest site is often flooded to a depth of a metre. A related species, *C. halophilus*, nests in earth banks fringing salt marshes on the east coast of England and the nest sites there are regularly flooded in autumn and winter with sea water.

Waterproof cell linings are not the only way that a female *Colletes* keeps her brood free from fungal attack. She also has a powerful chemical weapon at her disposal. All species of *Colletes* produce a heavy scent in a tiny gland at the base of each mandible. The scent is a substance called linalool, which is one of a group of chemicals called terpenes. Linalool is an effective fungicide and bacteriocide. A female *Colletes* sprays a newly lined cell with a fine mist of linalool. She does this by opening and closing her mandibles repeatedly, squeezing scent droplets from a tiny aperture in a membrane at the base of each mandible. Both sexes of *Colletes* produce this substance, which has several uses in the lives of these bees.

Species of the Central and South American anthophorid genus *Epicharis* use resin as well as their own glandular secretions to make a complete and waterproof lining for their cells. A female *Epicharis* cannot use her own secretion to cover the point in the cell closure through which the tongue protrudes into the cell, so she uses resin to bridge the gap. Several species nest in damp soil. *E. albofasciata*, for example, nests in alluvial sand banks of streams near the city of Goias in central Brazil. Many of these streams overflow their banks and at one particular locality the nest site is often under a metre of water. Drs D.W. Roubik and C.D. Michener record a similar circumstance in French Guiana, where *E. zonata* nests in small forest glades which are seasonally flooded. The females nest during the dry season and the completely waterproof cells enable the offspring to survive the rainy season.

THE BEE LOAF

The manner that the food is presented in the brood cells varies greatly among species. Some simply deposit and mix the food in the cell and then lay an egg on or near it. A female *Colletes* stores a liquid mixture of pollen and honey; she lays an egg on the cell wall above the level of the food (Figs. 8a–b). When the young larva hatches from the egg, it drops on to the food mass and begins feeding.

The cells of *Anthophora* are almost completely waterproof and the food store is a rather pasty mixture of pollen and honey. The female does not sculpt the pollen into any special shape. After laying her egg on the food mass, she partially closes the cell with compacted earth and then applies the cell lining material to as much of the inner surface of the plug as she can reach. This means that only a tiny area is unlined.

Most species laboriously sculpt the food into specialized shapes. Many Andrenidae, Melittidae and Halictidae fashion the food into shapes which are peculiar to the species. This work is a time and energy consuming activity and there must be a good reason for it to have evolved. Charles Michener has suggested that the shapes minimize the amount of food in contact with the cell

Fig. 21   Section through a brood cell of the Eurasian mining bee, *Dasypoda altercator* (Melittidae), showing how the pollen sphere is kept clear of the unlined cell wall by a 'tripod'.

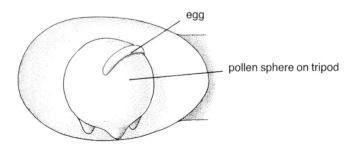

egg

pollen sphere on tripod

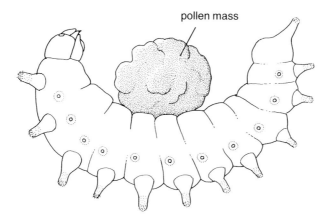

pollen mass

Fig. 22   A larva of the North American mining bee, *Perdita octomaculata*
(Andrenidae), nursing a pollen mass on its belly while resting on fleshy outgrowths
from its back, which minimize its contact with the cell wall.

wall which, apparently, reduces the risk of the stores becoming mouldy in the
incompletely waterproof cells of these species. This view is supported by our
observation that growths of mould on the pollen balls in *Andrena clarkella* cells
invariably spread from the point of contact between pollen and cell wall. The
mould probably develops from spores accidentally brought into the cell on the
feet of the female bee.

Despite their differences in nest architecture, females of the families Andrenidae and Halictidae have one thing in common: they take the trouble to
shape their pollen stores into nearly perfect or slightly flattened spheres. The
females of some Melittidae do the same.

The females of some genera of Anthophoridae from the Americas, such as
Paratetrapedia and *Exomalopsis*, also shape the food into pollen spheres. They
spread a waxy secretion on the cell wall, but not on the cell cap.

It is possible that some species minimize the risks of seepage from a rising
water table by making cells with a vertical axis. Such species also have specialized adaptations for limiting the amount of pollen in contact with the cell wall.
Females of the North American halictids, *Nomia triangulifera* and *N. heteropoda*,
shape the equator of the pollen ball into a rim, which is the only part of the
pollen store in contact with the cell wall (Fig. 14).

Not all species line their cells. The females of the melittid bee, *Dasypoda
altercator*, make no lining for their brood cells and have evolved an ingenious
way of keeping as much of the pollen store as possible away from the cell wall.
The female builds her pollen sphere on a tripod of smaller lumps of pollen, so
that the bulk of the food store is clear of the sides of the cell (Fig. 21).

In species of the North American andrenid genera *Nomadopsis* and *Calliopsis*,
the cell lining is very thin and is said to be permeable to water. The bees
overcome this problem, however, by covering the pollen ball itself with a
waxy, secreted layer.

Females of the North American genera *Perdita* (Andrenidae) and *Hesperapis*

(Melittidae) make no cell lining; they also cover the pollen ball instead. When the larva begins to feed, it breaches the cover but, nevertheless, much of the pollen remains protected while the larva is small. When the larva of *Perdita* reaches a certain size, it rolls over on to its back and cradles the remaining food mass on its belly (Fig. 22). Thus, while little of the original covering of the food remains, none of the food is in contact with the cell wall. In addition, the larva is adapted to minimize the amount of contact between itself and the cell wall: it lies supported by fleshy tubercles or outgrowths from its back. This is found in most, if not all, genera in the subfamily Panurginae.

As we have seen, most members of the Colletidae, especially *Colletes* spp., store a rather liquid mixture of honey and pollen in completely waterproof cells. This indirectly adds weight to the theory that specially sculpted pollen stores evolved to overcome the problem of contamination with mould from the walls of incompletely waterproofed cells.

The many ways which mining bees have evolved to avoid fungal infestation of their pollen stores is a good example of how diverse bees can arrive at different solutions to the same fundamental problem.

TWO EXTREME CASES

THE WET ENVIRONMENT

Unusual nests may reflect specialized life histories. Such is the case with the remarkable bee *Ptiloglossa guinnae*. It was discovered by Dr R. Roberts in Costa Rica, nesting in the soils of cool, wet, mountain forests, conditions normally shunned by bees.

P. guinnae is well adapted for life in this environment. The females forage in the cool, early mornings and often in rain. In the nest the female excavates between five and twelve branches, each ending in a vertical cell which is lined with a tough, brown, cellophane-like membrane. So far as is known, the species is unique in that the female leaves all the cells open after laying an egg in each one (Fig. 24). Apparently, this is an adaptation to the unusual food stored by these bees, which is watery, even by the standards of the Colletidae. Furthermore, the contents of the hundred or so cells examined by Dr Roberts were actively fermenting with bubbles of gas rising from the frothy slime at the bottom of the cells.

Roberts cultured two species of yeast from the provisions, which contained so little pollen that he concluded that the yeasts, rather than the pollen, were the major source of nutrients for the developing bee larvae.

The females of *Ptiloglossa* specialize in foraging on flowers belonging to the potato family, Solanaceae. Much *Solanum* pollen may lack cytoplasm and, therefore, has very little nutritive value. For this reason, it seems, the bees evolved an association with yeasts, though how and where the bees collect them is unknown.

As every home wine maker knows, the fermenting liquor emits carbon dioxide which must be allowed to escape and possibly the nesting bee leaves the cells open to prevent the build-up of this gas. However, the open cells impose problems of their own. Because the nests are excavated in damp soil in wet forest, there is always the danger of open cells being flooded. The females

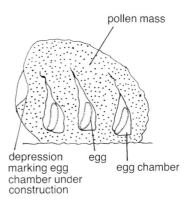

pollen mass

depression marking egg chamber under construction

egg

egg chamber

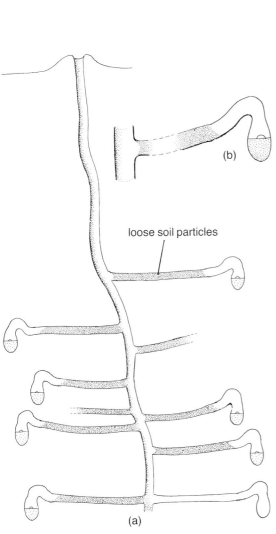

loose soil particles

(b)

(a)

Fig. 23 Section (*above*) through a nest cell of *Parafidelia pallidula* (Fideliidae); South Africa. (Redrawn after Rozen, J.G., 1877, *Am. Mus. Novit.*, No. **2637**.)

Fig. 24 Vertical section (*left*) through the nest of a solitary mining bee, *Ptiloglossa guinnae* (Colletidae); Costa Rica. (a) whole nest; (b) detail of side branch and cell. (Redrawn after Roberts, R.B., 1971, *J. Kans. Ent. Soc.*, **44**: 283–94.)

of *Ptiloglossa* reduce this danger by making the end of each side branch curve upwards just before the entrance to the cell; each cell is therefore furnished with a kind of sink trap (Fig. 19b).

The fully grown larva of *P. guinnae* spins a tough cocoon before pupation. This, too, is probably an adaptation to overcome the dangers inherent in unsealed cells. Cocoons are relatively rare among ground nesting bees and even where they occur they are usually very flimsy. Apparently, cocoons are redundant in the vast majority of ground nesting bees because of the protection afforded by the cell linings secreted by the mother.

The nests of *Ptiloglossa guinnae* are a good example of how nest architecture and larval behaviour have had to be modified to cope with the peculiar demands of fermenting provisions.

THE DRY ENVIRONMENT

Bees of the small and unusual family Fideliidae live in arid areas in South America and South Africa. Fideliids are related to the mason and leaf-cutter bees (Megachilidae).

The cell contents of *Parafidelia pallidula* are adapted to their extremely arid environment in an unusual manner. Dr Jerome G. Rozen Jr studied this species in Namibia, where the bees excavate nests in the coarse desert sand.

The cells are very large for the size of the bee, being about 35 mm long and 15–17 mm wide. The way in which the female stores the larval food is unusual. After placing several loads of nectar-moistened pollen in the cell she excavates a depression in it in which she lays an egg (Fig. 23). She then adds more pollen to seal the egg chamber. The process is repeated and the finished pollen mass contains three chambers, each containing an egg. The completed pollen mass is about 15 mm long, 12 mm high and 10 mm wide. The female then closes the cell with a heap of loose sand and fills the side branch leading to it with sand excavated as she digs the next cell.

The females of *P. pallidula* and other fideliids do not provide their brood cells with a waterproof lining. The enclosure of young stages in the pollen mass is presumably to prevent their desiccation in the dry desert conditions. The lack of a waterproof cell lining may restrict fideliid bees to arid regions. Moisture in the soil would cause liquefaction of the food, followed by destruction by mould as happened when Dr Rozen placed a food mass in a humid atmosphere. The nectar in the food rapidly absorbed water vapour and the whole food mass liquefied.

Just before pupation, the full-grown larva of *P. pallidula* eats sand grains, which it later extrudes from the anus mixed with a brown secretion. The larva plasters its immediate space in the nest with this material, which dries to form a tough cocoon. This is waterproof and is clearly an adaptation to prevent desiccation of the prepupa and pupa.

Chapter 5
Masons

The majority of mason bees nest in existing cavities. These range from irregular cavities under bark and rock, empty snail shells, hollowed-out gourds, insect borings in dead wood and disused cells of bees and wasps. Some species excavate nests in the soft pith of plant stems and others make nests on exposed surfaces such as rocks and walls; a few species dig their nests in the ground.

The great majority of cavity- and surface-nesting bees belong to the family Megachilidae. Members of this distinctive family line their nests with materials gathered from the environment rather than with their own secretions.

The term 'mason bee' is perhaps best suited to those bees which work in mud and pebbles. However, it is convenient to include all those surface- and cavity-nesting bees that gather soft, malleable materials, which they mould to some required shape and which harden to form durable structures. Materials include mud, resin, dung and leaf and petal pulp. Some species also incorporate unchewed pieces of petals, wood chips, twigs and small pebbles in their constructions.

It is remarkable that the use of these materials has evolved independently many times in the genera of mason bees. Thus, while the females of any given species use only one or, sometimes, a combination of two substances, the various species in a genus may encompass a wide range of materials mentioned above.

Mason bees can be classified according to the types of nests they build and the substances they collect for nest construction. Such a classification is convenient for our present purposes, but rarely coincides with the formal classification of the bees themselves, which is based on comparative anatomy and inferred, genealogical relationships.

The nests of mason bees may be built in (1) tubular burrows in wood or plant stems, as in *Osmia rufa* and *O. lignaria*, (2) irregular cavities and the abandoned nests of wasps and bees, (3) snail shells, (4) termite nests, (5) on exposed surfaces such as rocks or twigs and (6) excavations in the ground made by the bees themselves.

The nesting behaviour of several species of mason bees has been studied in great detail. This has been possible because of the readiness of the bees to utilize artificial nests called trap-nests. These can be bundles of drinking straws, hollow bamboo, or blocks of wood drilled with holes. The following accounts of two species of *Osmia* are based on studies of this type.

THE MASON BEES, *OSMIA RUFA* AND *OSMIA LIGNARIA*

In Britain and Europe, *Osmia rufa* is the commonest mason bee in spring. The female which is reddish brown and 10–13 mm long bears a pair of horns on the face (Fig. 25). The widespread North American species, *O. lignaria*, is similar in size, but darker. The hornless males of both species are more slender in build. The bees are active for about two months in late spring. They have

Nests of the Red mason bee, *Osmia rufa*, in bamboo trap-nests, England. The mud seals on completed nests are clearly visible (Family: Megachilidae).

Emerging (*above left*) from a mud source, a female Red mason bee, *Osmia rufa* (Megachilidae), carries a pellet of mud between her powerful jaws. She uses mud to partition and seal her cells. Several nesting females may find the same area of mud and their activities can create a distinctive hollow or 'quarry'. This widespread Eurasian species has a close relative in North America, *Osmia lignaria* (Family: Megachilidae).

A female Red mason bee, *Osmia rufa* (*above right*), carries a mud pellet to the nest she is building in a piece of bamboo. She uses the pair of horns, clearly visible on the front of her head, to tamp mud into position when closing a cell. The pollen scopa of stiff hairs on the underside of her abdomen, is characteristic of the family Megachilidae.

Fig. 25   Front view of the head of
the Red mason bee, *Osmia rufa*
(Megachilidae), showing the pair of
horns used to tamp mud during nest
building; Eurasia.

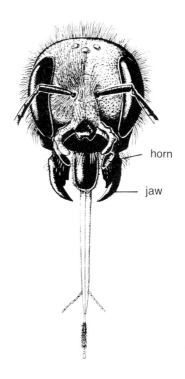

horn

jaw

similar life histories. After mating, the females search for a suitable cavity in
which to nest, which may take several days. For female mason bees, this is an
arduous and dangerous time.

Both species prefer to nest in cavities about 7 mm in diameter. However,
they are opportunists and nest in a wide variety of places as do many members
of the Megachilidae. They nest in cracks, old beetle borings and nail holes in
fence posts, logs and dead trees, and in old cells of solitary mining bees such as
Anthophora species. *Osmia rufa* often nests in the mortar of old walls, enlarging
existing nooks and crannies. The bees sometimes remove mortar from the
'frogs' or depressions of housebricks. This species has also been found nesting in
a variety of strange places, including holes in a piece of flint, door locks, a fife
lying in a garden shed and in the spout of an old teapot.

Despite this versatility, less than 50 per cent of *O. rufa* in southern England
survive to begin nesting. Presumably predation by birds takes its toll, but other
causes of death play a part. Females which have not discovered a nest site
spend the night in small cavities under bark or debris on the ground. The bees
become cool during the night and, while slow and torpid, are sometimes killed
by spiders in the morning. Females which spend the night in flowers are
attacked by crab spiders. However, once the bee has found a nest site, she is
safe at night.

We have made a special study of the nesting biology of *O. rufa*. On selecting
a suitable place, a female clears it of debris. The bee then searches for a source
of mud, usually at the edge of a pool or puddle. If mud is not available, she
selects some fine-textured soil and adds saliva to it to make a soft paste. When

A bamboo nest of the Red mason bee, *Osmia rufa*, split open to show a series of cells, each containing pollen, a single egg and separated from its neighbour by a mud partition (Family : Megachilidae).

several females return time and again to the same spot, the area comes to resemble a miniature quarry.

The bee scrapes together a small amount of mud with her jaws and moulds it into a pellet against the underside of her abdomen, which she bends forward between her legs. She adds more mud to the pellet. The whole operation takes about 40 seconds and a typical, completed pellet weighs about 11 mg. The female flies back to the nest with the mud held in her mandibles and often supports it with the front legs.

The bee uses the first loads of mud to build the back partition of the first cell at the blind end of the tunnel. When she has finished the partition, and before she begins to place food in the cell, she builds a small crescent of mud around part of the side of the tunnel at some distance from the partition. This marks the site of the next partition and thus defines the length of the cell. Probably it provides a reference point for the bee to assess how much food to store. This was first observed by the French entomologist, Jean Henri Fabre and is now called 'Fabre's threshold'.

As soon as the cell is ready, the bee begins to collect food to store in it. On her first return, she deposits pollen at the rear of the nest. After each subsequent foraging trip, she regurgitates honey on to the pollen of the previous trip, kneading it into a thick paste with her jaws. Next she scrapes the pollen from the scopa on the underside of her abdomen, using both hind legs simultaneously. In nests of narrow diameter she backs to the entrance in order to turn round so that she can back in again to deposit the pollen.

The stored food is a solid but friable mass, with a dusting of loose pollen over the surface. The bee lays her egg almost immediately after she has added the last pollen load. The egg is slightly curved, about 4.5 mm long and 2.1 mm wide. It is always laid with its posterior end in the pollen store.

After laying the egg, the female constructs a mud partition which she began with 'Fabre's threshold'. This wall seals the provisioned cell and forms the rear of the next one. To construct it the bee applies the first load of mud directly to

Feeding larvae of the Red mason bee, *Osmia rufa* (Family: Megachilidae).

the side of the tunnel in a tight spiral. She places the next pellet close to the spiral and nibbles off small pieces to add to the spiral foundation. She then adds a pellet in one piece to the centre of the partition, thereby closing it completely. Subsequent loads of mud are added directly to the partition. The female uses the pair of horns on the front of her head to tamp down and smooth the mud. The finished partition is approximately 1 mm thick, with a rough, convex inner surface and a smooth, concave outer one.

The bee goes on to repeat the process of building, provisioning and egg laying until the nest comprises a row of brood cells, each containing food and an egg and separated from its neighbour by a mud partition. She will complete between one and one and a half cells per day in good weather.

After the final cell has been sealed, the females of *O. rufa* and *O. lignaria* leave an empty space, called the vestibular cell, between the last brood cell and the nest entrance. This empty space is found in the nests of nearly all solitary bees and wasps which nest in tubular cavities. The vestibular cell is sealed with a thicker plug than an ordinary cell partition.

The bee spends a considerable time building this closure which plugs the nest entrance: it prevents another cavity-nesting species of bee or hunting wasp from utilizing the vacant space. The nest of another species might imprison the offspring of the first one and they would die in their cells.

The nests of *O. rufa* generally have four to six cells, and exceptionally up to ten in long reeds and bamboo canes. The females may complete four or five nests, with fewer cells in the later nests than in earlier ones. *O. lignaria* makes larger nests with eight to eleven cells per nest.

LARVAL DEVELOPMENT AND ORIENTATION OF THE COCOON

The egg of *O. rufa* hatches in about a week. The larva moults its skin three times during the thirty days it takes to complete its growth. Unlike the larvae of most solitary bees, that of *O. rufa* begins to defecate after the first eight days rather than at the end of larval development. The larva scatters the dry faecal pellets over the surface of the food but this seems not to contaminate it.

The larva spins a silk cocoon after it has finished feeding. At first, the cocoon is white but after a day or two it darkens to a reddish brown. There are two distinct layers of silk, an outer one of thick, coarse fibres and an inner one of fine, smooth threads. The cocoon is rounded at each end, with a nipple at the front.

Before the larva is fully grown and ready to spin a cocoon, it must be able to detect in which direction the nest entrance lies, for in most nests the mature larva and adult bee will be too large to be able to turn around. Correct orientation of the cocoon is important for the survival of the adult bee. If it is mis-directed and cannot turn around, the bee will bite its way out into the adjacent, inner cell and injure the occupant. Ultimately, it may die in a vain attempt to chew its way out through the solid wood at the rear of the nest tunnel. This applies to all wasps and bees which make linear rows of cells in pre-existing cavities.

Various explanations have been offered to account for the fact that larvae of cavity-nesting species nearly always align themselves correctly relative to the nest entrance. Probably the geometry of the mud partition provides orientation cues for the larvae. The inner surface is rough and convex, the outer one smooth and concave. Apparently, the larva uses these surfaces to detect the direction of the nest entrance.

PUPATION AND EMERGENCE OF THE ADULT BEE

In *O. rufa* pupation occurs about 56 days after the egg hatches and the bee remains in this state for a further 48 days before becoming adult. Hence, the bees complete their development from egg to adult in about 15 weeks. Towards the end of September the cocoons contain adult bees which remain quiescent during the winter.

The next spring the bees emerge from their nests. The silk of a megachilid cocoon is very tough to protect the dormant bee. In order to bite through it more easily, the bee produces an enzyme from the mandibular glands which softens the silk.

Because of the linear arrangement of cells in the nests of *O. rufa*, *O. lignaria* and related species, the youngest bee in each nest emerges first, followed, in sequence, by the progressively older bees, the oldest leaving last. However, as may be expected, the oldest bees, in the deepest cells, often awaken from their winter dormancy first. An older bee is thus likely to meet with a still-dormant bee in the next cell between it and the nest entrance. The problem is solved as follows: when the bee has bitten through the partition into the rear of the next cell, it then bites its way through the cocoon of the bee in front. If the occupant is inactive, the bee nips the rear of its abdomen. This awakens the second bee, which begins to vibrate its wings. Nipping is repeated until the bee in front is active and begins to bite its way out of its own cocoon and through the partition into the next, anterior cell. If necessary, this bee will awaken its neighbour in front, until the bee nearest the entrance starts to bite its way through the nest closure.

The first bees to emerge each spring from the nests of *O. rufa* and *O. lignaria* are normally males. This reflects the non-random distribution of the sexes in the nest: the outer series of cells are occupied by males, while the inner cells contain females. In 37 nests of *O. rufa* which were examined and which con-

Not all female mason bees use mud as a building material. Here (*above left*), a snail-nesting mason bee from Israel, *Hoplitis lhotelleriei*, chews a piece of leaf into a mastic which she uses to seal her cells. Back at her nest in an old snail shell (*above right*), the female *Hoplitis lhotelleriei* makes a final seal to complete her nest by embedding pieces of snail shell into a matrix of leaf mastic (Family: Megachilidae).

tained both sexes, only 3 had females in cells anterior to the males. The segregation of the sexes in this way is found in nearly all bees and wasps where the nest comprises a linear row of cells.

MORE NEST SITES AND BUILDING MATERIALS

TUBULAR NESTS

Many hundreds of mason bees share the habit of *Osmia rufa* and *O. lignaria* in making nests in insect borings in dead timber or the hollow stems of plants. Some species excavate their own tubular nest cavities in the soft pith of plants such as elder or sumac.

Many other mason bees use mud to build cell partitions and nest closures. They include *O. cornuta*, *O. taurus*, *O. cornifrons*, *O. tricornis* and *Hoplitis adunca* in Eurasia, *Osmia glauca* and *Prochelostoma philadelphi* in North America and *Chalicodoma lanata* and *Ch. rufipennis* in the West Indies.

Some species of *Chelostoma* use a mixture of soil and honey for the building of cell partitions and nest closures. *Ch. campanularum* is found in much of Europe where it nests in the galleries of woodworm beetles (Anobiidae) in old stumps and fence posts and sometimes in roofing straws and dry, dead reeds. The seven native species of North American *Chelostoma* are confined to the west of the Rockies. One of them, *Ch. minutum*, makes cell partitions out of a mixture of pitch and fine gravel. The females also line their cells with what appears to be a secreted varnish.

Some species of *Osmia* and *Hoplitis* use a mastic of chewed leaf tissue rather than mud when building cell partitions and nest closures, though in other respects their nest architecture resembles that of *Osmia rufa* and *O. lignaria*. These include *O. leaiana* and *Hoplitis leucomelana* in Britain and Eurasia and *Osmia cordata* and *O. georgica* in North America.

Several North American mason bees build with a mixture of mud and leaf mastic. Among them are two western species, *O. californica* and *O. marginipennis*. Although identical in appearance, Dr F.D. Parker found that *O. californica* nests in tubular borings in wood, whereas *O. marginipennis* constructs irregular nests in rock fissures. This is a good example of how details of nest architecture may be used to distinguish between closely related species.

Resin-producing plants abound in the drier parts of the world and many bees have adopted this substance as a building material. The bees collect the resin which oozes from wounds in plants such as pine trees, plum trees, American creosote bush (*Larrea tridentata*) and many other woody plants. It is remarkable that the bees can manipulate and transport this sticky substance. We still do not know how the bees work with it and clean it from their jaws afterwards. It is unlikely that they secrete a solvent because all known resin solvents are highly toxic. The hazards resin bees face are well demonstrated by the many insects which became trapped in resins and subsequently preserved in amber.

Notwithstanding the dangers, resin is an ideal building material. A small amount can be drawn out into a thin but tough, waterproof membrane, which provides a suitable matrix in which to embed other materials such as sand grains or fine gravel. Moreover, it is likely that the strong smell of fresh resin acts as a deterrent to intending robbers such as ants and small beetles.

Resin-building bees are not uncommon in the drier parts of the tropics. Some African species of *Heriades* collect the sap of the spurge *Euphorbia angularis*. The females of the widespread *H. spiniscutis* excavate tubular nests in the branches of plants and construct cell partitions and nest closures of resin. Dr C.D. Michener found that many nests of this species in Kenya and South Africa are unusual in having a string of compacted food masses in an open cavity without any cell partitions. Sometimes completed nests without cell partitions were guarded by the mother bee.

Many species of *Chalicodoma* also nest in tubular cavities and use resin. This genus is also in the Megachilidae, but is only distantly related to the *Osmia*-like mason bees. Some East Asian species construct partitions of pure resin. In Japan, *Chalicodoma disjunctum* uses resin of mango trees, while the widespread species *Ch. monticolum* collects resin from pine (*Pinus thunbergii*) and she-oak (*Casuarina sticta*). The females line the entire cell wall with resin and seal each nest with a pair of heart-shaped pieces of leaf. They then apply a film of resin to the leaf closure.

Resin bees are relatively rare in cool, temperate climates. However, the Eurasian species *Heriades truncorum* nests in reed stems or beetle borings in wood, making cell partitions and nest closures with resin collected from pine trees. In North America, *H. carinata* has a very similar life history and visits a wide range of plants, though it has a preference for staghorn sumac (*Rhus glabra*). Other Eurasian species, such as *Chalicodoma ericetorum* and *Ch. flavipes*, line their cells with mud before applying a layer of resin, while *Ch. sculpturale*, which nests in bamboo stems, makes cell partitions out of a mixture of resin and sawdust.

All the native *Chalicodoma* of North America use resin as a building material and nest in insect borings in dead timber. Several species including *Ch. exilis* and *Ch. campanulae*, make the cell partitions of resin, but also embed other materials like pieces of leaf, bark and wood chips, in the resin of the closing plug.

IRREGULAR CAVITIES, ABANDONED NESTS OF WASPS AND BEES

Many mason bees use irregular cavities rather than the tubular cavities of insect borings in dead wood. The females seek out a variety of sites such as small holes and fissures in rocks or the hollows under stones. They use much the same range of building materials as those which nest in regular, tubular burrows, though resin seems to be less common. They use rather more material because each bee constructs the whole of each cell, rather than just the end partitions.

Both the European Red Mason Bee, *Osmia rufa*, and its American counterpart, *O. lignaria*, sometimes build their mud cells in irregularly shaped cavities. Both are recorded from old cells of the mining bee *Anthophora*. Other mud-building mason bees which nest in irregular cavities include the European *Osmia cornuta* and *Hoplitis lepeletieri* and the North American *Osmia tanneri*.

Hoplitis anthocopoides usually builds free-standing mud nests on exposed surfaces but, in the volcanic Auvergne region of France, females of this species nest in holes in the local pumice stone. They seal their nests with a light grey mud, identical in colour to the lichen which encrusts the rocks in irregular blotches. The nests are therefore beautifully camouflaged.

The builders in leaf mastic which use irregular cavities include *Osmia inermis* from Europe and North America, and the American *O. emarginata*, *Anthocopa abjecta* and *A. elongata*. All of these bees nest in cavities under stones. *Osmia uncinata*, a recent addition to the wild bee fauna of Britain, makes mastic cells in nooks and crannies in the bark of pine trees in the highlands of Scotland.

Some mason bees use the abandoned nests of wasps or the persistent cells of mining bees. *O. texana* is widespread in North America and nests in old cells of *Anthophora occidentalis*. The female makes cell partitions and nest plugs out of a mastic made by chewing the leaves of the mallow *Malva neglecta* and *Sphaeralcea coccinea*. In the desert *wadis* of Israel, *Osmia latreilli* regularly nests in old cells of *Proxylocopa rufa* and some *Anthophora fulvitarsis*.

The exposed nests of mud-dauber wasps of the genus *Sceliphron* persist long after the wasps leave the cells. They are a common sight in warm temperate countries and most parts of the tropics.

In the deserts of the south-western United States, the mason bee, *Hoplitis biscutellae*, nests only in the abandoned cells of *Sceliphron caementarium*. The females build urn-shaped cells within those of the wasp. The cell walls, partitions and nest closure are made out of a mixture of flower parts, leaves and resin, all collected from the creosote bush, *Larrea tridentata*. The bee sometimes incorporates remains of the cocoons of the mud-dauber into the cell walls. *Hoplitis biscutellae* is the only one of the 45 North American species of this genus which builds with resin. In North America, *Osmia lignaria* has also been recorded from *Sceliphron* nests.

The tough, persistent nests of mud-dauber wasps and the cells of *Anthophora* and other mining bees are clearly valuable resources for mason bees. Utilization of these nests is geographically widespread in the genera *Osmia*, *Hoplitis*, *Anthocopa* and *Chalicodoma*, suggesting that it has arisen independently many times. It is hardly surprising that these opportunists *par excellence*, the mason bees, should exploit ready-built nests that offer an economy of labour. Moreover, a nest that has successfully protected the development of mud-dauber wasps or *Anthophora* might be considered to have a proven safety record.

SNAIL SHELLS

Empty snail shells, like mud-dauber nests, offer suitable nesting cavities and provide mason bees with a prefabricated home. Indeed, many bee species in at least five genera nest exclusively in old snail shells.

Naturally, these bees are commonest where the snail populations are highest. Snails require large amounts of calcium in their diet in order to secrete their protective shells and are especially common in limestone regions of Eurasia. Chalk downlands and sand dunes are also good habitats for snail-nesting bees. At the coast, the snails feed on plants which obtain their calcium from the breakdown of marine shells.

In the United States, *Osmia conjuncta* and one species of the exclusively American genus *Ashmeadiella* are the only known snail-nesters. There is no obvious explanation for the apparent dearth of snail-nesters in North America; snails are no less common in the New World than in the Old. Likewise, there is only one Japanese snail-nester, *Osmia orientalis*.

The nesting biology of *O. aurulenta* is typical. This species is widespread in Europe and is common in the extensive dune systems of the west coasts of England and Wales. Here it nests in shells of *Cepaea nemoralis* and also uses those of the larger *Helix aspersa*. The bees are 10 mm long and clothed with a dense, golden red covering of hairs, which soon fades to a pale silvery grey. The species is active from late April to late June or early July. Males emerge about a week before the females and seek out empty snail shells. Apparently, a female mates with a male which holds a territory containing a snail shell. This interesting male strategy is discussed in greater detail in Chapter 13.

Having accepted a snail shell from her mate, the female *O. aurulenta* inspects the interior and spends long periods sitting at the nest entrance, occasionally leaving the shell to make short orientation flights. If the shell is upside-down, she rights it before she begins nesting activities. This places the entrance in a position less exposed to the elements.

The bees are often very numerous and at Kenfig Burrows on the Welsh coast we estimated a density of 5133 occupied snail shells per hectare, or 61 per cent of the available shells. In Britain, the number of cells per nest ranges from one to six, while up to ten per shell have been recorded from continental Europe, where larger shells are available.

The bees partition their cells with a mastic of chewed leaves. In Anglesey, this is derived from yellow-horned poppy (*Glaucium flavum*), rest harrow (*Ononis repens*) and creeping willow (*Salix repens*). *Osmia aurulenta* may also use leaves of cultivated strawberries. The females scrape the leaves with their jaws and chew small pieces into a pulp, building up a pellet of material in much the same way that *O. rufa* builds up a pellet of mud.

The bee plugs the completed snail shell nest with a mixture of mastic and relatively unchewed leaves and makes no attempt to conceal it. As in *O. rufa*,

A female mason bee (*above left*), *Chalicodoma siculum*, collects silty sand from a track in Israel. She mixes it with saliva to make a cluster of exposed, durable mud cells on a rock or on the branch of a shrub. She puts the finishing touches to a cell (*above right*) before going on to store food in it.

After foraging at flowers (*above left*), she backs into her cell and uses her hind legs to scrape pollen from her abdominal scopa, depositing it on top of the pasty mixture of pollen and nectar from previous foraging trips. Back at her nest (*above right*), she applies another load of mud to a cell under construction. She has covered completed cells in the background with a protective outer layer of mud, which will eventually cover the whole nest, obscuring the shape of the individual cells (Family: Megachilidae).

the full-grown larva spins a cocoon comprising an outer layer of coarse, thick, brown fibres and an inner, pinkish layer of fine, smooth fibres.

The distribution of sexes in the cells is similar to that of *O. rufa*. The bee achieves this arrangement in the tapering interior of the snail shell by building larger cells, end to end, for females towards the back of the nest, and outer cells, side by side, nearer the mouth, for the males.

As with all solitary bees, the major part of the life span of an individual is spent within its natal nest. However, a nest in a shell lying exposed on the sand is subject to the wide fluctuations in temperature which are characteristic of dunelands. The developing larvae, in particular, must be able to withstand mid-summer surface temperatures of about 36°C (97°F) during the day and then the chilling effects of dew at night. Although severe frosts are rare on the west coast of Britain, we have found live, overwintering adults of *O. aurulenta* in frost covered shells in winter.

The inland species, *O. bicolor*, like the coastal *O. aurulenta*, also constructs leaf mastic nests in snail shells. However, other species use different materials. Several species of *Hoplitis* nest in snail shells; the widespread European species, *H. spinulosa*, uses sheep or rabbit dung as a building material. In southern Britain, it nests in shells of *Cepaea nemoralis* and *C. hortensis*. Another Eurasian species, *Hoplitis sybarita*, uses a mixture of leaf mastic and snail shell fragments as a building material. In Israel, the pan-Mediterranean species, *H. lhotelleriei*, uses the same mixture of building materials in the shells of *Theba pisana*.

Although only distantly related to the *Osmia*-like mason bees, some members of the anthidiine genus *Rhodanthidium* nest in snail shells. *R. septemdentatum* is found throughout the Mediterranean region, the Caucasus and Asia Minor where it nests in the shells of *Theba pisana*, *Helix lucorum* and the Roman snail, *H. pomatia*. The females make cell partitions out of resin and the nest closure comprises a layer of snail shell fragments embedded in resin.

Several snail-nesting species go to great lengths to conceal the shells containing their completed nests. The female of *Osmia bicolor* collects pine needles or stiff pieces of grass, which she piles on top of the snail shell. She glues 20–30 needles together with a sticky secretion, presumably of salivary origin. The pieces are up to five times longer than the bee, and a bee sometimes carries a piece of dry grass nearly a foot long (30 cm). It is not difficult to find the nest by following such a conspicuously laden female.

The bees expend much time and energy on this task, but the covering is washed away by rain and persists for only a few weeks at most. It is ineffectual in concealing the nest from the guild of wasps and bees which prey on the nests of *O. bicolor* because these enemies attack open cells in the process of being provisioned, long before the female covers her nest. Nevertheless, concealment of the nest seems to be important, for the females never omit their little tents of pine needles. We can only suggest that the covering may hide the shell during development of the bees. The potential predators may be thrushes in search of a juicy snail. In support of this, we have seen a songthrush breaking open the unconcealed nest of *O. aurulenta* and consuming the contents.

When the female of *Hoplitis sybarita* has completed her nest, she excavates the sand around the shell until it is eventually buried. Other snail-nesters take different steps to conceal their nests. *Osmia rufohirta* and *O. rufigaster* are widespread in central and southern Europe. Before they start nesting or immediately after the nest is completed, the females of these species transport their shell nests to a safe place, usually a dense grass tussock or a hollow under stone. Before moving the shell, a female sticks patches of leaf mastic to it to provide roughened areas on which her feet can gain purchase. Another Mediterranean snail-nester, *O. tunensis*, also moves her nest. According to the great French naturalist, Charles Ferton, the females use only mud-spattered shells, the mud serving the same purpose as the mastic applied by *O. rufohirta* and *O. rufigaster*. The behaviour of these species led Ferton and others to attribute them with 'intelligent foresight'.

The females of *O. rufohirta* are good mineralogists. They fashion their cell partitions and nest closures from a mixture of leaf mastic and chips of quartz crystals. *O. rufigaster* goes one stage further in the protection of her nest by covering it with a layer of snail shell fragments embedded in a mixture of glutinous leaf mastic. Other Eurasian mason bees which nest in snail shells and use leaf mastic as a building material include *O. balearica*, *O. versicolor*, *O. melanogaster* and *O. ferruginea*.

SURFACE NESTS

The mason bees which build exposed nests on surfaces such as rocks, cliff faces or the branches of shrubs, must use durable, weather-proof materials. Some species use resin but many more use pebbles embedded in a mortar of their own making. A female makes her mortar by mixing saliva with fine silt. The female of the Mediterranean species, *Chalicodoma siculum*, impregnates her mortar with the secretion from the Dufour's gland in her abdomen. This makes the finished mud nest totally water-resistant, so that it is not softened by the infrequent but nevertheless torrential winter rain storms characteristic of the region. The finished nests are extremely tough and can be broken open or prized off the substrate only with great difficulty, even with the aid of a stout knife or chisel.

Species of *Chalicodoma* are, in fact, the best known surface-nesting mason bees in Europe and are familiar to many naturalists through the observations of the Frenchman, Jean Henri Fabre (1823–1915). Fabre was a school master who lived in Serignan, a village in the dry, vineyard country of Provence. His imagination was captured by the wealth of the region's insect life, especially the rich fauna of bees and wasps. His writings are among the classics in the literature of natural history. However, he was not the first to write extensively on mason bees. In 1742, another Frenchman, M. Réaumur, inventor of the thermometer that bears his name, published a detailed account of the nest-building behaviour of a *Chalicodoma* species. Without access to correctly identified museum collections, both Réaumur and Fabre made their own decisions on the names they used for the various species they observed. The species they both knew as *Ch. muraria*, and appropriately called 'Mason Bee of the Walls' in the English translation of Fabre is in fact *Ch. parietinum*. Fabre also studied the biology of *Ch. siculum* ('Mason Bee of the Sheds'). Fabre also describes the biology of two other species of *Chalicodoma*, but there is uncertainty as to their true identity: much of his collection has proved to be inaccurately named.

Chalicodoma parietinum and *Ch. siculum* both make cells with calcareous clay mixed with sand and saliva to make a mortar-like paste. Unlike the Red Mason Bee, *Osmia rufa*, a female *Chalicodoma* does not gather her building material from the damp margins of puddles. Rather, she collects dry material and moistens it with her own saliva, making a pellet which she transports back to the nest. *Ch. parietinum* gathers dry earth rich in small fragments of gravel; *Ch. siculum* collects silt along the margins of tracks and well-trodden paths in sandy areas. Unlike *Ch. parietinum*, this species does not regularly incorporate pebbles into its mortar constructions.

Ch. parietinum is active during April and May. Both sexes are handsome insects. The females are 16–20 mm long and clothed in a dense, sooty black pile, while the wings are a dark, smoky violet. The males are slightly smaller and bear a dense coat of tawny hairs.

The female selects a large stone or the south facing wall of a house on which to build. She then seeks a source of soil and pebbles. According to Fabre, the female first lays a foundation course of mortar, which she gradually builds up in layers, with small, angular pebbles embedded separately on the outer face. The finished cell is a vertical cylinder about 2–3 cm high. On a vertical structure, such as a rocky cliff face or a stone wall, the cell resembles half a thimble. While the outer surface of the cell is rough in texture because of the angular pebbles, the inner surface is smooth, covered with a layer of mortar.

When the cell is built, the bee collects pollen and nectar. On her return, she enters the cell head first and regurgitates honey into the bottom. She then leaves and re-enters backwards in order to scrape off the pollen from her abdominal scopa. She again enters the cell head first to mix the pollen and honey using her mandibles. When the rather runny food store occupies about half the volume of the cell, the female backs into it, and lays an egg on the food. She then leaves to gather material with which to seal the cell. The seal consists of mortar alone.

After completing the first cell, the female builds and provisions several more, following the same pattern. Completed nests comprise six to ten cells. The female then applies a protective coat of mortar over the whole cluster of cells. The coating is about 1 cm thick and completely obscures the outline of the cells. When the outer coat is finished, the whole nest resembles a hemispherical dome about the size of an orange.

The egg hatches in a few days and larval development is rapid. The prepupa spins a thin cocoon and by early July the cell contains a pupa. The adult stage of *Ch. parietinum* overwinters.

The mortar and pebble nests of *Ch. parietinum* are very persistent and females often re-use nests of a previous year before they start building their own. Before re-using an old cell, the female inspects it with much antennation, and clears out the tattered remains of the former occupant's cocoon.

The females of *Ch. parietinum* seem to have a preference for siting their nests on imposing human architecture. We have seen them on ornately carved walls at Schlöss Hellbrun and the Belvedere in Vienna and we have had specimens sent from the Parthenon in Athens, where the females collected their building materials unnoticed at the feet of tourists toiling up a dusty track.

Chalicodoma siculum lives in much of southern Europe and throughout North Africa and is active during April and May. The females are tolerant of each other and nest gregariously in large numbers, up to several thousand at a single site, often on rock heaps or around the bases of fence posts. They often use old cells from previous generations. These are very persistent, being rendered water-resistant by the admixture with mud of a secretion from the Dufour's gland. Females of *Ch. siculum* also sometimes nest in shrubs and trees,

Always opportunists, female mason bees often use nests built by previous generations of their own and other species. Here, a female of a species of *Hoplitis* removes debris from a vacated cell of *Chalicodoma siculum* in Israel (Family: Megachilidae).

building their nests in the crotches of branches and twigs. Wherever the nests are situated, the females always coat the finished cells with a protective layer of mortar and each globular nest is the size of a large walnut.

Britain has only one, rare, mason bee which builds exposed mud nests. *Osmia xanthomelana* is widespread in much of Europe where it is active in May. The nest is made of 3–4 cells arranged in a cluster, in a grass tussock or exposed on a rock or cliff face. The cells are about 15 mm high and made of mud pellets glued together with saliva. The bee adds a lining of smooth mortar to the inner wall of the cell, but the outer surface is left rough.

Another mason bee, *Hoplitis anthocopoides* (*Osmia caementaria* of older literature), makes exposed cells of mud. This bee is widespread in Europe, but not found in Britain. Dr George Eickwort of Cornell University recently found it in New York State. The species is communal in that bees of adjacent nests cooperate in the construction of the final coat of mortar.

The genus *Dianthidium* includes several species from the western United States to central Brazil which build exposed nests out of pebbles and resin. *D. pudicum* constructs nests on rocks or in the crotches of twigs.

GROUND-NESTING MASON BEES

Many of the genera mentioned above have a few species which excavate their own nest burrows and cells in the ground. In a sense, they are mining bees. However, they differ from the majority of the 'true' mining bees of Chapter 4 in that they do not secrete a nest cell lining substance from the Dufour's gland. Instead, they are typical mason bees in that they collect nest building materials from the environment.

Two Eurasian species of *Anthidium* nest in the ground either in pre-existing hollows under stones, abandoned subterranean runs of ant nests or in cavities excavated by the bees themselves at the end of a short tunnel. According to Fabre, *A. laterale* (called *A. quadrilobum* by Fabre) builds a cluster of up to twelve freestanding cells out of resin.

The female incorporates small lumps of dry earth and the heads of ants into the resin. The bees do not decapitate worker ants, but pick up the head capsules from desiccated corpses which abound in the dry Mediterranean habitats where the bees live. They may collect them from middens which build up from time to time near the entrances to ant nests. Ants are fastidious housekeepers and regularly bring out their dead. Presumably, the habit of using tough ant heads became fixed in the nest-building behaviour of *A. laterale* soon after the use of dry pellets of earth: so far as the bee is concerned, both structures are probably similar in their handling.

Species of the primitive megachilid genus *Trachusa* line their underground cells with leaves and resin. There are only four species *T. byssina* lives in Europe and nests gregariously in patches of bare soil in July. The females excavate nearly horizontal tunnels 8–10 cm (3–4 in) long. They line their linear series of cells with strips of willowherb leaves (*Chamaenerion angustifolium*) embedded in an outer wall of resin. The German bee specialist, Dr H. Friese described how he found an aggregation of forty nests of *T. byssina*. Females often returned to their nests carrying pellets of resin 2–3 mm in diameter, clasped between their front legs. They collect pollen from *Lotus corniculatus*.

The three other species of *Trachusa* – *perdita*, *gummifera* and *manni* – live in the western United States and have a similar life history.

Chapter 6

Leaf-cutters

Gardeners are often alarmed in early summer to find circular and oval pieces missing from the leaves of their rose bushes. These excisions betray the activities of leaf-cutter bees, which belong to the genus *Megachile*. Like the mason bees of the previous chapter, they are members of the Megachilidae.

Leaf-cutter bees use pieces of leaf to line their nests. They nest in almost any ready-made cavity, though they prefer beetle tunnels in timber, hollow plant stems and crevices under the bark of dead trees. They also nest in nooks and crannies in old walls and in a range of other man-made structures. We have found nests in garden hoses and door locks, and others have reported nests in the radiators of abandoned motor cars. Someone once sent us a nest of *Megachile* from Kenya, made of *Acacia* leaves built in the nasal sinuses of a wildebeeste skull. A few species of *Megachile* nest in the ground.

Megachile is a cosmopolitan genus with about 1,500 species in both temperate and tropical regions. In the Americas the genus ranges from Alaska to Tierra del Fuego. Despite the diversity of habitats and nest sites exploited by these bees, they differ little in structure and nesting behaviour and are often very difficult to identify.

Two Eurasian species, *Megachile willughbiella* and the slightly smaller *M. centuncularis*, are common from June to August in suburban gardens in Britain. The first species uses the leaves of roses, willowherb, lilac and beech trees to line its cells. The second is called the rose leaf-cutter because of its partiality for rose leaves. It is also common in many parts of North America. It nests in almost any dry cavity in wood, preferring tunnels with a diameter of 7–8 mm. The female is mostly black, with some pale hairs and a bright orange scopa.

There are 118 species of *Megachile* native to North America. The widespread and common ones include *M. coquilletti*, *M. mendica*, *M. relativa*, *M. frigida* and *M. brevis*. Another species, *M. rotundata*, is an important pollinator and has the distinction of being the best known leaf-cutter bee to the American public.

A nest of a leaf-cutter bee, *Megachile centuncularis* (Family: Megachilidae), in a length of bamboo.

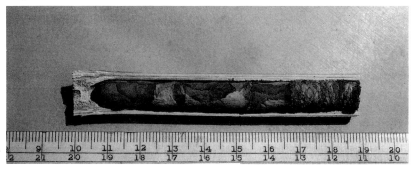

A female *Megachile versicolor* returns with a piece of leaf to the nest she has made in a length of rubber hose in a greenhouse in Warwickshire, England. This unusual nest site reflects the opportunist nature of many megachild bees.

Using her powerful jaws, a female leaf-cutter bee, *Megachile willughbiella*, cuts a piece out of the margin of a rose leaf in an English garden. She lines and partitions her cells with pieces of leaves of appropriate shapes and sizes (Family: Megachilidae).

Having detached a piece of leaf (*above*), the female *Megachile willughbiella* flies off with it gripping the edges to hold it against her body. After removing the piece of rose leaf, she alights briefly (*below*) to adjust her load, pulling it forward to grasp it with her jaws and the first two pairs of legs. It seems that all species of *Megachile* stop to adjust their loads in this way (Family: Megachilidae).

All the species mentioned so far have very similar life histories and the following account is generally applicable.

After a female *Megachile* has mated and found a suitable nest site, she searches for leaves of the correct texture. They must be smooth on at least one side and reasonably stiff. She alights on the leaf and investigates it with her antennae, occasionally nipping the edge of the leaf with her jaws. If the leaf is suitable, she straddles its margin with her legs and rapidly cuts out a piece with her heavily built, toothed jaws, which act like a pair of scissors. She always positions herself with her head pointing towards the base of the leaf and the whole operation takes no more than two or three seconds.

Just before the leaf fragment becomes completely detached, the female vibrates her wings rapidly, so she is already in flight as soon as the leaf is free. She then flies a short distance and lands on the ground, a stone or a tree trunk while she adjusts her load. If the leaf fragment is longer than broad, she uses her feet to fold it lengthways, so she straddles the leaf with its convex surface towards her. She flies back to the nest carrying the leaf in this way.

When a female *Megachile* finds a source of leaf material, she returns to it time and again, so that nearly all of the leaves in a small area of, say, 2–3 sq m (2.4–3.5 sq yd) may have pieces cut out of their margins. We estimate that a nest of *M. willughbiella*, comprising eight cells, uses a total leaf area of 0.5 sq m (5.38 sq ft). Very often, the source of leaves is close to the nest site and collecting trips may take less than a minute.

Female leaf-cutter bees use at least two and sometimes three different shapes of leaf fragment. The first three or four pieces a female brings to the nest are about the same length as the bee herself and are elongate, almost rectangular in shape. She uses these as the foundation lining for the rear of the cell. The female places them at the rear of the nest tunnel, with their ends and sides overlapping to make a cup-like end lining. She sticks the leaf fragments together by crimping the edges of the leaves so that sap oozes out and this, possibly with a glue of salivary origin, acts as an adhesive.

Once the female has lined the rear of the cell, she lines the side walls with oval-shaped leaf pieces which are usually longer than her body. She always positions the leaves so that their smoother, shiny surface faces into the cell. *Megachile* sometimes use hairy leaves, but the hairy surface always faces outwards. If the diameter of the nest tunnel is too large, then the bee uses additional pieces as a loose packing until she achieves the preferred diameter of the species and only then does she stick leaf pieces together to form the rigid, inner lining.

The female next provisions her cell with pollen and honey. The food store of *Megachile* is more liquid than that of most mason bees, with the consistency of a damp paste. It takes the females of *M. centuncularis* and *M. willughbiella* about 18 foraging trips to provision one cell. The completed food mass occupies about two-thirds of the volume of the cell. The female lays an egg on the food and then seals the cell with a series of four to twelve, perfectly circular pieces of leaf. She positions the plug so that the side walls of the cell extend beyond it. Thus, the plug and the protruding side walls of the first cell form the base for the foundation leaf pieces of the next cell. In this way, the female builds a linear series of cells which ultimately occupies the full length of the nest tunnel.

Unlike those mason bees which nest in similar, tubular tunnels, leaf-cutter bees rarely make vestibular cells before they seal the completed nest. The nest closure comprises a compacted series of leaf discs like those used to close a cell. The number of discs varies greatly, but is always more than in a cell closure.

The fact that females of *Megachile* use leaf pieces of different sizes and shapes at different stages in the building of a cell testifies to their high level of behavioural complexity and integration; a female 'knows' where she is at any stage of the process and behaves accordingly.

M. centuncularis and *M. willughbiella* make six to ten cells in a nest. The building, provisioning and sealing of one cell takes six to eight hours, so, assuming good weather, a female can complete only one cell per day. A female spends about four-fifths of her time foraging for pollen and nectar to provision her cells. When at rest, or during the night, the female sits at the nest entrance, facing outwards. She bites any other bees, ants or earwigs which try to enter.

The eggs hatch in 12–16 days and the larvae begin to feed immediately. They defecate after feeding for 6–12 days and spin cocoons after 17–18 days. The cocoon resembles that of the mason bees in that it is made up of two layers, an outer one of thick, coarse fibres, and an inner, membranous layer in a matrix of fine fibres. The larva incorporates faecal pellets into the outer layer of the cocoon which it applies closely to the inner leaf layer of the cell wall.

OTHER SPECIES

In Jamaica, *Megachile concinna* is widespread and relatively common. On the coastal plains it nests all the year round. The bees nest in all manner of places, including cracks in wooden window frames, in old nests of the mud-dauber wasp, *Sceliphron assimile*, and in the tunnels of ship worms, *Teredo*, in driftwood stranded above the tide line. They line their cells with the leaves of Senna and *Cassia* species and the pink bracts of *Bougainvillea* flowers. The bees forage at flowers of heliotrope, *Bidens pilosa*, *Sida* species and *Tribulus cistoides*.

Although the nesting behaviour of leaf-cutter bees varies little between species, there are, nevertheless, some interesting exceptions. *Megachile bombycina*, a Eurasian species, incorporates sawdust into its cell linings from the beetle burrows in which it nests. *M. sericans* mixes a mastic of chewed leaves with leaf pieces to make its cells and *M. analis*, also Eurasian, uses strips of birch bark instead of leaves.

Several species of *Megachile* nest in the ground. *Megachile umatillensis* is widespread in the Western United States, where it nests in light sandy soils, and sometimes in partially stabilized sand dunes. The nest consists of two to four cells built in a tunnel about 28 cm (11 in) long. Each cell has up to 32 pieces cut from the petals of a species of evening primrose, *Oenothera pallida*. The bees do not cap their cells with circular pieces. Instead, they simply fold over long side pieces. The petals overlap loosely and do not appear to be stuck together. In this respect, they resemble the untidy looking cells of another ground-nesting leaf-cutter bee, *Megachile maritima*, found in much of Europe, including Britain.

Megachile oenotherae has a more easterly distribution than *M. umatillensis*, ranging from New Jersey and North Carolina to Oklahoma and Texas. This species nests in the burrows of the mining bee, *Andrena macra*, in sandy soil, and uses *Oenothera laciniata* as a source of both food and cell-building materials. The cell walls are made of pieces of leaves, but the bees use petals to cap each cell.

A few species of *Megachile* depart from the normal nest cell structure. In

Jamaica, *M. zaptlana* makes nests of five to seven cells in beetle borings in timber. They are unusual in that the females make cell partitions of leaf fragments and leave the sides of the cells unlined. The species is active throughout the year.

An American species, *M. policaris*, has further reduced its nest-building activities. Instead of a series of separate cells, the nest consists of a single large brood chamber, the rear of which is sometimes lined with a thin layer of gummy leaf pulp. The bee lays 2–16 eggs, each in a pouch in a more or less continuous food mass. The larvae share their communal food store without any signs of aggression. However, the behaviour of this species is variable, for a female sometimes makes a single cell in which she lays one egg. The partitions between brood chambers comprise layers of whole leaflets separated by thin layers of gummy leaf mastic. Krombein identified leaflets of mesquite (*Prosopis* species), cat claw acacia (*Mimosa biuncifera*) and kidneywood (*Eysenhardtia polystachya*).

THE MIXERS

Creightonella is another genus of leaf-cutting bees, similar in appearance to *Megachile*. Restricted to tropical and warmer parts of the Old World, all known species nest in the ground and use leaves, mud and resin to line the cells.

Females of the African *Creightonella cornigera* excavate a tunnel in a vertical bank. They layer their cell lining as follows: they bond an outer wall of roughly cut leaf fragments with resin to an inner layer of coarsely chewed leaf pulp which is itself lined with an inner layer of black resin. The roughly cut leaf pieces contrast with the neatly shaped work of *Megachile* species.

Layered cell linings are also built by the best-studied species, *Cr. frontalis*, a handsome black bee, with dark, smoky wings. It ranges from the Malay Archipelago to the Solomon Islands. The bees excavate their nests, 40–150 mm deep (0.6–6 in) in clay banks and lawns, and seems especially fond of well-kept tennis courts. Each nest contains up to six near-horizontal cells.

The cell wall comprises three layers: an outer one of 11–16 leaf pieces, a middle layer of well-smoothed mud 0.5–1.5 mm thick and a thin, inner layer of leaves. Internally, the cells are 13–16 mm long and 8–10 mm wide.

The cell closure is a cap with an inner layer of one or two leaf discs, followed by a layer of chewed leaves, then two or three more discs and a final, outer layer of mud or a mixture of mud and leaf mastic.

The females are well adapted to a wet, tropical climate: they continue to cut leaves and to forage in all but the most torrential of downpours. The species is unusual in that the females do not spend the night in their nests. Instead, they sleep on vegetation, hanging from stems by their mandibles. These aggregations of females are often large and sometimes contain males.

Chapter 7
Carpenters

Carpenter bees excavate their own nest tunnels in wood rather than use pre-existing cavities. They use both sound and rotten timber, preferring softwoods, but hardwoods are by no means ignored. Even the softest wood, such as pine, is much tougher than any of the nesting substrates used by the bees mentioned so far and carpenter bees therefore have very powerful jaws. The habit has evolved independently in two unrelated families, the Anthophoridae and the Megachilidae.

Although the wood-boring habit has evolved more than once among bees, carpenter bees have several features in common. Apart from the obvious requirement of strong jaws, the females are much longer-lived than those of other solitary bees; they usually survive long enough to see their own offspring become adult and some even interact socially with their sons and daughters.

Longevity in carpenter bees may be related to the slow, laborious process of excavating burrows in solid wood. It may also be connected with another feature of carpenter bees, the laying of a few, very large eggs. If the excavation

A female carpenter bee (*below left*), *Xylocopa nigrita*, in Kenya, leaves a legume flower with a dusting of pollen on the upper side of her thorax. This is a typical part of the bee's body where large flowers of this family of plants deposit pollen. A male of *Xylocopa nigrita* (*below right*) feeds on nectar on the same species of legume as the previous female. The anthers of the flower swing forward to brush pollen on to his thorax. When he next visits a flower of this species, the pollen will brush on to the stigma, effecting pollination. His very different colouring is typical of the sexual dimorphism found in many species of *Xylocopa* (Family: Anthophoridae).

of cells is very costly in terms of time and energy, then it probably pays a female carpenter bee not to spread her investment too thinly. Some species lay as few as eight eggs and each one represents a much greater proportion of her total investment than that of a bee which lays two or three times this number of smaller eggs. This probably led to the evolution of another behavioural trait, namely the guarding of the unsealed nest until the offspring have completed or nearly completed their development.

THE GIANT CARPENTER BEES: *XYLOCOPA*

There are more than 730 species of *Xylocopa*, the large anthophorid carpenter bees. Most are tropical and subtropical, though a few are found further north. They include some of the largest bees and all have a very similar life cycle. The bees use both sound and rotten wood and some tropical species nest in the hollow internodes of bamboo stems and the petioles of large palm leaves.

Both sexes of many species, like the Eurasian *X. violacea*, are entirely blue-black and have blackish wings. However, there is often considerable sexual dimorphism in colour, with the males entirely clothed in yellow hairs (see photographs on page 83), while conspicuous banding patterns of black with white, yellow or even pale blue are often seen among the females. Both sexes of *Xylocopa* are long-lived.

The structure of *Xylocopa* nests varies little throughout the genus. Generally, a female excavates a tunnel in solid wood, usually a dead branch. The entrance tunnel may be at right angles to the grain of the wood, but the main tunnel runs along the grain. The bee may use the nest of a previous generation, clearing out the remains of cell partitions, dead bees and any remaining pollen.

Several species nest in hollow stems or culms of herbaceous plants (Fig. 26). The female of *X. cyanescens* (recorded as *X. iris* by Dr S.I. Malyshev) protects the nest entrance from the weather by cutting the stem above the nest tunnel and breaking it off to make a kind of lid. In Israel this species builds its nests in the stems of *Ferula gummosa*.

Typically, the *Xylocopa* nest comprises a linear series of cells, the first cell being at the back of the main tunnel. Females of *X. sulcatipes* line their cells with a waterproof secretion from their abdominal glands which presumably pro-

Fig. 26 Nest of the African carpenter bee, *Xylocopa caffra* (Anthophoridae) in a length of bamboo. (Redrawn after Skaife, S.H., 1952, *J. Ent. Soc. S. Africa*, **15**: 63–76.)

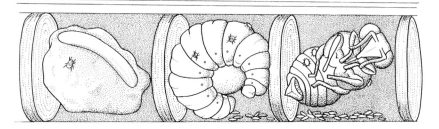

tects the cell contents from desiccation, a potential problem in the desert conditions which the species inhabits. Possibly other species of *Xylocopa* protect their cells in this way.

In a piece of wood there may be two or more parallel tunnels with a few cells in each. On returning to the nest, the female deposits the successive pollen loads at the back of the cell and later sculpts them into an oval mass. The shape of the finished pollen loaf may be characteristic for the species and attached to the cell wall at one narrow point (Fig. 26).

The female then lays her remarkably large egg on the pollen; in many species the egg is more than half the length of the bee. The process of egg-laying has been observed in the Afro-Asian species, *X. pubescens*, using a portable x-ray machine. The bee stands on the pollen loaf, facing the nest entrance, with her abdomen resting along the curve of the loaf. As she lays the egg she walks forward along the length of the pollen loaf. After depositing the egg, the bee seals the cell with a partition of concentric rings of wood fibres scraped from the sides of the tunnel.

In *X. caffra*, a species widespread in southern Africa, the egg hatches after 18 to 21 days and the larva feeds for about 15 days, until it is fully grown. The larva, which does not spin a cocoon, spends about 14 days as a prepupa and pupates over 36 to 40 days. The larva begins to defecate when it is five days old and the mid- and hindgut are therefore united relatively early in these bees.

Before pupating the prepupa faces the rear of the cell, which is the opposite of the situation found in other tunnel-nesting bees. However, the cells of *Xylocopa* are wide enough to allow the adult bee to turn around and make for the entrance. It is not known why the bees pupate facing the rear of the nest.

Female *Xylocopa* guard their offspring against a range of predatory insects and also from other female carpenter bees, which sometimes attempt to take over the nests of others. A successful usurper clears out the nest contents, including the brood, and constructs her own series of cells.

This is a simple outline of the nesting behaviour of a typical female *Xylocopa*, but it does not convey the complexity of the whole life cycle of giant carpenter bees. The nesting behaviour of most of the species which have been studied, encompasses some of the basic elements of social behaviour.

This is true of *X. caffra*, which has only one generation per year and the females live for a year or more. They nest in dry, decayed wood, old fence posts or, sometimes, in dead flower stalks of aloes and *Agave* species, plants introduced from America.

Both sexes emerge in summer, in January and February. Unlike most solitary bees, they do not mate immediately. Instead, the female cleans out the natal nest where she remains until early spring, in September. During this period brothers and sisters occupy the same nest amicably, in what is called a pre-reproductive assemblage.

Probably, as with other species of *Xylocopa*, the ovaries of the females remain undeveloped throughout this eight-month period. Both sexes spend most of their time in the nest, leaving it only intermittently to feed at flowers. Before the males are able to fly, however, their sisters feed them with regurgitated nectar which they have collected.

The males of *X. caffra* make a low, undulating buzzing noise while being fed and they solicit the donation of food by waving their front legs so as to tickle the female on any available part of her body. If the solicited bee is receptive,

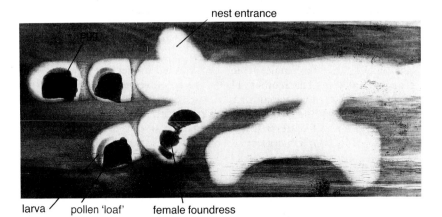

nest entrance

egg

larva   pollen 'loaf'   female foundress

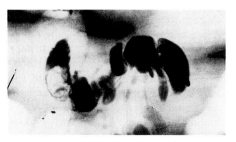

trophallaxis (food exchange) from
mother bee *(right)* to daughter *(left)*

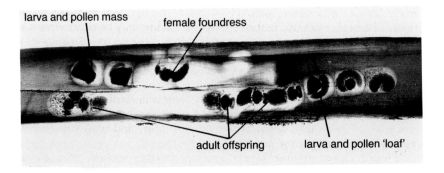

larva and pollen mass   female foundress

adult offspring   larva and pollen 'loaf'

X-ray photographs (*above*) taken in Israel of nests of the carpenter bee, *Xylocopa pubescens*, showing occupants (Family: Anthophoridae). (Courtesy of Professor Dan Gerling, University of Tel-Aviv.)

she lowers her mouthparts so that the male can drink the nectar regurgitated between her jaws. However, the females frequently ignore soliciting males and signal their unwillingness with short bursts of a shrill, piping buzz. The females cease to feed the males as soon as the latter can fly and forage for themselves. In early spring, the females eject their brothers from the communal nest. The males seek hollow stems or old, abandoned nests, where they roost communally.

In late spring, the females which were united in ejecting their brothers, become intolerant of each other. The most aggressive one of them succeeds in ousting her sisters and remains as the sole occupier of the natal nest. The fighting between females consists of butting inside the nest and never results in injury. The ousted females finally leave and seek nest sites of their own.

Occasionally, two females remain, but each provisions her own cells, sometimes extending one or more of the nest tunnels. There is no cooperation between them.

At about this time, the males adopt territories near the flowers where the females forage. They spend much of their time hovering in the territory, interrupted by agitated, darting flight. They maintain their territories during October and November, when mating takes place and the females begin to nest. By the end of December and the beginning of January, the males die and the females remain with their nests until just before the offspring are ready to emerge and begin a new cycle.

The first individuals to emerge break down the cell partitions and crawl over their nest mates until they reach the nest entrance, where they wait. Eventually, all the newly adult bees emerge and they then clean the nest of old cell partitions, faeces, dead larvae, pupae and adults, tossing this and any other debris out of the nest entrance. And so a new generation of brothers and sisters enters the communal stage.

In North America, x-ray techniques have been used to study behaviour of *Xylocopa virginica* within the nest. They showed there is a long juvenile stage in which brothers and sisters of the summer emergence remain with their natal nests through autumn and winter, occasionally leaving on warm days to feed at flowers. Some of the females, however, do not leave the nest. Instead, they feed on pollen provided by other females.

In addition to the newly emerged males and females, there may be one or more females of the same generation as their mother, that remain with the nest. These older females, in their second year of life, may be either virgins, or they may have mated the previous spring. In either case, they will not have nested, but will have remained with the nest of a sister. The overwintering community therefore comprises a female in her second year and her nephews and nieces in their first year.

In March and April, the males leave the nest voluntarily, set up territories near the nest site and mate with most of the females. By the end of May, the males die. The females begin to nest in early May, and most females have finished egg-laying by the middle of the month.

There are usually two or three females associated with a nest, although only one excavates, provisions cells and lays eggs. The egg-layer is an older female in her second year and the non-layers are likely to be her nieces. The nieces guard the nest while their aunt is away on foraging trips. They contribute to the welfare of their aunt's offspring, presumably because some of these nieces may remain in the natal nest the next year, when they will be egg-layers themselves. Although four or five females overwinter together, only two or three remain with the nest to found or guard a new generation of offspring. Thus, one or two females leave each spring to set up new nests of their own, without the help of non-breeding guard bees.

Xylocopa virginica regularly reuses nests of previous seasons. However, the continual extension of nest tunnels weakens a branch, which may eventually break off.

In Israel, *X. pubescens* has a similar life history in that a nest community comprises an older, egg-laying female and a small, temporary group of virgin females, which act as guards. However the association in *X. virginica* is between aunt and nieces, whereas in *X. pubescens* it is between mother and daughters. The mother continues to provision cells and lay eggs after the first three or four daughters become adult and break down their cell partitions. The daughters (and sons) remain in a teneral state for up to two weeks. That is, their wings remain soft, they cannot fly and their gonads are undeveloped.

During this time, one of the daughters defends the nest against intruders when the mother is absent on foraging trips. There seems to be a dominance hierarchy among the daughters, because the same one is on guard for most of the time. Where there is a shortage of suitable timber in which to nest, especially in the semi-desert areas, guarding is an adaptation to prevent seizure of the nest by other females which have failed to find nest sites of their own. Guarding also helps to protect the nest from the several predatory flies, beetles and wasps which attack the larvae of *Xylocopa*.

The nest guards, therefore, defend the nest and protect the developing brood. However, this is not without cost to the mother. When she returns to the nest, the guard allows her into the main tunnel, but blocks her passage to the cell being provisioned. Sometimes the guard is aided and abetted by some of her sisters. The mother may charge her daughters vigorously or try to take an alternative route to the cell. Usually, they prevent their mother from proceeding until she has regurgitated some nectar to feed them by direct, mouth-to-mouth contact (trophallaxis).

The degree of relationship between the egg layer and guards in *Xylocopa* is of particular importance in understanding the evolution of social behaviour in bees and we discuss this in Chapter 9.

DWARF CARPENTER BEES: *CERATINA* AND *PITHITIS*

The dwarf carpenter bees belong to the same subfamily as *Xylocopa*, but superficially look very different. They are rather flattened in appearance and range in length from 3–15 mm. The solitary species belong to the genera *Pithitis* and *Ceratina*, the latter also containing primitively social species. Dwarf carpenter bees are relatively hairless, dark in colour, though there are some strikingly metallic ones. Most species have pale ivory or yellow markings on the front of the head.

They excavate their nest tunnels in the soft pith of plant stems, tending to favour weedy plants associated with disturbed ground. Many species nest in the stems of bramble, *Rubus* spp. and the stalks of sunflowers, *Helianthus* spp. Because these bees are small, without powerful mandibles, the females nest only in stems which have had their ends broken off to expose the soft pith. Some species nest in stems damaged by bush fires.

Species of *Ceratina* live in Eurasia and in both North and South America, with most species being found in warm areas; the Mediterranean region is a centre of diversity. *Pithitis* is restricted to the Old World.

The life histories of solitary *Ceratina* species are similar. A mated female overwinters in a cavity she has excavated for a short distance into a pithy stem. The cavity is called, appropriately enough, an hibernaculum. The following spring, the female burrows deeper into the stem and provisions a linear series of about six cells. Each cell is separated from its neighbours by a partition of pith mixed with saliva. The female scrapes the pith from the walls of the nest tunnel. Some, possibly all, species line the walls of the cells with a waxy secretion from glands in the second and third segments of the abdomen. The food store in each cell is a loaf-shaped pollen mass, sometimes attached to the cell wall by a short stalk.

The female of *Ceratina* remains with the nest until her offspring are fully mature. She faces inwards and blocks the nest entrance with her down-curved abdomen. Some species defend their nests with the aid of a strong-smelling secretion from the mandibular glands. The smell has been likened to that of the crushed leaves of Lombardy poplar.

The innermost and oldest of the offspring emerges first and makes its way towards the nest entrance, pushing cell partitions and undeveloped bees to the back of the nest. The bees continue to emerge in age sequence and repeat this behaviour so that, eventually, all the adult bees are lined up in reverse order just behind the nest plug. That is, the sequence of bees is the opposite to that of the cells in which they developed. They thus form a pre-reproductive assemblage, rather like the giant carpenter bees, *Xylocopa* spp. Bees from nests constructed in late summer remain in this position through the winter. Their mothers die on guard duty, but the offspring are protected by the nest closure.

Some species have two generations per year and the offspring of the first remain in line behind the nest closure for about two weeks before they break down the final pith barrier and join their mother at the nest entrance. The females disperse, mate and establish nests of their own. Often, one female will remain and use her natal nest.

Ceratina cyanea is the only species of dwarf carpenter bee in Britain, where it is rather uncommon, nesting in bramble stems in the south. It is common and widespread in Europe, where there are 26 other species. One of them, *C. dallatorreana*, is also found in the western United States, where it was presumably introduced via accidentally transported nests. It is ironical that another dwarf carpenter bee was deliberately introduced into California from India, with no apparent success. *Pithitis smaragdula* is an important pollinator of leguminous crops and cucurbits in India and it was introduced into America in the hope that there it would increase seed-set in the same crops.

The American populations of *Ceratina dallatorreana* are unusual in that males are extremely rare and most females are able to lay fertile eggs without mating, that is, by parthenogenesis. In all Hymenoptera, males result from unfertilized eggs, but in *C. dallatorreana*, females, too, develop in this way. A few chalcids and other parasitic wasps and some sawflies have this ability. In bees, apart from *C. dallatorreana*, it is known only in a peculiar race of the honeybee, *Apis mellifera capensis*, found in the temperate, southernmost tip of South Africa.

In addition to *Ceratina dallatorreana*, there are 20 species of *Ceratina* native to North America. In the Old World tropics, there are many species of dwarf carpenter bees in genera such as *Allodape*, *Allodapula*, *Braunsapis* and *Exoneurella*. These are social bees and we discuss them in Chapter 9.

THE MEGACHILID CARPENTERS: *LITHURGUS*

In the Megachilidae, species of the genus *Lithurgus* are carpenter bees. They look very like the leaf-cutter bees, *Megachile* spp. There are 27 species, three in Europe and North Africa, four in sub-Saharan Africa, one in Japan and eleven in Australia. There are eight species in North America, including *Lithurgus chrysurus*, which was accidentally introduced from Europe into the eastern United States. Another species, *L. huberti*, although described from specimens collected in Brazil, belongs to an Old World species group and was probably introduced into South America in recent times via infested wood. Dr C.D. Michener has noted that this species is indistinguishable from the Old World species *L. atratus*. Their nesting biologies are very similar. The best known species is *L. fuscipennis*, which lives in continental Europe and which was studied by the Russian entomologist, the late S.I. Malyshev. An American species, *L. apicalis*, was studied by Drs F.D. Parker and H.W. Potter. The related genus *Trichothurgus* has eleven species in South America, but nothing is known of their nesting biology.

Both *Lithurgus fuscipennis* and *L. apicalis* nest in sound or slightly rotten wood and excavate short tunnels which radiate rather like the fingers of a hand. The female builds a series of cells in each tunnel. *L. apicalis* nests in dead branches and logs of cottonwood and is regarded as a pest in some areas of Arizona, where it burrows into doorposts. In Japan, *L. collaris* nests in weathered cypress wood.

The food store of *Lithurgus* is dough-like in consistency. *L. fuscipennis* collects pollen from knapweeds, *Centaurea* spp. Several species from both the Old and New Worlds have distinct preferences for flowers which produce very large pollen grains. Thus, in the United States, *Lithurgus apicalis* and three other species visit cacti such as *Opuntia* and *Echinocactus*; in Japan, *Lithurgus collaris* collect the large-grained pollen of the mallow family, Malvaceae.

The female of *Lithurgus* lays an egg in a chamber excavated in the pollen mass and she thus resembles that of the fideliine bees and *Osmia californica* (Chapter 5). She does not seal the cell with a conventional partition. Instead, she builds a temporary barrier out of loose chips of wood scraped from the sides of the nest burrow. When the larvae of adjacent cells begin to grow and move about their cells, they break down the barriers, so that they end up sharing a common brood chamber, not unlike that of *Megachile policaris* (Chapter 6).

The females of *Lithurgus apicalis* line the outer surface of the cell barriers with honey. They are unusual for *Lithurgus* in that they plug the nests with wood fibre, faeces and other debris from previous generations which have used the burrows. According to the Japanese entomologist, Dr K. Iwata, other species apparently do not seal the nest, but leave it open, with the female remaining on guard until her offspring are mature.

Chapter 8
Other Solitary Bees

In the last two chapters we saw that some mason and leaf-cutter bees subvert our simple classification of nesting types by excavating nests in the ground. Thus, they are both miners and masons or leaf-cutters. There are many other bee species which do not readily fit into our scheme of things and they are the subjects of this chapter.

CARDER BEES

> There is a sort of wild bee frequenting the garden campion for the sake of its tomentum, which probably it turns to some purpose in the business of nidification.

Thus wrote the Rev. Gilbert White in his celebrated *Natural History of Selborne* (1795, p. 348). Although he did not know the identity of the bee he observed, he was correct in surmising that it was gathering the down from leaves of garden campion, *Lychnis chalcedonica*, for building purposes.

The bee in question was *Anthidium manicatum*, the common carder bee of Britain and Europe. Both sexes are black, and liberally marked with yellow. It nests in a variety of ready-made cavities, including beetle burrows in dead wood and the tunnels in tree trunks made by caterpillars of the Goat moth, *Cossus ligniperda*. Females also nest in the hollow stems of plants and the soft mortar of old walls. Other nest sites we have come across include compost-filled plant pots and a lead water pipe. This species is yet another megachilid opportunist and it is not surprising that its nesting habits have led to its accidental spread to the United States and several countries in South America, including Brazil. In North America, *Anthidium callosum* has a similar nesting biology.

Anthidium manicatum builds a linear row of cells, each one being lined and partitioned with cottony down 'carded' from hairy leaves. The term 'carder' refers to the teasing out or carding of woollen or cotton fibres with a comb-like tool. The female of *A. manicatum* has five sharp teeth on each jaw and these are her carding tools. The bees collect the flock from the downy leaves of lamb's ears (*Stachys lanata*), hedge woundwort (*S. sylvatica*), cultivated Scottish thistle (*Onopordon acanthium*) and mullein (*Verbascum thapsus*). When collecting a load of down, the bee walks slowly backwards, shearing off the hairs with her jaws, leaving a bald trail up to 50 mm long and about 0.3 mm wide. She gathers the flock into a ball with her mid- and fore-legs, pressing it against the underside of her abdomen, which she arches forward between the legs. Often she readjusts the ball while hovering, before flying back to the nest.

A load of flock weighs about 1.4 mg and may be nearly as big as the bee herself. It takes her six or seven loads to make one cell. When lining a cell, she presses a portion of the flock against the sides of the tunnel with her head and cards it by repeatedly pushing in her jaws and then opening them to tease out the fibres over the cell wall.

It takes a female about 40 minutes to line a cell. She next begins to forage for food, but before leaving the nest she usually pulls some flock over the front of the cell, possibly to protect it against intruding ants and earwigs.

A female makes 19 or 20 foraging trips to provision a cell. The stored food is a viscous, liquid mixture of pollen and honey. A female spends up to $7\frac{1}{2}$ hours gathering food for a cell. Thus, with the forty minutes it takes to line a cell with flock, a completely provisioned cell is the result of a little more than eight hours' work. Weather permitting, a female may be able to complete one cell per day. At night, she rests just inside the nest entrance, facing inwards, with her abdomen curved down to block the entrance. When she has completed a cell and laid an egg in it, the female closes it with a plug of flock. She closes a completed nest in the same way. She may then add grass, twigs, grit or pellets of dry soil to the nest closure.

The eggs and subsequent larvae are more than half submerged in the liquid food mass. The egg hatches in about 12 to 18 days and the larvae begin to defecate at about day 14. After 23 days the larva spins an oval cocoon which is twice as long as broad, with a very small nipple at the front end.

Our attention was drawn to one nest in a Warwickshire garden, where a female *Anthidium manicatum* had built between the overlapping horizontal slats of a wooden garden fence. The full length of the nest was visible from the top of one of the slats when the female had finished it. She then collected small pebbles and pellets of dry earth and dropped them through the gap, one by one, until the nest was completely obscured. This was an extension of normal nest-closing behaviour and shows that the behaviour of female solitary bees is sufficiently plastic to be able to cope with unusual situations.

Many more species of *Anthidium* and related genera are to be found in the warmer, drier parts of the world. The Mediterranean, Middle East and arid areas of the south-western United States are centres of diversity for these bees.

A. florentinum, found in central and southern Europe, nests in rushes and lines its cells with the fluffy down of dandelion seed heads, *Taraxacum* spp. The dandelion seeds are often still attached when the female applies the down to her cell wall. This species also uses light, downy feathers as a lining material. According to the Russian entomologist, S.I. Malyshev, females of *Anthidium florentinum* often use old nests of the previous generation. They do not bite away or clear out the remains of the cell partitions, but merely push their way through any available opening. *A. diadema*, another European species, uses dead, dry leaves and stems rather than the downy substances preferred by other carder bees.

In Africa, the tiny black and yellow carder bees of the genus *Micranthidium* build downy nests attached to the underside of leaves. The nest is made of a mass of dense flock, composed of plant hairs, roughly square in outline, with sides 2.5 cm long and about 6 mm (0.23 in) thick.

Another African species, *Serapista denticulata*, makes impressive, exposed nests built on and around twigs. Both sexes are blue-black. Unlike the pigmented spots of the carder bees mentioned so far, the pale markings of *S. denticulata* are patches of dense, short, velvety hairs. Dr Charles D. Michener has examined a nest of this species in Malawi which contained eleven cells. Apparently, the bee first constructs the outer envelope of greyish white down, so densely woven as to give the appearance and texture of felt. She weaves animal hairs into this felt layer. The envelope is 8.5 cm (3.3 in) long and tapers toward each end. Within the chamber the bee next constructs up to eleven cells of white down, without animal hairs. The cells are roughly vertical, with walls 1–3 mm thick. Internally, the cells are 13–15 mm long and 8–10 mm wide. The yellow, pasty provisions are packed tightly into the bottom of each cell.

TERMITE NESTERS

Chalicodoma pluto is the largest, and until recently one of the most enigmatic of bees. With a body length of up to 39 mm, a wingspan of 63 mm, only the largest of the giant carpenter bees (*Xylocopa* spp.) rival the female of this species in size. No other bee has so large a head, which is 13 mm wide, and boasts jaws worthy of a stagbeetle. The female is clothed with a velvety black pile, with white hairs on the lower half of the head and on the first abdominal segment.

Until recently, the species was known from only two specimens. One was collected in the 1850s on the island of Bacan (= Batchian in older atlases) in the Moluccas group of islands at the eastern end of the Malay Archipelago. The collector was the famous Victorian naturalist, Alfred Russell Wallace. Recent reports of forestry activities on Bacan gave rise to concern that the bee might become extinct before yielding up the secrets of its biology. However, an American biologist, Adam Messer, has found populations of *Ch. pluto* on another Moluccan island, Halmahera and has established that the bee still survives on Bacan, in remnants of the original forest. Messer also found the hitherto unknown males. These are smaller than the females, being 25–30 mm long.

The nesting biology of *Ch. pluto* turns out to be as remarkable as its appearance. We are grateful to Adam Messer for allowing us to quote his information, which was laboriously gathered under trying conditions.

The females of *Ch. pluto* nest in association with colonies of wood-eating termites, a species of *Microcerotermes*. The termite nests are built of carton-like material made of cellulose cemented together with saliva. This is a light but durable material and the termites usually build their nests attached to the trunks and branches of forest trees. The females of *Chalicodoma pluto* burrow into the termite carton. Each nest consists of a horizontal entrance tunnel and a vertical main tunnel. The bees excavate their large cells off the main tunnel.

The main nest tunnel is wide enough for two females to pass one another and more than one female may share a nest. Messer found several such nests, the largest of which was shared by six females. Of the 157 cells, 24 contained larvae or pupae and three cells were open and being provisioned. The remainder of the cells were sealed up and abandoned.

At the very least, *Ch. pluto* may be communal, that is, nesting bees share a common nest entrance and main tunnel, but each builds and provisions her own cells without cooperation. However, there were twice as many nesting bees as open cells so the species may be quasisocial or subsocial (See Chapter 9). Only further research will clarify this question.

The bees line the main nest burrow and their cells with a mixture of resin and wood chips. Their huge jaws are an adaptation for this task: just how the bees collect resin is a good example of how natural selection can shape two or more body parts to function together in a specialized role. The jaws are not the

The world's largest bee, a female of Wallace's giant mason bee, *Chalicodoma pluto*, from the Moluccan island of Bacan. This is the type specimen, collected by Alfred Russell Wallace and housed in the Oxford University Museum (Family: Megachilidae).

only structures which are unusually developed. The labrum, too, is greatly expanded into a triangular flap between the bases of the jaws. A female lands at a wound or fissure in a tree trunk which oozes resin. She scrapes together a small ball of resin with her jaws. Then she walks forward, compressing the ball of resin against the labrum. She repeats this procedure until she has accumulated a ball of resin approximately 5 mm in diameter. The expanded labrum exerts tension on the load, preventing it from dropping out while the female flies with it back to the nest.

Each cell lining is 1.5 mm thick on side walls and up to 4 mm thick at the base. The resin is white when collected and applied, but blackens with age. The females also gather chips of wood, which they use as a filler to extend the resin, in much the same way that builders may add gravel to cement. A completed cell containing a male was 33 mm long and about 15–18 mm wide. One built for a female was 42–44 mm long and 18–22 mm wide.

Analyses of pollen taken from cells show that the females of *Ch. pluto* collect pollen from a wide range of flowering plant families, but the rose (Rosaceae) and eucalyptus families (Myrtaceae) are dominant. When the food store occupies about half the volume of the cell, the female lays an egg on it. The egg is pearly white and about 7 mm long. The female then seals the cell with a cap 5.5 mm thick, made of resin and wood chips.

When fully grown, the larva spins an amber-coloured, papery cocoon. This is thinner and more delicate than the coarse cocoons normally spun by mason bees. Presumably, a thicker cocoon is unnecessary with the protection afforded by the tough resin lining the cell.

The females of *Ch. pluto* often reuse vacated cells of a previous generation. They apply a new layer of resin within the cocoon of the previous occupant. Thus, in sectional view, a reused cell is easily recognized because of the double thickness of resin, the two resin layers being separated by a thin, amber layer representing the original cocoon. Because of the large difference in size between the sexes of *Ch. pluto*, it is likely that when reusing an old cell a female builds a smaller male cell inside a larger vacated female cell.

By excavating nests in the substance of termite nests, females of *Ch. pluto* probably gain substantial protection for their provisions and brood from the high humidities prevalent in the forests of tropical South East Asia. Wallace's giant mason bee is a very impressive animal and it is reassuring that it still survives in the Moluccas. Let us hope that enough forest land is left intact so that the association between bee and termite may endure; we have much more to learn about them.

Some South American species of *Centris* also associate with the nests of termites. They excavate their nests in the compacted clay forming the termite mound. They include *C. thoracicus*, *C. sponsa* and *C. derasa*. Their larvae spin tough cocoons which are strong enough to withstand the attacks of termite workers.

MASKED BEES

Masked bees belong to the Colletidae. This family consists largely of mining bees such as *Colletes* and *Ptiloglossa* (Chapters 3 and 4). The masked bees are placed in a separate subfamily, the Hylaeinae.

Rather few of these species are mining bees. Instead, they resemble the opportunist Megachilidae, the masons and leaf-cutters (Chapters 5 and 6), and nest in pre-existing cavities. But there the resemblance ends. They do not collect substances from outside the nest to use for building, as do the mason and leaf-cutter bees. Rather, they secrete their own cell linings, either from the Dufour's gland or, possibly, from the enlarged thoracic salivary glands; the exact source is unknown. As in *Colletes*, the cell linings are transparent, like cellophane.

Masked bees are so-called because both sexes are largely black, with distinct patches of white, ivory or orange pigment on the front of the head. These pale markings are always more extensive in the males than in the females; in the latter, pale markings are usually restricted to a pair of wedge-shaped flashes, one on either side of the face.

The principal genus is *Hylaeus* (= *Prosopis* of older literature), which is world-wide and has many species. It is the only hylaeine genus in the Americas and Eurasia. They are all relatively hairless and many species are small and slender. Australia has the greatest diversity of hylaeine bees, with at least 320 species in eleven genera. Many Australian hylaeines are associated with the flowers of *Eucalyptus*.

Although they have the short, blunt, bilobed tongue characteristic of the Colletidae, the females differ markedly from all other nesting species of bees: they do not have specialized hairs for the transport of pollen. Instead, they swallow their pollen, which is mixed with nectar in the crop. On return to the nest, the female regurgitates the runny mixture into the cell. The Eurasian species *Hylaeus cornutus* is an exception. It does transport pollen externally, but not on the hind legs. The female of this species carries pollen in a large bowl-shaped concavity on the front of its head, between two projecting horns.

In the absence of a pollen scopa, *Hylaeus* and its relatives resemble the cuckoo bees (Chapter 14), which have secondarily lost these structures because they have no use for them. The females of *Hylaeus*, however, almost certainly never had them and their absence is therefore a primitive character. Indeed, the absence of pollen scopae contributes much to the wasp-like appearance of *Hylaeus*, which led some early authors to classify them as sphecid wasps.

The ready-made cavities used as nest sites by hylaeines include beetle borings in dead wood, the hollow stem of dock, reeds and abandoned insect galls. *H. communis* is common in Britain and Europe and the females forage at the flowers of bramble (*Rubus* spp.) and hogweed (*Heracleum sphondylium*). We have found nests in the stems of hogweed and the reeds of roofing thatch. In North America, where there are 50 species, *H. mesillae* is widespread and nests in pithy twigs of plants such as *Symphoricarpos* spp. The females have been recorded from more than 120 species of flowering plant.

If the females of *Hylaeus* are generalists in their sources of pollen, a few are specialists in their choice of nest site. Thus, *H. confusus*, common in southern Britain and Europe, nests in vacated oak marble galls, which are caused by the gall wasp *Andricus kollari*. The bee builds cells in the feeding chambers and exit burrows formed by the wasp.

Hylaeus pectoralis is another, extreme specialist, found in southern Britain and Europe. This bee nests exclusively in old galls induced in the flower heads of the reed *Phragmites communis*, by larvae of the chloropid fly, *Lipara luscens*.

Hylaeus signatus is one Eurasian species which does nest in the ground. In southern England, we know of two disused sandpits, where females of this species excavate burrows in the vertical cliffs of the old workings. They not only excavate their own burrows, making a linear series of cells, but also use the old nest tunnels of *Colletes daviesanus*, even to the extent of adding their own cell lining to the old lining of the *Colletes* cell. *Hylaeus signatus* is very widespread and extends into desert areas of North Africa and Israel, where, as in western Europe, it forages only at flowers of various species of mignonette, *Reseda* spp.

Chapter 9

The Road to Sociality

At its simplest, social behaviour in bees involves a female living long enough to guard her eggs and feed her larvae. A next step involves two or more females sharing a nest and cooperating in the rearing of their young. Social behaviour of one sort or another has arisen so often among the bees that it is clearly very important. Indeed, it has evolved independently at least eight times in the bees, twice in the wasps, and once each in the ants and termites.

All species of termites and ants are highly social, so we can only guess at the evolutionary stages they underwent. But when we turn to bees, the trail is still warm: many life styles persist which are intermediate between the extremes of the solitary bees and the highly social honeybees and their allies. These intermediate life styles give us clues as to how sociality may have evolved among the bees, but they do not necessarily indicate which pathways led to particular types of social behaviour in particular species.

The bees with these interesting, intermediate levels of sociality belong to three families, the Halictidae, Anthophoridae, and Apidae. Only in some of the Apidae has sociality reached permanent and sophisticated levels.

THE KINDS OF SOCIALITY

In discussing the stages of sociality intermediate between the solitary and highly social states, entomologists have inevitably defined a confusing number of behavioural categories. As we shall see, the confusion is compounded by the fact that the colonies of some species pass through several kinds of social organization during their establishment and growth and, in some circumstances, may revert to simpler levels of organization.

The first, minimum step towards sociality is mutual tolerance between two or more females. Even genera of strictly solitary bees such as *Colletes*, *Andrena*, *Dasypoda* and *Chalicodoma*, which nest in dense aggregations or villages (Chapter 3), show this trait to some extent.

COMMUNAL NESTS

Occasionally, several female bees share a common nest entrance, although each bee has her own individual group of cells within the nest. This situation is not unlike that in an apartment block, where many occupants share a common groundfloor entrance, but each has his or her own suite of rooms. Bees with this very simple level of sociality are said to be communal. Despite their proximity, communal females do not cooperate, and do not normally tolerate other females near their cells. In almost all respects, therefore, they resemble solitary bees, differing only in their mutual tolerance within a shared burrow system. Mason bees, such as *Osmia rufa*, may form communal associations in which several females share a cavity, each with its own cluster of cells.

Many species are only occasionally communal, with most individuals being strictly solitary. *Andrena scotica*, a common and widespread Eurasian species, is a good example. Communal nests of this species in Britain have 9 to 16 females. In North America, two females of *A. erythronii* occasionally share a communal nest, as do those of *Nomia punctulata* in Japan and *Eucera longicornis* in western Europe.

The factors which lead some females to associate in this way and others of the same species to remain solitary are unknown. In some circumstances, a local shortage of soil exposures of suitable texture may be important. With some species, such as the South American halictid *Augochloropsis diversipennis*, a communal association of two or three females results from individuals remaining with their natal nests, extending the burrow system and excavating their own cells.

In some bees, the communal habit is a fixed characteristic of the species. Thus all known populations of the Eurasian *Andrena bucephala* and *A. ferox* are communal. A nest of *A. bucephala*, studied near Oxford in southern central England, contained 234 females. Curiously, twelve females of the closely related *A. scotica* shared the nest too. The nest was active for about four weeks, with heavy traffic of outgoing and incoming foragers at the nest entrance. This and several other neighbouring nests of *A. bucephala* were perennial, persisting for at least four years. That is, the single generation of each succeeding year used the same nest entrance and probably many of the same tunnels as previous generations. On continental Europe, communal nests of *A. ferox* may contain more than 2,000 females.

In communal nests, the females, being of the same generation, are sisters. As we shall see, the levels of kinship between nestmates is crucial to our understanding of how social behaviour is maintained in colonies of bees.

QUASISOCIAL BEES

A quasisocial colony of bees is impossible to distinguish visually from a communal one: all the observer sees are several to many female bees using a common nest entrance, all of them foraging for nectar and pollen. Only by examining the nest contents can one see how they differ.

Like communal bees, all the females belong to the same generation, and are mated; they have enlarged, functioning ovaries and are therefore egg layers. The main difference lies in the number of open, incomplete cells. At any given time, there are fewer cells being built and provisioned than there are bees. In other words, the building, lining and provisioning of a cell involves the work of more than one female. With this simple level of cooperation, we have the beginnings of true sociality. However, only one female gets to lay an egg in any one cell.

In Chapter 3, we saw that a solitary female performs a stereotyped sequence of behaviours in making a cell, provisioning it and laying an egg: the completion of a particular task is the stimulus for beginning the next one in the sequence. We suggest that in quasisocial and other primitively social bees, this sequence of behaviours is less fixed and the bees are more flexible: a female is stimulated to perform a particular task when she finds a cell requiring a particular piece of work. For example, if a female with a full Dufour's gland encounters an incompletely lined cell, then she is stimulated to add some lining material to it. With this scheme, it does not greatly matter if a female works on a particular cell, but does not get to lay an egg in it. Other things being equal, she can be sure that when she does lay an egg in a cell, she will have not done all the work on that cell. We can call this 'delayed reciprocal altruism'.

There are relatively few good examples of quasisocial bees. It is thought that some Indian species of *Nomia* are quasisocial. The French entomologist, E.P. Deleurance, described how he found three females of a mason bee, *Osmia emarginata* which, between them, built 23 cells out of leaf mastic, 21 of which were sealed, each with an egg. This was almost certainly a quasisocial group of females.

Species of *Exomalopsis*, a genus in the family Anthophoridae are probably quasisocial. The bees are common in tropical regions of the New World and several species reach the United States. In a common Jamaican species, *E. globosa*, a nest contains up to 19 adult females that are only vaguely divided into egg-layers and non-egg-layers; all act as workers. There is no queen as such and the bees are probably sisters, daughters, and nieces.

It is possible that species of Central and South American orchid bees are quasisocial. In Costa Rica, the American entomologist, R.B. Roberts, found an association of eight females of the large, brilliantly metallic green *Euglossa imperialis*. All had enlarged ovaries and the nest contained fewer than eight open cells, which is strongly suggestive that they were being cooperatively provisioned and that the bees were quasisocial.

Because quasisocial colonies are rarely reported, it is possible that they are more usually a temporary stage in the development of colonies with higher levels of sociality.

SEMISOCIAL BEES

As with communal and quasisocial bees, semisocial colonies comprise a group of females of the same generation. Although the bees are outwardly identical, if one examines the ovaries of females from such a nest the differences are immediately apparent. Some females have enlarged, active ovaries and are egg layers; others have slender ovaries, and rarely lay eggs. Some of the latter may also be unmated. Often, there is only one cell being built or provisioned at a time, so there is cooperation between individuals. But the main difference here is the beginnings of a division of labour: a caste of egg-layers which do little or no foraging, and a caste of foragers which do little or no egg laying. It is possible that for an individual bee these roles are not fixed. It is also likely that semisocial colonies may, from time to time, become quasisocial and vice versa. Even species such as *Augochloropsis diversipennis*, which are sometimes communal, may occasionally have semisocial nests.

Although being semisocial seems to be an option for species which are normally communal or quasisocial, there are some species for which semisociality is the norm. Examples are the large, metallic halictid mining bees of the genus *Pseudaugochloropsis* and *Augochloropsis sparsilis*, both from the neotropics. As we shall see, colonies of other, primitively social halictids, go through a semisocial phase during the course of their development.

So, our first three categories of primitive sociality are superficially similar, at least in comprising associations of females from the same generation. They are often referred to as being 'parasocial', a convenient collective term. The new generation of females in a parasocial colony usually overwinter in their natal nests and remain with them in the following season. In tropical areas, there may be two or more generations per year, with little or no overlap between them. In either case, a proportion of females in a new generation leave their natal nests and excavate new ones of their own, where they may be joined later by other females.

SUBSOCIAL BEES

A subsocial colony is a family group comprising a female bee and her immature offspring. She guards her eggs and feeds the larvae progressively when they hatch from the eggs. Typically, the mother dies when the offspring become adult. A subsocial nest differs from parasocial nests in that there is direct association between the adult females and the immature stages of the next generation, in the form of some sort of maternal care.

The dwarf carpenter bees of the anthophorid tribes Ceratinini (*Ceratina* spp.) and Allodapini (e.g. *Allodape* and *Exoneurella* spp.) are among the best-studied examples of subsocial bees. Members of both groups nest in pithy stems. Female *Ceratina* partition their cells with pith, while those of the allodapines have open-plan nests, without partitions.

We saw in Chapter 7 that females of solitary species of *Ceratina* remain with their nests as guards. Subsocial species such as *C. japonica* and *C. calcarata*, take things one step further: a female regularly breaks down the cell partitions, inspects her developing larvae, and removes their faeces, dead larvae and other debris. She then carefully rebuilds the partitions between cells.

These species were studied in Japan by Dr S.F. Sakagami and his colleagues. They found that in some nests of *C. japonica*, two or more females shared a nest. They were usually sisters and some of the colonies were quasisocial in that the females cooperated in brood care and all were mated egg layers. Other colonies were semisocial in that some females were mated, had enlarged ovaries and presumably laid eggs, functioning as queens while other females were often unmated, had small, undeveloped ovaries, and, presumably, laid few or no eggs and functioned as foraging workers. In the semisocial colonies, the presumed workers were on average smaller than the presumed queens. There is a possibility that some nests of *C. japonica* contained adult females of two generations, in which case they could be said to be eusocial (see below). The remarkable thing about *C. japonica* is that, within one species, we have a range of behaviours covering the whole gamut from solitary to semisocial and possibly primitively eusocial.

The biology of the allodapine bees is just as remarkable. The nesting behaviours of species have been unravelled in southern Africa, in south-east Asia, and in Australia. Some species are solitary but others are subsocial, such as the typical *Allodape mucronata* from Africa. The nest is always started by a lone female. She selects the dead hollow stem of a plant, often a gladiolus or aloe, cleans it out and builds a constricted nest entrance which she can defend effectively.

The foundress next lays a batch of eggs, and it is here that her behaviour is unusual. She does not build cells, but attaches her eggs in a line or a ring to the wall of the cylindrical cavity, without even a covering to make a communal cell. Another way in which she differs from most other bees is that she feeds her offspring continually with very small meals. The lack of cells, progressive feeding, and the resulting frequent contact with her larvae are typical of ants, but not the sort of behaviour associated with bees.

Because the larvae are not confined in cells, there is a danger that they could roll about the open nest, lose contact with their meal and starve. They overcome this dilemma in a novel way: each larva has false legs or pseudopodia with which to hold its food. The larva lies on its back and its mother regurgitates a drop of liquid food on to its belly between the pseudopodia. In one African species, *Allodapula dichroa*, the female lays her eggs in a ring around the tube-shaped nest. When they hatch, the larvae remain attached to the wall by their dorsal surface, their sides pressed against their neighbours, while the mother provides a communal meal in the centre.

When the bees of the first egg batch reach adulthood, one or more of them normally remains behind to help the mother raise the next generation. If this happens, then the colony has passed from the subsocial to the eusocial level (see below). The number of adult bees in a nest is usually two, but there may be up to six. The additional bee or bees are usually workers that do not mate but collect most of the colony's food. Occasionally the number of bees in a nest may reach twenty or more, but the majority leave to found nests of their own instead of helping in the old nest.

PRIMITIVELY EUSOCIAL BEES

A eusocial colony comprises an egg-laying queen and two or more generations of adult females which function as workers. The latter excavate, line and provision cells. They forage at flowers and, in many species, one or more function as guards at the nest entrance.

A primitively eusocial colony is always founded by a single, mated female, and thus passes through early solitary and subsocial phases. In some cases, a founding female may be joined by other females of the same generation and the colony may pass through a semisocial phase until the original female has asserted dominance and the joiners cease to lay eggs.

Because primitively eusocial colonies pass through solitary and subsocial phases, it may be more accurate to refer to them as temporarily eusocial, to distinguish them from the highly eusocial or permanently social stingless bees and honeybees (see Chapter 10).

The most important primitively eusocial bees are the so-called sweat bees and the bumblebees, *Bombus* spp.

The sweat bees, Halictidae   The sweat bees figure prominently in studies of primitive sociality. They belong to the family Halictidae and are called sweat bees because they are often attracted to human perspiration. The most important genera are *Lasioglossum* and *Halictus*.

Sweat bees are moderately common in most parts of the world but, because they are so small, they are often overlooked. Many are only 4 mm long. The species are notoriously difficult to identify, and students of the group often have to use characteristics of the nest architecture to identify the species. Most species excavate nests in earth, though some tropical species nest in rotten wood. Some species are solitary, while others exhibit varying degrees of social behaviour. Every nest is founded by a lone female. In the social species, the daughters remain with the natal nest, construct new cells and forage for food.

Sweat bees have an important feature which may have made it easier for them rather than other mining bees to develop social behaviour. The females of all species, whether solitary or not, mate before hibernating for the winter. This means that, unlike female solitary bees of other families, those of halictids do not have to mate before founding a nest in the following spring. The females of some species raise a first generation that consists entirely of daughters. These cannot mate and, in the case of social species, they are 'predisposed' to remain with their natal nest and act as non-reproductive workers. In a sense, therefore, by producing no males among the first generation, a female manipulates the behaviour of her daughters in such a way as to make it likely that they will remain to help rear later generations.

In the northern hemisphere, most halictid colonies produce males only in the last generation of offspring, in late summer and early autumn.

One of the best-understood primitively eusocial halictids is *Lasioglossum zephyrum*, which is common in the Mid-west of North America. Charles D. Michener and several of his students, notably Suzanne Batra, Denis Brothers, G.R. Buckle and Les Greenberg, have studied the social biology of this bee over many years in Kansas. They made direct laboratory observations of activities within artificial nests in soil between two plates of glass.

The colonies of *L. zephyrum* are annual and have 4–45 females. Some individual females, however, remain strictly solitary. The life cycle is as follows: females mate in the autumn and then hibernate, usually in their old nests. They re-emerge in the spring, around mid-April and each one founds her own nest. She excavates a burrow in an earth bank in which she constructs three or four cells, providing each with a sphere of pollen lightly moistened with nectar; she lays a single egg in each one and, during this period, behaves exactly like a solitary bee. She then waits for her offspring to grow, and adults of both sexes emerge in late spring. During this stage, the colony is subsocial.

Her daughters remain in the nest, enlarging it, building more cells and provisioning them. The colony is now at a simple eusocial level of organization. During this time, the foundress queen asserts domination over her daughters by nudging them frequently with her head. This presumably inhibits the development of their ovaries.

The queen is the most active bee in the nest, frequently inspecting cells. She also spends time waiting just behind the nest entrance, or near branches in the nest burrow, where she is most likely to meet workers. When she encounters a returned forager, she backs away, leading the pollen-laden bee to a cell which needs provisioning. The queen therefore directs the activities of the workers to some extent.

Because the first brood of offspring contains both sexes, some of the workers are mated and may occasionally lay eggs. However, the ovaries of such bees are not as enlarged as those of the queen. Among the workers, though, there is variation in the size of the ovaries. Within a colony, the worker with the most developed ovaries tends to spend most of her time on guard duty at the nest entrance. She deters bees from other colonies which mistakenly try to gain entry and lets only her own nestmates into the nest. She recognizes nestmates by their smell, which is characteristic of the colony. She also attempts to deter, not always successfully, enemies such as the wingless females of mutillid wasps, sometimes known as velvet ants.

In June, the foundress queen dies and some of her mated daughters and,

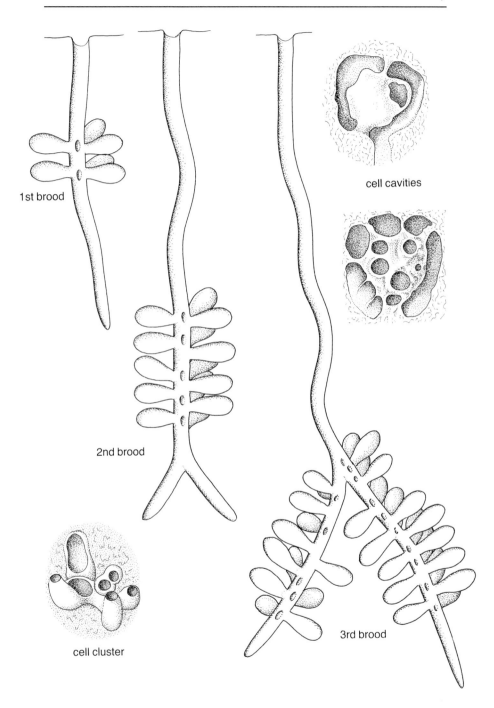

1st brood

2nd brood

cell cluster

cell cavities

3rd brood

Fig. 27   Sections through nests of a primitively eusocial mining bee, *Lasioglossum malachurum* (Halictidae); Eurasia. (Redrawn after Michener, C.D., 1974.)

possibly, granddaughters begin to lay eggs. They are called replacement queens. The colony therefore assumes a quasisocial or semisocial state, with the foundress's female offspring rather hazily divided into house bees, egg layers, and foragers.

Even when the foundress queen is at the height of her powers, the division of labour is very vague. In any individual colony, the queen is, on average, larger than most of the workers, with the principal guard often being the largest of the workers. Even so, in the population as a whole, there is no absolute size difference between queens and workers and there may be a confusing overlap, with the largest workers being bigger than the smallest egg layers.

A bee generally works in the nest when younger and forages and lays eggs when older, but foragers occasionally lay eggs and the bees seem to switch quite readily from one task to another. After three or four generations have been produced throughout the season, the organization of the colony breaks up and several of the younger females mate and hibernate. They will become active the following spring and begin the cycle anew.

Lasioglossum malachurum is widespread in Eurasia, including southern Britain and often nests in dense aggregations. This bee was studied in France by Drs Gerd Knerer and Cecile Plateaux-Quénu. The foundress queens are distinctly larger than their worker daughters. The foundress excavates a near-vertical burrow in spring. She constructs a dense cluster of six to seven cells several centimetres below the entrance (Fig. 27). Here she rears her first brood of workers. Each successive generation of workers develops in deeper and larger cell clusters. The second cell cluster contains 19–26 cells, while the third contains 60–97 cells. In a departure from the norm, the cells are open during larval development, being sealed by workers only at the time of pupation. There is usually a guard worker stationed at the nest entrance.

There are two to three generations of workers before the production of males and new queens in the late summer and autumn, when the foundress queen, now worn and flightless, dies. The new queens mate and hibernate until the following spring.

The soil at the nest entrance and that lining the upper reaches of the main burrow is impregnated with Dufour's gland secretion, the same secretion used by the bees to line the brood cells. Dr Abraham Hefetz of Tel-Aviv University studied this bee in Israel and showed that, as in all halictid bees, the Dufour's gland secretion comprises a mixture of chemicals called macrocyclic lactones. Each individual has its own unique blend of lactones, giving it a kind of chemical 'fingerprint'. Each worker contributes to the secretion impregnating the nest entrance and upper tunnel areas, so that the glandular deposits contain the sum of individual variants of lactone blends in the colony. This imparts a unique nest odour to the entrance, which no doubt enables returning workers to recognize their own nest among the many hundreds that form the dense nesting village. It also gives the guard bee(s) a unique reference basis on which to recognize nestmates on their return. It may also be the basis of individual recognition of social status between nestmates. These little bees clearly operate at a level of chemical discrimination that is quite beyond that of the human nose. It is more than likely that other primitively social halictids do likewise.

Lasioglossum marginatum is another well-studied species. It is common in southern central Europe, the Mediterranean Basin and the Middle East. Dr

Cecile Plateaux-Quénu investigated this species in France. As in *L. zephyrum* and *L. malachurum*, a lone female founds each colony and behaves like a solitary bee until her first brood emerges to help run the nest. In a manner not yet fully understood, the queen inhibits the ovarian development of her daughters, and they remain as workers. From this point, the colony's destiny differs from that of *L. zephyrum*. There are no guard bees and there is more than one generation per year. The first generation of workers excavate and line all the brood cells before provisioning them with food. When provisioning is finished, the bees block much of the nest tunnel with soil and the queen walks about the nest and lays a single egg in each of the provisioned cells.

L. marginatum is unusual in that the workers do not seal the cells; these remain open throughout larval life, during which time the workers do no foraging. They presumably inspect the developing brood and remove faeces. The cells remain unsealed even during the pupal stage.

Unlike the foundress queen of *L. zephyrum*, that of *L. marginatum* does not die after her first generation of daughters reach maturity. Instead, she lives from five to six years and thus presides over a perennial colony. Towards the end of the first year, she loses her ability to fly and becomes a full-time egg layer. She eats food deposited in cells by the workers. All offspring that survive to the beginning of winter hibernate in the nest and resume their chores the following spring.

Communication among bees in a nest seems to be minimal. The organization of tasks needed to be done seems to be indirect, the stimuli being the cues received from the work accomplished. For example, a cell constructed by one bee stimulates one or more of the foragers returning to the nest to deposit food in the empty cell. This may then trigger another to construct a pollen ball.

A colony produces males only in its fifth and sixth years. During this period, the colony, including males, often exceeds 200 bees; the largest nest on record contained 486 workers. All of the younger females appear to be identical, but towards the end of the colony's life a number leave the nest to mate and hibernate, before founding colonies of their own in the following spring. *Lasioglossum marginatum*, with its perennial colonies and the clear behavioural distinction between queen and workers, is regarded as the most socially advanced of the halictid bees.

The bumblebees, *Bombus* To most of us, the bumblebees, *Bombus* spp. are the most easily recognized bees after the honeybee and, because bumble-bees are larger, furrier, and generally more 'bee-like', they are sometimes mistaken for them. Although both are members of the same family, the Apidae, and have many structural features in common, their social lives are very different.

Bombus species are typical of temperate climates, and are common throughout Eurasia and North America. Some species live in more extreme environments, like the cool slopes of the Himalayas, while others thrive in the tropical forests of the Amazon. They are absent from Africa south of the Sahara, however, and they were deliberately introduced into New Zealand in the late 1800s and early 1900s (See Chapter 11). Bumblebees are primitively eusocial and, like *Lasioglossum zephyrum* and other social halictids, each colony has a solitary and subsocial phase.

In northern, temperate areas, queens and males are reared in late summer.

A nest of the bumblebee, *Bombus pascuorum*, showing workers adding nectar and wax to the haphazard clump of storage and brood cells (Family: Apidae).

In the autumn a queen mates, eats enough food to build up a fat reserve to last through the winter, and then finds a quiet, dry nook in which to hibernate. The warm spring weather awakens her from dormancy and she leaves to find food. She drinks nectar for energy and eats pollen to obtain the protein she needs to develop her eggs. Suitably refreshed, she begins the search for a nest site. Some species always nest underground, often favouring an old mouse nest. Other species nest above ground, collecting a pile of dry grass and moss to cover the cells.

Using wax secreted by glands in her abdomen, the queen builds a single wax cell in which she lays up to a dozen eggs. This is not typical of bees generally, for the vast majority lay only one egg per cell. She also builds a small wax pot in which she stores honey. Although she must leave the nest to gather more food, most of her time is spent lying on top of the cell to keep her offspring warm and hasten their development into adults. She incubates her brood by generating heat within her body by chemical means (See Chapter 11).

Although the eggs were laid in a clump in a single cell, the queen soon surrounds each growing larva with its own wax cell, which is enlarged with the addition of extra wax. Just before pupation, the larva spins a whitish cocoon of silk, after which the queen or, later, the workers, remove the wax of the cell to use elsewhere. Before the daughters of her first batch emerge to help in the nest, the queen lays a second batch of eggs.

Sometimes the queen's first daughters are so small that they cannot fly and they confine themselves to work in the nest. The queen continues to forage until a brood of larger daughters emerges. These will release the queen from other duties to carry out the more important task of egg laying. Her daughters are mere workers. They lay very few eggs and these are eaten by the queen.

As the season progresses, the colony enlarges and the number of workers increases because they are raised faster than the older ones die. The later workers are generally larger than the earlier ones because of the larger food

Workers of the bumblebee, *Bombus lucorum*, tending larvae. The latter are visible through feeding holes in the wax brood cells (Family: Apidae).

supply they enjoyed as larvae. With time, the colony becomes more affluent, with plenty of workers to raise the new queens. It is still not clear, but it seems that the main difference between the workers and the new generation of queens depends on the amount of food that they are given as larvae. All of them are sisters and thus are genetically related to each other.

Some species of bumblebee are called 'pouch makers', because of the way the workers supply food to the larvae. They construct a pouch at the side of the cell containing a growing larva and place the food in it. The larva eats the food directly from the pouch, which is periodically replenished by workers.

In other species, the workers bite a hole in the cell wall and regurgitate the food directly into the cell, after which they seal the breach. Bees in this group are called 'pollen storers' because they store surplus pollen in old cells. The bees extend the walls of these cells as more pollen is added and columns occasionally 8 cm (3 in) high are characteristic features of their nests. The apparent advantage of this method of feeding larvae is that it is easier for the workers to assess larval needs. Even in the pouch-making species, the larvae that are destined to become queens are supplied food directly, without the construction of pouches.

The eventual size of the colony depends not only on the species but also on the climate. Nests of the North American *Bombus terricola* and *B. fervidus* and the European *B. hortorum* and *B. pascuorum* usually have 100 or more workers while *B. impatiens* in North America and *B. terrestris* in Europe may have more than 400. The largest bumblebee nest ever found was produced by the Mexican *B. medius*, and contained 2,184 workers.

A mature colony contains many workers and the number of eggs laid by workers increases. Inevitably, some of the eggs escape detection by the queen and, once they have hatched, the larvae are unmolested. Since the worker does not mate, her eggs are unfertilized and all her offspring will be males. Most of the males in bumblebee colonies are produced in this way, while the queen continues to lay daughter eggs. Males are only necessary at this stage to mate with the young queens and this is a very economic way of producing them.

The young queens and males leave the nest. They mate several times, after which the males die. After feeding up, the queens go into hibernation, and the cycle begins again the following year.

WHY BE SOCIAL?

One of the reasons postulated for the evolution of nest-sharing behaviour in bees is that it provides an opportunity for defence against predators, especially cuckoo bees and wasps. Thus, either the coming and going of foragers at the nest entrance acts as a deterrent, or some bees can remain on guard at the nest entrance while others leave to forage.

This supposed advantage may not apply for communal associations such as that of *Andrena bucephala* near Oxford: despite the heavy nest entrance traffic of bees, many females of the cuckoo bee *Nomada bucephalae* were seen to gain successful entrance to the nest.

Moreover, the evidence, at least from the quasisocial *Exomalopsis globosa* and *E. similis* in Jamaica does not support this suggestion either. About half of the *Exomalopsis* young die in their cells, giving a survival rate no better than that in many solitary species. The implication here is that nest defence is not very effective. However, there is a big difference between the lives of these quasi-social species and solitary bees. After solitary bees have emerged from their nests, at least half of the females die before they even begin nesting. This is said to be because they cannot find suitable nest sites or are killed by predators while searching for a nest site. As many as 66 per cent of female *Osmia rufa* never survive after emergence to found nests. In contrast, 80 per cent of adult females in nests of *Exomalopsis* survived to continue working in their natal nests. Some of those that left must have gone to found new nests.

Our personal view is that primitively social associations, either communal or of the several types described above, may arise not for reasons of defence, but for another reason: by remaining with her natal nest, a female avoids high post-emergence, pre-nesting mortality.

There may well be another advantage. If a nest has served a female well in rearing her offspring, then it is likely to be a good site in the following year for another generation of bees, so it will pay some of her daughters to remain with it and excavate and provision their own cells. To use the jargon of evolutionary biology, the females which remain with their natal nest are said to increase their inclusive fitness, that is, they maximize their chances of surviving to reproduce themselves.

If being social is so advantageous, an obvious question is why are not all bees social? There are several possible answers. There may not be enough flowers to provide food for increased numbers of bees, and thus it may pay the bees to specialize in their diet rather than develop more sophisticated forms of social behaviour. A further possibility is that in cooler climates the summer may not be long enough or reliable enough for the bees to invest in a big social nest which persists for several generations. In fact, the vast majority of social bees, especially the highly eusocial species, with perennial nests, live in the tropics.

Inherent in the question 'Why are not all bees social?' is the assumption that the less social bees, such as many of the Halictidae, are in some way inferior to the highly social honeybees, that they have failed to make the grade. And it is tempting to look among the Halictidae, with their varied types of simple sociality, for an evolutionary sequence of increasing complexity, culminating in the honeybees as some sort of evolutionary pinnacle. But we should remember that, as Michener has pointed out, only a minute fraction of the Halictidae have been studied; there undoubtedly remain many more types of sociality to be discovered among these fascinating bees. In the meantime, it remains imprudent to draw general conclusions about the evolution of sociality in bees based only on a few, well-studied examples.

Each species has its own unique evolutionary history and its level of sociality (or lack of it) is more reasonably thought of as being the optimum for that species, at this point in its history. Thus, we can say that something like the primitive social behaviour seen in halictid bees may have preceded the permanent, highly social organization we see in honeybees and stingless bees, but no one suggests that the halictid bees are on the same direct evolutionary line as the apids.

We saw earlier that some of the euglossine bees, for example *Euglossa imperialis*, are quasisocial. All known species of the related genus, *Eulaema*, are at the least communal or perhaps semisocial. The euglossines are closely related to the bumblebees, *Bombus* spp. and both groups are in the same family as the stingless bees and honeybees. It is among the euglossines, then, that we should look for further clues as to the evolution of sociality in apids. There are at least two lines, one leading to the stingless bees, the other to the true honeybees, *Apis* spp. But, as we noted in Chapter 1, p. 19, highly social bees are of great antiquity: the recently discovered fossil in mid-Cretaceous amber of *Trigona prisca* is clearly very closely related to modern species of the same genus. Moreover, as Michener has recently suggested, the evolution from solitary to highly social may proceed rapidly, with few or no intervening 'primitive' stages.

He envisages this happening in species which are normally solitary but which under some circumstances form eusocial colonies. Examples are Japanese species of *Ceratina*. Michener suggests that in such species, eusocial behaviour may become fixed. There is no reason why this could not have happened in some early, euglossine-like apids, giving rise eventually, to the permanent eusociality found in stingless bees and the honeybees.

KEEPING IT IN THE FAMILY: DARWIN'S DILEMMA SOLVED?

We have discussed the pressures which may have led some female bees to have started sharing nests or led daughters to remain with their mother in their natal nest. In some cases, this leads to females abandoning their reproductive capacity and becoming workers, helping to rear and defend the offspring of others. We are faced then with a problem. How is this system maintained? Natural selection has favoured a particular trait which is fixed in a caste of non-reproductives, which, by definition, have no descendants and cannot therefore pass the trait on to subsequent generations.

In the case of worker honeybees and some worker ants, the workers are prepared to sacrifice their lives for the well-being of the colony. How can a gene for such altruism be passed on to future generations via a non-reproductive caste?

A female of an orchid bee, *Eulaema* sp., drinks from mud on a damp path in Peru. Orchid bees are the closest living relatives of the bumblebees (*Bombus* spp.) and several species of *Eulaema* are primitively social (Family: Apidae).

These questions posed a real dilemma for Charles Darwin. With his typical candour, he recognized that the social Hymenoptera might well subvert his theory of evolution by means of natural selection operating on variable, but inherited characters. In the *Origin of Species* he confronted this dilemma and concluded that the social insects were a special case, with natural selection operating on the colony as a whole rather than on individuals.

Social behaviour has evolved 12 times in the insects, 11 of them in the Hymenoptera. There must be some quality about the ants, wasps and bees which predisposes them to develop sociality. In 1964, the British biologist W.D. Hamilton came up with a theory which satisfactorily explains the evolution of social behaviour or 'altruism' in this group.

Since the nineteenth century, it had been known that in bees and wasps females are derived from fertilized eggs and males are derived from unfertilized eggs. We now know that the fertilization of an egg is under the conscious control of the female. To fertilize an egg, she releases sperm from the spermatheca as the egg passes down the oviduct. By withholding sperm, she lays an egg destined to become a male. It follows that a female receives genetic material from both her father, via the sperm, and from her mother, via the egg. She therefore has the normal or 'diploid' number of chromosomes. By contrast, a male receives genetic material only from his mother. He has a single, maternal grandfather, but no father. In fact, he has half the normal number of chromosomes and is said to be 'haploid'.

It was Hamilton's great insight to recognize the consequences of this, the haplo-diploid method of sex determination and how they affect the likelihood of sociality evolving in the Hymenoptera. And how, in fact, the apparently 'selfless' behaviour of workers has nothing to do with altruism, but rather a lot to do with the way haplo-diploidy distorts the genetic relationships between females in a family group.

Because a male bee is haploid, all his sperm are genetically identical. If a female mates only once, then all her female offspring will receive an identical set of genes from their father. But, because the mother is diploid, her daughters have in common only one half of the maternal genes.

If we now add up the genes received by a female bee from her father and mother, we can see that hymenopteran sisters have a very special relationship. They share, on average, 75 per cent of their genes by common descent, i.e., 50 per cent from the father and 25 per cent from their mother. Thus, when a female bee or wasp has daughters, she passes on only 50 per cent of her genes to the next generation. But if she gives up reproduction and helps to rear sisters, some of which will become reproductive queens, then in so doing, she helps to pass on, via her sister, a set of genes which are, on average, 75 per cent identical to her own. Because the shared genes are identical, it does not matter whether they are in the female's own eggs or in those of her younger sisters. By being a worker, she reproduces by proxy, the pay-off being the extra 25 per cent of genes which are perpetuated in this way.

This is the so-called theory of 'kin selection' and it offers the most elegant explanation for the evolution and maintenance of sociality in the Hymenoptera, especially the highly social (eusocial) forms such as the honeybees and stingless bees, which are the subjects of the next chapter. It also solves Darwin's dilemma and gives us an important new insight into social behaviour in bees, wasps and ants: far from being a selfless altruist, the worker hymenopteran is, or rather its genes are, utterly selfish.

Chapter 10
The Highly Social Bees

Social behaviour in bees has reached its highest levels in the honeybees and stingless bees in the family Apidae. Members of the two groups are similar both in some adult structures and in their social organization. In colonies of both, there is a clear distinction between a single queen and hundreds or thousands of sterile workers. In both, the queen is totally dependent on the workers for her food, and new colonies are organized by the workers; both store honey and build nests of wax.

The common or western honeybee, *Apis mellifera*, is perhaps the insect best known to man, and is undoubtedly one of the best understood of all animal species. It occurs naturally in Africa, the Middle East, and Europe and has been introduced into many other parts of the world where beekeepers maintain populations in artificial nests called hives.

From time immemorial, people have been interested in honeybees (Fig. 28). Honey was once the only sweetener. The earlier puzzle of how to obtain honey without provoking the wrath of bees has been replaced by wonder at the sophisticated society of the bees and investigation into how that society functions.

Fig. 28   A Bushman cave-painting from the Eland Cave in the Natal Drakensberg of South Africa, showing a man climbing a ladder to rob a nest of wild honeybees. Nearly 80 examples of Bushman cave art depicting honey-gathering activities are known. The paintings were made in the last 2,000 years, up to recent times. The Bushmen are the true aboriginals of Southern Africa and reached a stage of cultural development equivalent to that of the Late Stone Age people of the European Mesolithic Period. (After Pager, H., 1973, *Bee World* **54**(2): 61–8.)

Worker honeybees, *Apis mellifera*, adding honey to storage comb (Family: Apidae).

Deep in a Peruvian rain forest, worker stingless bees, *Trigona* sp., tend larvae and adults of the sap-sucking bug *Aetalion reticulatum*. Like many sap-suckers, these bugs exude sweet honeydew, which bees and ants find irresistible (Families: Apidae and Fulgoridae).

There are six other species of *Apis*, all more or less oriental in distribution. These are *A. dorsata*, *A. laboriosa*, *A. cerana*, *A. koschevnikovi*, *A. florea* and *A. andreniformis*.

Stingless bees are placed in the subfamily Meliponinae and are found throughout the tropics. There are about 300 species, nearly two-thirds of them occurring in Central and South America. As the most primitive and most advanced species both occur in the Neotropics, this is where stingless bees probably originated.

The largest species of stingless bees are slightly bigger than the common honeybee, while the smallest are among the smallest of all bees, being only 2 mm long. Moreover, the number of individuals in a colony varies greatly among species. *Melipona* nests usually have a few hundred occupants and the smaller nests resemble those of bumblebees. Likewise, some nests of *Trigona* contain only a few hundred individuals, but in others there are thousands. Colonies of one widespread South American species, *Trigona spinipes*, are among the most populous of any bees, some of them achieving 180,000 workers.

THE NEST

In the wild, most species of *Apis*, including the common honeybee, *A. mellifera*, nest in dry caves and hollow trees. The nest of the giant honeybee, *Apis dorsata* of East Asia, is a single exposed comb hanging from a branch or a rock.

The honeybee comb is a thin sheet of wax covered with hexagonal cells on both sides. It hangs from the roof of the nest cavity and has a high strength-to-weight ratio: it can support 40 times its own weight of honey.

An array of hexagonal cells is the most efficient way of using enclosed spaces for storage. The bees build the cells side by side and back to back so that every wall is common to two cells and the amount of building material needed is halved. Thus, the bees use less wax and the comb is lighter in weight. Apart from wax, honeybees use propolis as a building material. They make this by mixing wax with resin they collect from sticky buds and plant wounds. The bees use propolis to glue honeycomb to the substrate and also to plug gaps in the sides of the nest.

Workers of the giant Oriental honeybee, *Apis dorsata*, drinking from damp sand on a river bank in a Malaysian rainforest. By drinking this water they probably replace body salts, a vital activity in a hot, humid climate (Family: Apidae).

Many Central and South American stingless bees, like this Costa Rican species of *Trigona* (*above left*), build turrets at their nest entrances. In the Neotropics, the turrets may afford some protection from the seven species of cleptoparasitic stingless bees of the genus *Lestrimelitta* and army ants of the genus *Eciton* (Family: Apidae and Formicidae). Workers of a *Trigona* sp. (*above right*) collect resin oozing from a wound in a tree trunk in Kenya, the result of a wood-boring insect. The bees transport the resin back to their nest in their pollen baskets, where they use it as building material (Family: Apidae).

Many stingless bees nest in cavities in tree trunks, some build exposed nests attached to branches, while others nest in the ground and a few occupy parts of termite nests.

The meliponine nest is always enclosed in a special covering called the batumen, which is equivalent to the propolis of honeybees. An exposed nest or one built underground is completely covered with batumen. When the nest is located in a hollow tree trunk, the batumen is restricted to sheets above and below to shut off the nest from the rest of the unwanted space. A tube of the same material connects the nest cavity with the outside world.

The nest usually has two parts. The brood chamber contains the queen and the cells in which the larvae are reared. This chamber is surrounded by another, called the involucrum which literally envelops the brood cells. Some species build nests without an involucrum. Honey and pollen are stored in groups of larger cells outside the brood chamber. In some species, the honey and pollen pots are intermixed while in others they are segregated. In a few species, the two are different shapes, the honey pots being oval and the pollen pots like stalactites hanging above the brood cells.

In localities where stingless bees are common, they are often seen visiting trees that are secreting resin from recent wounds. The bees collect the resin, take it to the nest in their pollen baskets, where they add wax to it to make cerumen. This name is also used for human ear wax, which gives an idea of the colour and texture of the material which the bees use to build cells.

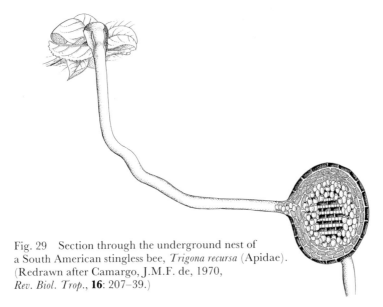

Fig. 29   Section through the underground nest of
a South American stingless bee, *Trigona recursa* (Apidae).
(Redrawn after Camargo, J.M.F. de, 1970,
Rev. Biol. Trop., **16**: 207–39.)

To make the tougher batumen, used for the outer covering of the nest, the
bees mix wax with various amounts of other materials, such as resin, mud and,
sometimes, animal faeces, mineral oil, grease, and even fresh paint. It is a
strange sight to see a stingless bee alight on wet paint, gather up a portion and
place it in the pollen baskets on her hind legs to carry to the nest. The bees
remain perfectly clean and look very pretty as they carry off the paint.

The brood cells are oval or cylindrical. In the nests of some species they are
in a more or less irregular cluster (Fig. 29). However, many species build the
cells in groups forming horizontal sheets. In some nests, cells are so close
together that they resemble one side of a honeycomb. The horizontal comb of
the infamous firebee, the *tataira*, forms an overlapping ever-widening spiral.
An African stingless bee, *Dactylurina*, produces vertical combs with the cells
back to back on the same plan as the comb of the common honeybee.

Because honeybees are more familiar than stingless bees, we consider their
social organization first and later see how that of the meliponines differs.

HONEYBEES

The major division in a colony is between the queen and her workers. In
normal circumstances, only the queen lays eggs, up to 2000 per day, and she
does little else in the hive. The other tasks are carried out by the workers, all of
which are more or less identical in size and appearance. Each one can, at some
stage of her life, do all of the necessary jobs in the colony.

A honeybee colony may contain 40–80 thousand workers. This is a very
large work force and clearly needs a great deal of organization if it is to
function properly. Given that there are always several different jobs to be
done, the principal part of the organization exists in job specialization, more
commonly called division of labour, so that the various tasks are suitably
distributed among the members of the work force.

The allocation of tasks is age-related. During the first half of her adult life of six weeks, a worker functions in the nest as a 'nurse' or house bee. She spends the latter half of her life initially as a guard at the entrance, then as a field bee or forager. This is also common practice among the stingless bees and bumble bees.

The main reason for this division lies in the physiological state of the bee, especially the activity of certain glands (Fig. 30). These are the abdominal wax glands and the glands in the head which secrete royal jelly, a special food fed to larvae. The glands are generally functional only when the bee is young. Hence the bee remains in the nest to build cells with the wax she produces and to feed the young larvae on royal jelly. This sequence of carrying out chores in the nest followed by foraging activities has been known since the time of Charles Butler; he wrote in his book, *The Feminine Monarchie*, published in 1609: 'The young bees . . . not only work abroad but also watch and ward at home whereas the labour of the old ones is only in gathering.'

The progression was neatly investigated by the German Donhoff in 1855. In a colony of a black strain of honeybees, he replaced the old black queen with a young yellow one. This enabled him to distinguish between the offspring from the two queens. When the first yellow workers appeared, they worked in the hive and did not go out to forage until they were at least fifteen days old.

During the first day or two of her adult life, the young worker bee moves about the hive eating pollen and honey but does little work. The head glands that secrete royal jelly and the wax glands in her abdomen develop and then she is ready to nurse larvae and to build new comb. She performs these tasks for up to three weeks, mixing the chores with tending the queen, cleaning the interior of the hive and receiving nectar brought in by the foragers.

After she has taken nectar from these other workers, she finds a quiet part of

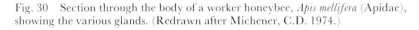

Fig. 30   Section through the body of a worker honeybee, *Apis mellifera* (Apidae), showing the various glands. (Redrawn after Michener, C.D. 1974.)

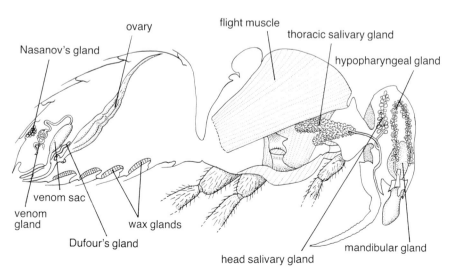

the nest. Here she sits and repeatedly opens and closes her mouthparts, exposing the nectar to the air. This allows water to evaporate from the nectar. The nectar gradually becomes thicker and the sugar concentration increases. In this way, nectar is ripened into honey. After about 20 minutes, the worker places the nectar into a cell. The ripening continues for several more days; other bees help the evaporation process by fanning their wings to create a stream of drying air over the honeycomb. Worker bees may carry out fanning duties at almost any age.

Although there is marked specialization in the colony, the ability of a house bee to be a jack-of-all-trades and her instinct to search out work is the basis of the efficient functioning of the colony as a whole. She spends much of her time walking about in the hive carrying out a job here, and a job there. On some days she may spend half her time looking for work, but the key to success is that recruitment to any particular task is fast and effective.

Cells containing larvae are always left open, and nurse bees feed them. Each one receives 140 or more small meals from the team of young nurses. After six days, when the larva is fully grown, it begins to spin a cocoon and, at this stage, the workers seal the cell with a wax cap. The cap must be a more intricate structure than it at first appears for the workers make well over 100 visits to construct each cap and spend more than six hours in the process. The mature larva takes about two days to spin the cocoon and to moult into a pupa. Three weeks after the egg was laid the young adult bee emerges from her cell.

Frequently, honeybees clean the cells of refuse and reuse them to rear more broods, but in growing colonies the lower edge of the comb is extended as new cells are built on to it, and it is here that the queen lays eggs. The workers store honey in the older cells above. With the location of the young brood in newer cells, there is a clear connection to be seen between the supply of food to the

Full-grown larvae of the honeybee, *Apis mellifera*, in their cells (Family: Apidae).

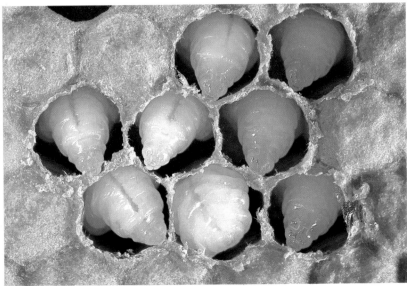

colony and its subsequent growth, for the house bees must be well-fed in order to secrete wax and royal jelly.

Another function of the house bees is to meet the returning foragers and receive the nectar that they have collected. The forager regurgitates the liquid and the house bee sucks it into her honey stomach with her tongue. The forager leaves to collect more and the house bee walks to the top of the comb and regurgitates the nectar into a cell. The first stages of conversion of nectar into honey will have already started in the honey stomach of the house bee. If, by chance, there is no more available space to store honey the house bee must retain the dilute honey in her stomach for a while. Eventually, the food will be digested, which enables the bee to secrete more wax. Hence the lack of storage space enables the bee to alleviate the problem by transforming food stores into construction material.

A forager returning with pollen finds it less easy to shed her load. Pollen cannot be transferred to a house bee. The pollen-laden forager jostles her way to the part of the comb near the brood, where she deposits her own loads in pollen storage cells. When pollen is in short supply, the nurse bees take great interest in any returning pollen gatherer, often removing and eating the load as soon as the forager enters the hive.

It is not known what stimulates the forager to collect pollen, but ease of disposal must encourage the forager to bring back more. On the other hand, a bee that must wander around the crowded hive looking for somewhere to dump its pollen load is less likely to repeat the process.

The ease with which bees change from one task to another is not entirely lost when they become foragers. If a colony is divided so that one contains only the younger workers and the other the older ones, some of the latter redevelop their wax and mandibular glands and return to house work.

STINGLESS BEES

Stingless bees differ from honeybees in some important details. One of the more obvious differences is the way they feed their larvae. Honeybees practise

Some *Trigona* spp. are aggressive foragers. Here, workers from two different colonies fight over a source of resin in Trinidad. Fights of this kind often result in injury or even death to individuals by biting. The glistening brown resin can be seen on the pollen baskets of several of the bees (Family: Apidae).

progressive feeding in open cells, whereas stingless bees mass provision the cells as solitary bees do: they put the larva's entire food supply into the cell before the egg is laid. The nurse bees have enlarged head glands and the food provided for the larvae resembles the royal jelly or 'bee milk' of honeybees.

When a cell is built, several workers fill it with food. The queen is very soon attracted to the little group of workers. One of the workers lays an egg in the cell and the queen eats this, with a little of the food in the cell, before turning around to lay her own egg. The queen of a stingless bee colony receives much of her food in this way, although the workers also feed her directly. The queen then departs, leaving the workers to seal the cell. The offspring is left to complete its development entombed with all the food that it needs.

The division of labour in stingless colonies has not been much studied but seems to be similar to that in honeybees. It is based on the age of the worker, each one passing through stages where she performs particular tasks, the sequence of which is based to a large extent on the state of development of the glands that produce the materials she uses.

In *Melipona quadrifasciata*, for example, the worker's peak of honey production occurs before she is a nurse bee. In other species, however, the sequence is like that of honeybees, where house duties are mixed, but are done before the work outside the nest. In several species of *Trigona*, workers spend about the first four weeks of work caring for the brood, laying trophic eggs to be eaten by the queen, and building cells. During the fifth week, workers begin to secrete wax and build cells, although some adopt other duties such as nest defence.

The workers of the different species of *Trigona* may spend different amounts of time pursuing tasks with greater or lesser degrees of overlap. Nevertheless, it seems that the stimuli for recruitment among the members of a stingless bee colony are much the same as in honeybees, depending on the number of recruits available and the tasks that need to be done. As in honeybees, older bees that are foragers can return to house duties when there are too few nurse bees and when their head glands which secrete royal jelly regenerate. Some of the *Trigona* species are tiny, yet the workers live considerably longer than those of the honeybee. The South American *T. xanthotricha* works for about six weeks in the nest and then for about the same length of time in the field, a lifespan about double that of a honeybee.

CONTROL OF CONDITIONS IN THE NEST

Because the western honeybee, *Apis mellifera*, builds in an enclosed space, the bees are able to control the temperature and humidity within the nest very accurately. They take particular care to control the temperature of the air surrounding the brood. The young larvae develop faster at 35°C and commonly die at temperatures below 32°C and above 36°C. In an active colony, the workers maintain the temperature around the young at 34.5–35.5°C. The temperature is raised with their own body heat, generated by shivering the wing muscles. It has been calculated that 10,000 worker bees can produce at least 40,000 joules.

High temperatures can be disastrous in a nest built of wax. Beeswax melts at 63–65°C, but long before it reaches this temperature it becomes too soft to support the weight of honey stored in the comb. Honeybees use two methods to lower the temperature within the nest. In the simplest, bees stand at the nest entrance and fan their wings to draw the cooler air into the nest. When this method is not effective, the bees gather water to spread over the comb. The water gatherers find the house bees eager to receive water from them, while nectar gatherers may have difficulty in discharging their loads. Very quickly, foragers change to collecting water which the house bees distribute as droplets in the brood cells. If the delicate larvae become overheated, they die.

Stingless bees are not as efficient as honeybees in controlling nest temperature. Maybe the dangers of high temperatures are not so great for stingless bees which use very little pure wax in nest construction. Some species are better at temperature regulation than others. In southern Brazil, workers of *Trigona spinipes* maintain the temperature of brood chambers at 33–36°C, while outside temperatures vary from less than 8°C to 30°C. The bees raise the temperature in the brood chamber by shivering as honeybees do, and lower the temperature by fanning their wings at the nest entrance.

COMMUNICATION OF FOOD RESOURCES

The success of highly social bees is largely based on the workers' ability to recruit colleagues to sources of food. Foraging for food is the most time-consuming task undertaken by the bees and it occupies most of the work force of an active colony. Worker bees usually begin foraging after working for some weeks in the nest.

A worker does not leave the hive to look for food at random. She waits for the scouts to tell her where forage is to be found. This communication occurs via an amazing form of behaviour. The famous dances of the common honeybee were unravelled by the Austrian entomologist, Karl von Frisch. It is still not understood how the dances and the ability to interpret them evolved. However, if we examine the dances of three species of *Apis* we may obtain some insight into the evolutionary path taken. All three species have made enormous leaps in communication. Each dance is a symbolic re-enactment of the foraging trip just completed.

The small honeybee of south-east Asia, *A. florea*, builds a nest of one exposed, vertical comb, which is widened at the top to form a horizontal platform. A worker, having discovered a food source, returns to the nest and goes to the platform where she performs a dance surrounded by her sister workers. The dance entails a few walking steps in a straight line while shaking her abdomen, and this is repeated several times over. The direction that the dancer follows in the straight line of her dance is the direction in which the new source of food lies. Any bee about to look for food watches the dance and then flies off to find it.

The giant honeybee, *A. dorsata*, also from south-east Asia, has taken this one stage further. The bees dance on the sunny side of the single vertical comb. When the source of food is directly towards the sun the critical part of the bee's dance, when she walks in a straight line, is directly upward. When the food lies 20 degrees to the left of the sun's direction, she walks 20 degrees to the left of the vertical and makes similar compensations for other directions. The attendant bees interpret the direction of the food from the position of the sun.

The common honeybee, *A. mellifera*, which nests in dark cavities, has made several advances in its dance language. The workers can convey not only the distance and direction of the food source, but also its quality. This information

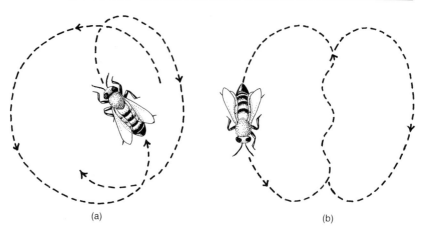

Fig. 31   The dance language of the Western honeybee, *Apis mellifera* (Apidae):
(a) the 'round dance', which alerts other foragers to a source of food within 25 m
(80 ft) of the nest; (b) the 'waggle dance', which indicates to other foragers the
direction and quality of food sources further than 100 m (330 ft) from the nest.

is imparted in the darkness of the hive and is perceived by several 'followers'
which always attend a dancer, inspecting her closely with their antennae.

Foragers returning from a food source within 25 m (80 ft) of the hive perform the 'round dance' (Fig. 31a). This is a series of circular runs with more or
less frequent changes in direction. The rate of direction changes increases with
the sugar concentration of the food.

A worker indicates a food source at a distance of 25–100 m (80–330 ft) by
performing a figure intermediate between the round dance and the 'waggle
dance'. The 'waggle dance' is a contracted figure-of-eight (Fig. 28b) and
indicates food sources at distances greater than 100 m. She waggles her abdomen from side to side during the straight run between the two semicircles at
the ends of the figure. She indicates distance by the duration of the straight run
and the frequency of waggles which accompany it. She indicates direction by
the angle from the vertical of the straight run; this corresponds to the angle
between the direction of the food source and the sun, as seen from the entrance
to the nest.

The dancing bee is able to give accurate directional information because she
remembers the position of the sun as she dances in the darkness of the hive; she
has a sense of time and compensates for the ever-changing position of the sun
by adjusting the angle from the vertical of her straight runs. The German
honeybee specialist, Dr Martin Lindauer, found that a bee which dances for
thirty minutes will move the direction of her dance by 7 or 8 degrees of arc to
compensate for the equivalent amount of change in the sun's position.

It is likely that the waggle dancer imparts information on the quality of the
food by the intensity of waggling and the high frequency buzzes of 250 cycles
per second which accompany it.

The bees recruited by the waggle dancer perceive and interpret all this
information in the darkness of the hive, by touching her with their antennae.
They are also sensitive to sound vibrations transmitted via the comb. It is
likely that the specific scents of flowers on the body of the dancing bee may also

impart information. Just how the recruits interpret this information from what is clearly a multi-channel system of communication, is still not understood.

Dr von Frisch found that workers of *A. mellifera* have 'dialects'. Italian honeybees, for instance, change from the round dance to the waggle dance when the forage is about 35 m (115 ft) from the colony, whereas Austrian honeybees do so at 80 m (260 ft). He mixed the two types of bee in a hive and found they had considerable difficulty in understanding each other when the food was between 35 and 80 m away.

The speed at which stingless bees exploit new sources of food suggested that they also communicate among the members of the colony. However, it was not until 1953 that the Brazilian entomologist, Dr Warwick Kerr, demonstrated that these bees do communicate. Since then, he and his group have investigated the behaviour of several *Trigona* and *Melipona* species in Brazil and have constructed a very plausible explanation of their methods of communication.

In a primitive form, communication is achieved simply by a bee passing food she has gathered to her nest mates. She also vibrates her wings and this may help in drawing attention to herself. Her sisters leave the nest and search for the food source. Apparently, the bees recognize the food by its odour as they are unable to find a dish of plain sugar syrup unless a scent is added. These bees cannot communicate directional information.

Kerr's group found that four *Trigona* species can direct their nest-mates with some accuracy to a new food source and their system is as efficient as that of honeybees. When a field bee finds a new food source, she makes a few trips bringing food to the nest; then she dallies on her return, alighting every few metres on leaves, twigs, and stones. Each time she does so, she nibbles the surface to deposit a droplet of liquid from her mandibular glands. The secretion is strongly scented to the human nose and contains a number of aromatic compounds, the mixture differing according to the species of bee. The scents are quite distinctive, resembling a mixture of burnt sugar and strong blue cheese.

The species of bees that use scent in this manner have larger mandibular glands than other species. One forager of *Trigona postica* was observed by Martin Lindauer to deposit scent at thirty-two points along a trail of 40 m (130 ft). The points lay closer together nearer the food source, presumably to improve the trail's accuracy. The bee flew up to the nest but did not alight. She was seen by others at the nest entrance and they followed her back along the trail to the food.

Many species of *Trigona* live in tall forests 30–40 m tall and the advantage of using scented trails lies in their ability to communicate the height of the food source as well as the distance and direction, an ability that honeybees do not have.

The workers of *Melipona* use a very different method. They are not known to use scented trails, but nevertheless their method of communication has a special interest. To recruit nest mates to a new food source, a worker makes a buzzing sound, presumably by vibrating her wings. The length of time that the sound lasts indicates the distance from the nest. Hence in *M. quadrifasciata* a sound of half a second indicates that the food source is very close to the nest, for one second it is 200 m (650 ft) away and for precisely one and a half seconds, it is 700 m (2300 ft) away. Having given this information, the bee leaves the nest and flies towards the food source followed by recruits. However, she only flies

10–20 m (30–60 ft) whereas the others fly on to find the food.

One cannot help wondering whether the dances of *Apis florea* might have evolved from a situation like that in *Melipona*, by shortening the communication flight until it is a ritual walk.

REPRODUCTION AND SWARMING: HONEYBEES

As the colony becomes more populous, the workers make provision to divide it by producing swarms. The emission of a swarm may seem to be impulsive, but the plans are set in motion some weeks before the event.

As we have already shown, honeybees produce a substance called royal jelly. As the bulk of it is fed to the workers, it is really inappropriately named, and some entomologists prefer the term 'bee milk'. It consists of a mixture of two liquids produced by the head glands of the nurse bee. One is colourless and originates in the hypopharyngeal glands, while the other is white, a little thicker in consistency and is produced by the mandibular glands.

Larvae destined to be workers are fed for two days on a mixture of one-third or less of the white component and two-thirds of the colourless liquid. On the third day, the white food is replaced with a mixture of pollen and honey, but they still receive the colourless liquid.

Larvae destined to become queens are fed equal parts of the two bee milk constituents throughout their entire development. It is this food that has been called royal jelly. The time needed to rear a worker is between twenty and twenty-two days. Despite her larger size, a queen completes her development in seventeen days, the reason being that royal jelly is very rich in body-building amino acids, vitamins, and sugars.

The eventual caste of the adult female has nothing to do with the constitution of the egg. When the old queen lays a female egg it has all the potential to become either a new queen or a worker. The fate of the offspring is decided by her adult worker sisters who decide whether the larva will receive the richer diet and become a queen or the poorer one used to rear a worker. Generally, this decision is made when the bees are building cells and some time before the egg is laid. Queen cells are larger than worker cells and hang vertically, usually from the lower edge of the comb (Fig. 32). To the mother queen, however, they are all cells for daughters. She takes her cue from the diameter of the mouth of the cell and, although the queen cell is larger inside, it is oval, with its opening narrowed to the same size as a worker cell.

Cells in which drones are to be reared have a wider mouth than female cells and this induces the queen to lay an unfertilized egg that will become a male. Hence, the workers decide which types of cells to build and what the larva will be fed. Thus, new queens are only produced when the colony needs them. The question remains as to what stimulates the bees to rear queens or, rather, what usually prevents them from doing so.

The queen is always surrounded by a court of a dozen or so workers who constantly touch her. The queen secretes a powerful pheromone in her mandibular glands which inhibits development of the workers' ovaries. It is called trans-9-keto-2-decenoic acid or, simply, queen substance. The workers remove this substance and distribute it to bees throughout the colony. This is achieved by the constant turnover in the bees that make up the 'court', three-quarters of which attend the queen for less than a minute. Each obtains a small amount of queen substance and leaves to make way for another and to distribute the substance among her nestmates. Every bee in the colony needs to receive one millionth of a gram (0.001 mg) of the substance each day.

The bees are surprisingly sensitive to the presence of their queen. If she is removed they begin to search for her within fifteen to thirty minutes. The workers spend much time feeding each other, and the queen substance and probably several other pheromones are distributed with the food. This behaviour is called trophallaxis, from the Greek *trophos* (= food) and *allaxis* (= exchange).

When the queen dies, it is vital that the workers quickly notice her absence. No more eggs will be laid and they have only a few days to revise the feeding programme of some of the eggs in the cells to rear a new queen. This is a risky time for a colony. Even after the new queen emerges, she must leave the nest to mate, running the gauntlet of waiting predators. The investment of egg-laying responsibility in one individual in a colony of tens of thousands is a safe policy while the queen remains secure in the nest, but is a great risk on the occasions when she must leave.

The bees also rear more queens under different circumstances. As the colony expands, it may occupy all the space in the nest cavity or hive. Even with enough space for expansion, it may become so large that increasing numbers of workers receive less than their daily requirement of 0.001 mg of queen substance. Either situation stimulates the bees to rear other queens. While they are rearing new queens their behaviour towards the old queen changes. They bite her, pull her limbs and are generally aggressive towards her. The queen also changes, and lays fewer eggs.

After two weeks, the new queens emerge. The first one to appear seeks out each of her royal sisters, stinging each one to death while still in their cells. The young queen leaves the colony to mate and very soon after her return, the old queen leaves with a substantial swarm of workers to start a new colony. If more than one young queen emerges they may fight to the death in the hive, or the more submissive ones may leave, each with a group of worker bees in an 'after swarm'.

On leaving the old nest, the swarm normally flies only a few metres and

Fig. 32   Cell of a queen honeybee, *Apis mellifera* (Apidae): (a) in section; (b) outer view.

(a)   (b)

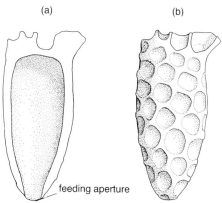

feeding aperture

A queen honeybee, *Apis mellifera* (*top right*), laying an egg (Family: Apidae).

A swarm cluster of the Africanized honeybee, the so-called 'killer bee' of South America, in a tree in Brazil (*above left*). During this phase, scout bees seek new nest sites and communicate to nestmates the distance and direction of the new site by means of the 'waggle dance' (Family: Apidae).

Honeybees (*above right*) exchanging food (Family: Apidae).

settles. Scout bees look for a suitable place to start the new colony. They may find several places and, on returning, each bee dances to communicate the location of likely sites. Eventually, one location wins favour and the whole swarm takes to the air again and moves to the new nest site. The ability of the bees to communicate the whereabouts of a suitable home was proven by Martin Lindauer who, on three occasions, watched the dancers, and was then able to arrive at the new site before the swarm!

REPRODUCTION AND SWARMING: STINGLESS BEES

The stingless bee queen flies only once in her life. Her general shape differs from a worker's in having a smaller head and thorax and larger abdomen.

In all stingless bees, apart from the genus *Melipona*, the rearing of queens and workers is similar to the method used by honeybees. The house bees construct larger cells, usually at the margins of the worker comb, and fill them with royal jelly. After the queen has laid an egg in the cell the workers seal it. Again, the workers control the production of new queens by constructing larger cells and providing the occupants with more food. In stingless bees, the production of a queen apparently depends entirely on the amount of food that the larva is given, and any fertilized egg can become a queen or a worker.

In *Melipona* the situation seems to be more confusing, for the cells in which queens, workers and males develop are all of the same size and the three types of offspring are intermixed in the brood comb. *Melipona* often rear large numbers of queens in times of plenty, up to a quarter of the females being queens. This high proportion led Warwick Kerr to suggest that the production of queens might be genetically controlled and not rely simply on the amount of food that the larvae are given.

The fate of an egg which has the potential to become a queen rests with the house bees and depends on the quantity of food the larva eats. The more food the nurse bees eat, the more royal jelly they secrete and this is reflected in the provisioning of cells; a full cell for a queen and less food for a worker. When the bees have little royal jelly, less is deposited in the cell. They never recruit additional bees to fill the cell and raise a queen.

Although the fate of three-quarters of the female eggs of *Melipona* is determined genetically, the situation in the remaining 25 per cent is not unlike that of *Apis*, where the female eggs have the potential of becoming queens or workers depending on the food they are given by the nurse bees.

In *Melipona* and *Trigona* nests there are usually young virgin queens present in addition to the mother queen. This is seemingly an insurance against the possibility of the old queen dying without leaving her orphans the means to continue the life of the colony. In some species, the young queens are allowed to roam about the nest, but in others, the workers trap the young queen in a corner or in a cell. She is totally enclosed and visited only to be fed. As new queens are raised, the workers usually kill the imprisoned ones.

The first indication that a colony is about to reproduce is that scout bees select a suitable nest site not too far from the parent colony. Next, the bees carry cerumen and honey from the old nest. They begin to build the new nest, constructing the protective coverings, the brood chamber and some food pots, and they begin on the first brood cells. A young virgin queen accompanied by a group of workers flies to the new nest. This is the nearest equivalent to a swarm in stingless bees. A crowd of males from neighbouring nests flies around the entrance to the new nest; in the smaller species they resemble a swarm of gnats. Soon the young queen leaves briefly on a mating flight. She returns to begin laying, while the workers continue building and begin foraging. They often continue to bring materials from the old nest, as the Brazilian entomologist, Dr Paulo Nogueira-Neto, discovered by adding dye to the old nest and noting that it was carried to the new one.

The strategies employed by stingless bees and honeybees to establish new colonies are very different: the former gradually establish a new nest, while there is a rapid break-up in the latter. Nonetheless, they achieve the same major objective. The difference is explained by the mobility of the laying queens. The old stingless bee queen has lost the ability to fly so she remains in the old nest, whereas in *Apis*, the old queen accompanies the swarm, leaving the old nest to her daughter. Hence, in both honeybees and stingless bees, the young queen becomes the head of an established nest.

Chapter 11

Bees and Flowers

Flowers are the sex organs of plants. And pollination is the flower's equivalent of the mating process; it is the process by which the male spores or pollen grains are transported from the flowers of one plant to those of another. Being rooted, literally, to the spot, flowers cannot themselves bring the sexes together. Thus, they rely on other agencies to do it for them.

Some flowers are adapted for pollination by wind, some by water, others by birds, or bats, or mice. But the vast majority of the 300,000 known species are specialized for pollination by insects; of these, most are pollinated by those highly efficient agents of proxy mating, the bees. Bees are the most effective pollinators simply because they and their offspring are entirely committed to a diet of food collected from flowers. Bees therefore make repeated visits to flowers, ensuring a high rate of pollen transport from flower to flower.

If flowers are the sex organs of plants, then the hedgerow in spring, the primrose wood and the traditional English cottage garden are awash with rampant sexuality. And this testifies to the importance of sex in the success of

A spring mining bee, *Andrena armata*, forages at a gooseberry flower. Like many solitary bees, this species is an important pollinator of soft fruits. This female has an incomplete load of pollen on the scopae on her hind legs (Family: Andrenidae).

flowering plants. Why else would they invest so much of their energy resources in producing showy and often large flowers?

In the process of forming the male and female sex cells and in their fusion to make a new individual, genes are reshuffled, often in novel ways. This maintains variability in the population, ensuring that new combinations of genes are exposed to natural selection in each generation. Some individuals in a population will have more beneficial traits than others and will, on average, leave more offspring than less-well-adapted individuals. In this way, the beneficial genes spread in successive generations and new adaptations to an ever-changing environment appear and become fixed. Evolution, then, is an opportunistic process, based on the differential survival of genes; it is not enough to succeed, others must fail.

Most flowering plants have an additional adaptation, which enhances the benefits of sexual reproduction. If pollen lands on the female parts of the same flower, it fails to germinate and fertilization does not occur. This is called self-incompatability and is the plant's equivalent of the incest taboo. If self-fertilization was the norm, then variability within a population would decrease and evolutionary stagnation would set in. Self-incompatability necessitates out-breeding and the transport of pollen, by insects or other agencies, to other individuals, i.e., cross-pollination. This is a principle well-understood by growers of apples, pears, cherries and apricots. They often arrange for local beekeepers to station hives in the orchards to ensure cross-pollination.

We saw in Chapter 1 that some time in the early Cretaceous, certain sphecid hunting wasps became bees by adopting a vegetarian diet: they began to rely more and more on the pollen of plants as a source of protein for themselves and their offspring, as an alternative to insect prey. In so doing, they accidentally transported pollen on their bodies to other plants of the same species, bringing about pollination. The stage was set for the evolution of ever-closer mutual adaptations of bees and flowering plants. In particular, flowers began to reward bees for their unwitting role in their sex lives by providing richer sources of pollen and an additional food, nectar. This chapter deals with the products of this evolutionary history.

ADAPTATIONS OF PLANTS TO BEES
Why are so few flowers green? In a world of green vegetation, green flowers would be overlooked by foraging bees. Brightly coloured petals, offering a contrast to the background, are an obvious way for flowers to advertise their presence. This exploits the fact that bees have not only colour vision, but the ability to learn, remember and generalize: spots of colour on a green or brown background signal a source of food and may be worth exploring.

The spectrum of colours visible to bees is shifted towards blue, so that, unlike us, they are sensitive to ultraviolet light. Bees are red-blind and see red as black, although some red flowers reflect ultraviolet and do attract bees. Otherwise, they see blue, green, yellow and orange much as we do.

Scent is another attractant used by plants to advertise their presence. Flowers secrete scents from special glands which are usually situated on the petals. It is a fortunate accident of evolution that bees and people find the same scents attractive!

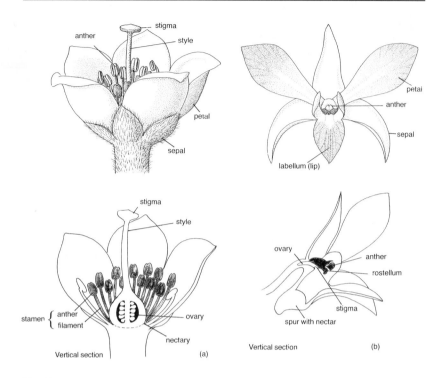

Fig. 33 (a) section through a simple, open-access flower such as a buttercup, *Ranunculus* sp., showing the relative positions of the male and female parts; (b) the same for an orchid, e.g. *Dendrobium* sp.; S.E. Asia.

Heavily dusted with pollen, a female mining bee, *Agapostemon* sp., visits a flower of the Hedgehog cactus, *Echinocereus fendleri*, in the desert of New Mexico, USA (Family: Halictidae).

A female solitary bee, *Anthidium laterale*, probes for nectar (*above left*) in flowers of the Sea holly, *Eryngium maritimum*, in France. She will return to deposit the food in her nest of resin cells built in some sheltered cavity (Family: Megachilidae).

Yellow pigment is a nectar guide in flowers of horse chestnut, *Aesculus hippocastanum*, and leads a worker honeybee, *Apis mellifera*, to the nectaries (*above right*). The nectar guides of the flowers on the left have turned red, indicating that they are pollinated and no longer secrete nectar. The colour change is accompanied by a change in scent (Family: Apidae).

On arrival at the flower, a bee confronts another adaptation of the flower which is geared to increase the likelihood of pollination: the pollen-bearing male parts (anthers) and the receptive female part (stigma) are so arranged that when a bee scrabbles about gathering pollen, she becomes dusted with thousands of tiny pollen grains. When the bee next visits another flower of the same species, she cannot avoid brushing against the stigma, and depositing pollen grains on it. The stigma secretes a sticky fluid to make this more likely. The relative positions of male and female parts in a simple flower such as a buttercup, *Ranunculus* spp., are shown in Figure 33a.

Pollination, often confused with fertilization, is only a prelude to the latter. After being deposited on a receptive stigma of the correct species, a pollen grain germinates and a microscopic tube grows down to one of the ovaries. The pollen tube contains three cell nuclei, two of which are so-called sperm nuclei, the equivalent of an animal's sperm cells. One of these nuclei unites with the nucleus of the egg in the ovary and fertilization is complete.

Some plant species, such as anemones (*Anemone* spp.) and poppies (*Papaver* spp.), produce copious quantities of pollen and rely on this as the sole reward for the pollinating services of bees. But most other plants offer nectar as an additional reward. Nectar is a liquid solution of sugars, mainly sucrose, fructose and glucose. Flowers secrete nectar from special glands called nectaries, which are usually situated at the base of the petals. The positioning of nectaries is usually such that the bee has to make an effort to find them, and in so doing brushes against the anthers and the stigma.

Nectar is an energy-rich food and it fuels all the activities of bees. Bees are very energy efficient: a worker honeybee has a fuel consumption of 700 km/cc – or, in more familiar car-owner terms, 2 million mpg!

131

The flowers of many plant species provide special markings on the inside of the petals which indicate to the bee the direction of the nectaries. These markings are called nectar guides and may be a series of spots, as in foxgloves, *Digitalis* spp. or clear lines, as in some species of *Geranium*. In these plants, the nectar guides are visible to the human eye, but many plants have adapted to exploit the bees' ability to perceive ultraviolet light. In meadow cranesbill, *Geranium pratense*, for example, the nectar guides are barely visible to the human eye, appearing as faint lines radiating from the centre of the flower, but to a bee they are distinct. This is because the entire surface of the petal reflects ultraviolet light, except for the nectar guides, which appear to the bee as black lines on a pale background. A 'bee's-eye' view of the flower can be shown in a photograph by photographing it using a filter which excludes all but ultraviolet light.

ADAPTATIONS OF BEES TO FLOWERS

Almost all pollen-collecting bees are densely clothed in branched or plumose hairs, amongst which the pollen grains become trapped. The effect is enhanced further by static electricity. A flying bee builds up an electrostatic charge of at least 45 pC, equivalent to a potential of 450 volts, on its body. Most floral structures, including the anthers, are well-insulated and pollen is attracted to the bee from the anthers, jumping an air gap of 0.5 mm. It seems that the stigma of a flower is better earthed than other floral structures, so that pollen grains on an incoming, highly charged bee will be attracted preferentially to the stigma rather than to other parts of the flower.

Although a bee may become covered with thousands of pollen grains during a foraging trip, they are not much use to the bee scattered about among its body hairs. Back at the nest, the bee must be able to remove pollen efficiently in a highly confined space. The best way to do this is to concentrate the pollen before returning to the nest.

Bees have evolved several ways of transporting compacted pollen back to the nest. Almost all solitary and primitively social mining bees carry compacted pollen in the scopa, a patch of modified hairs on the hind leg. Species of *Colletes* and *Andrena* may have an additional scopa on the thorax, on the sides of the propodeum. Bees of the family Fideliidae and the family comprising the mason, leaf-cutter and carder bees, the Megachilidae, have the pollen scopa in the form of dense fringes of stiff bristles, on the underside of the abdomen.

All members of the Apidae, the orchid bees, bumblebees, stingless bees and honeybees, have a pollen basket proper, rather than a scopa. The basket, often called the corbiculum, is formed from the slightly concave outer face of the hind tibia, fringed by stiff hairs.

Whatever method of transport is used by a bee, she has to be able to gather together the pollen from her body and concentrate it. Bees do this by using stereotyped grooming movements of the front and middle pairs of legs. The undersides of the basitarsi and tarsi are covered with comb-like arrays of stiff bristles. The bee uses her forelegs to rake up pollen from her head, passing it back to the midlegs and thence to the pollen scopae or corbiculae. She uses her midlegs, which have a wide field of rotation, to gather pollen from her thoracic body hairs. Megachilids simply run the pollen-laden basitarsi of the hind leg through the bristles forming the abdominal scopa, so dislodging the pollen.

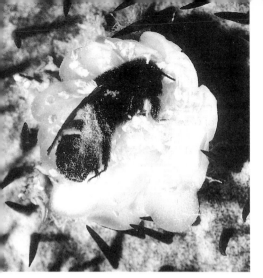

A female of an as yet unnamed species of leaf-cutter bee, *Megachile* (*above left*), feeds at a cactus flower in the Atacama Desert of Chile. The pollen scopa on the underside of the abdomen, characteristic of the Megachilidae, is clearly visible.

A worker honeybee, *Apis mellifera*, probes the nectaries (*above right*) of a quince flower, *Cydonia oblonga*. The pollen baskets or corbiculae are full and clearly visible (Family: Apidae).

All of these complicated pollen manipulations are performed in flight, testifying to a high degree of co-ordination for an animal with so small a brain. It seems to us to require the same degree of dexterity and co-ordination as a man rolling a cigarette in each hand, while running on the spot.

Bees inherited sucking mouthparts from their wasp ancestors. As in the wasps, the tongue is adapted for imbibing liquid food, but in almost all bees, it is longer than that of wasps (Fig. 1). There are exceptions to this rule: some solitary hunting wasps have tongues which are much longer than those of the shorter-tongued bees.

Longer tongues enable bees to probe nectaries in search of nectar. Another adaptation for feeding at flowers is the greatly distensible crop, sometimes called the honey stomach. This enables a female to collect and transport nectar in quantities far greater than those required to meet her own fuel needs; she is, after all, collecting food for her offspring as well.

We saw in Chapter 1 that nesting bees build up a mental map of their surroundings so that they can find their way back to the nest. Female bees use the same ability to memorize the location of good patches of flowers, knowledge which honeybees communicate through dance movements described in Chapter 10.

SPECIALIZED BEE–PLANT RELATIONSHIPS

The simple, buttercup-type flower (Fig. 33a) is often called an 'open access' flower. This is because the flower forms a radially symmetrical, shallow dish shape, which attracts not only short-tongued bees, but also flies, wasps and a wide range of other insects. Typically, open access flowers have a relatively low nectar reward. Although such flowers may be most frequently visited by bees, they are not particularly specialized for pollination by them.

This worker bumblebee, *Bombus lucorum*, swings her tongue forward as she is about to enter bodily a tubular flower of foxglove, *Digitalis purpurea*. The pollen basket on her hind leg contains an incomplete load of pollen. Spotted nectar guides and guard hairs are clearly visible on the lower lip of each flower. The guard hairs deter smaller insects from entering the flower (Family: Apidae).

A mêlée of bumblebees, *Bombus* spp., and cuckoo bumblebees, *Psithyrus* spp., feed peaceably at Woolly thistle, *Cirsium eriophorum*, in southern England (Family: Apidae).

Examples of open access, low-reward flowers in Eurasia and North America are those of hawthorns (*Crataegus* spp.), blackthorn (*Prunus spinosus*), apple (*Malus sylvestris*), brambles (*Rubus* spp.) and hogweed (*Heracleum* spp.). They are visited by short-tongued bees and bees with tongues of medium length. The tongues of short-tongued bees are 0.5–3 mm long; those of medium length are about 3.5–5.5 mm. Short-tongued bees include species of *Hylaeus*, *Colletes* and *Andrena*; bees with tongues of medium length include *Melitta*, *Dasypoda*, *Halictus* and *Lasioglossum* spp.

Dark lines on the petals of this mallow flower, *Malva* sp., are nectar guides, indicating to the bee where the nectaries lie. The bee is a female of a solitary mining species, *Tetralonia malvae*. As its name suggests, it specializes on *Malva* pollen and has widely spaced hairs on its pollen scopae in order to accommodate the large, sticky pollen grains of this plant (Family: Anthophoridae).

Females of the British subspecies of the solitary mining bee, *Colletes cunicularius celticus*, specialize in collecting pollen from male catkins of creeping willow, *Salix repens*. However, this bee will contribute nothing to pollination, because the male catkins of this plant have rich nectaries and she has no need to visit the female catkins (Family: Colletidae).

Many flowers are specialized to attract bees with long tongues. Such flowers have the petals fused to form a tubular corolla and typically are 'high reward' flowers, offering more nectar than open access flowers. Only bees with long tongues can reach the nectaries at the bottom of the tube. The pay-off for the flowers is that they enjoy the pollination services of a restricted, but specialized group of pollinators. The advantage for the bees is that they have access to higher rewards than are available to short-tongued bees. Long-tubed flowers and long-tubed bees evolved together in an evolutionary spiral: by evolving ever-longer tubes, the flowers screen out all but the longest-tongued bees.

Typical long-tubed flowers from temperate regions are primroses (*Primula* spp.), lungwort (*Pulmonaria officinalis*), deadnettles (*Lamium* spp.), sages and claries (*Salvia* spp.) and the North American beard tongues (*Penstemon* spp.). The long-tongued bees which pollinate them are mainly bumblebee (*Bombus* spp.), with tongue lengths of 9–18 mm and the many fast-flying species of *Anthophora*, with tongues 9–20 mm long. Members of the mint and deadnettle family, the Labiatae, provide bees with a landing platform in the shape of a modified petal. These flowers are bilaterally rather than radially symmetrical.

In Central and South America, the long-tongued bees are anthophorid genera such as *Centris* and *Epicharis* and the euglossine bees. They visit the showy, long-tubed flowers of tropical forest trees such as *Jacaranda* spp., lianas such as *Bignonia* spp. and the boxwoods, *Tabebuia* spp.

It is no coincidence that long-tubed flowers yield a high nectar reward: long-tongued bees are larger and much faster flyers than the short-tongued bees and have higher calorific needs. Some flowers are specially adapted for pollination by bumblebees and often have their nectaries at the ends of long, tubular spurs. Columbine, *Aquilegia vulgaris*, is a good example. Other bumblebee flowers, such as the monkshoods (*Aconitum* spp.) and the 100 or so species of lousewort (*Pedicularis* spp.), require physical strength to prize apart their modified petals in order to enter and reach the hidden pollen and nectar. The dependence of these plants on bumblebees is underscored by their distributions, which coincide exactly with that of their pollinators.

Foxgloves (*Digitalis* spp.) are bumblebee flowers and have corolla tubes which are wide enough for the bee to crawl into, out of view. A dense array of stiff hairs inside the tube forms an insurmountable barrier to smaller, short-tongued bees.

Because female bees work in the dark of sometimes complicated nests, they have to be able to develop three dimensional mental maps of where they are in space. Flowers such as deadnettles, monkshood and louseworts, exploit this. The bees have to learn the structure of the flower in order to harvest its nectar rewards. By taking advantage of the bees' behaviour in this way, the flowers greatly increase the likelihood that the bee's next visit will be to another flower of the same species and that cross-pollination will occur. Having learned a particular flower structure, it pays the bee to specialize on that species of flower for so long as the rewards make it worthwhile. The temporary specialization in one flower species is called flower constancy. It is a feature of all large, long-tongued bees, especially bumblebees. Worker honeybees show the same trait and an individual may concentrate on one plant species for up to 12 days.

Flower constancy is a temporary affair and is a property of individuals. There is another kind of bee–flower specialization which is more extreme. Some species of bees specialize exclusively on one plant species or a group of related species as a source of pollen, though they may visit other plants for nectar. This is called oligolecty, and, unlike flower constancy, is a permanent affair and is a property of a species rather than an individual. Oligolectic bees time their emergence as adults to coincide with the flowering period of their pollen plants. They probably do this by being sensitive to the same cues as are the plants, such as increasing day length or soil temperature. Typically, oligolectic bees are solitary and highly seasonal. One would not expect social bees to be oligolectic because their long periods of activity greatly exceed the flowering periods of most plants.

Oligolecty is common in species of *Colletes* and *Andrena*. In Eurasia, including Britain, *Colletes succinctus* is oligolectic on heathers, *Erica* and *Calluna* spp. In *Andrena*, members of the subgenus *Chlorandrena* are oligoleges of yellow-flowered members of the daisy family, Asteraceae. As the name implies, the dapper females of the little mason bee, *Chelostoma campanularum*, specialize on the pollen of bellflowers (*Campanula* spp.). Also appropriately named is the Eurasian bee, *Tetralonia malvae*, which collects pollen only from mallows, *Malva* spp. In all of these examples of oligolecty, the bee–plant relationship is one-sided. Although the bees have evolved total dependency on their food plant species, the plants are not dependent on the oligolectic bees for pollination, although there can be no doubt that much of their cross-pollination is achieved by these bees.

However, there are some examples of plants which are largely dependent for cross-pollination on their oligolectic visitors. Examples in North America are some evening primroses, *Oenothera* spp., pollinated by species of *Andrena* (subgenus *Onagandrena*), and sunflowers, *Helianthus* spp., visited by species of the anthophorid genus *Melissodes*. However, for the levels of pollination required in the commercial growth of cultivated sunflowers, the introduced honeybee is infinitely more efficient than the native species of *Melissodes*.

There are instances of oligolecty where the bees contribute nothing to pollination. Thus, the British populations of the mining bee *Colletes cunicularius*, are oligolectic on creeping willow, *Salix repens*. As with all species of willow, the male and female catkins are on separate plants. The male catkins, apart from producing vast quantities of pollen, also have nectaries. The females of *Colletes cunicularius* obtain all the pollen and nectar they need by visiting the male catkins. They rarely, if ever visit the female catkins and so contribute nothing to pollination.

The extreme specialization of oligolecty is an efficient way of harvesting pollen quickly, especially in unpredictable climates. It is also well-developed in extreme environments. Thus, more than 60 per cent of bees in the deserts of North America are oligolectic. However, as with all extreme adaptations, oligolecty works well so long as there is long-term stability in the environment. Major shifts in climate or the flora could be fatal.

Some bees subvert the normal bee–flower relationship by robbing flowers of nectar. Short-tongued bumblebees, such as *Bombus terrestris* and *B. pratorum*, often bite a hole near the base of the corolla tube of flowers such as comfrey, *Symphytum officinale*, gaining direct access to the nectar. Because the bees by-pass the anthers and stigma, they do not pollinate the flowers. The same species of *Bombus* also bites into the long nectar spurs of columbine, *Aquilegia vulgaris*. Other bees, such as worker honeybees, often use the holes made by nectar-robbing bumblebees.

A worker bumblebee, *Bombus pascuorum* (*above left*), forages at a flower of Comfrey, *Symphytum officinale*. This bee has a tongue which is long enough to reach the nectaries at the base of the deep-tubed flower. In so doing, she contacts the anthers and stigma and can effect pollination. Bees which do this are termed 'legitimate' visitors (Family: Apidae).

Using a hole made by a worker honeybee (*above right*), a male bumblebee, *Bombus pratorum*, robs nectar from a Comfrey flower. Only very long-tongued bumblebees can reach the nectaries by the direct, 'legitimate' route. Honeybees, with their shorter tongues, often bite holes into long-tubed flowers to get at the nectar and other species follow them. Illegitimate visits of this kind contribute nothing to pollination. (Family: Apidae).

OIL-COLLECTING BEES

The flowers of some plants provide oils rather than nectar as a reward, and bees in three families are adapted to exploit them. In Central and South America, species of the anthophorid genera *Centris*, *Epicharis*, *Tetrapedia* and *Paratetrapedia* collect oils from flowers of the Malpighiaceae, especially *Malpighia* spp.

In tropical Africa and Asia, species of *Ctenoplectra* (Family: Ctenoplectridae) collect oils from flowers of the melon and squash family, Cucurbitaceae, while in both Eurasia and North America, species of *Macropis* (Family: Melittidae) collect oils from loosestrife, *Lysimachia* spp.

The flowers produce the oils in special, thin-walled glands called elaiophores. The bees rupture these glands with pads of modified hairs and/or spines on the undersides of the foretarsi. (See electron microscope photographs.) These pads, which in the case of *Macropis* are velvety, absorb oil

138

A worker honeybee, *Apis mellifera*, gains illegitimate access to the nectaries of a bluebell flower, *Endymion nonscriptus*, by another kind of robbing. Instead of biting through the petals, she uses her jaws and tongue to prize them apart (Family: Apidae).

Seen through a scanning electron microscope, modifications for collecting plant oils: (*below left*) a pad of special hairs on the underside of the foretarsus of a female *Macropis europaea* (Family: Melittidae), which collects oils from yellow loosestrife, *Lysimachia vulgaris* and (*below right*) a rake of modified spines on the underside of the foretarsus of a female mining bee, *Centris* sp. (Family: Anthophoridae), which collects oils from flowers such as boxwood, *Tabebuia* spp., in South America.

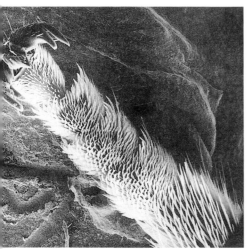

droplets which the bee passes back to the pollen scopae on the hind legs; here the oil is mixed with pollen.

In females of *Ctenoplectra*, the underside of the abdomen is armed with paired pads of special brush-like hairs. Using a side-to-side waggling motion of the abdomen, the bee walks over the oil glands, rupturing them with the pads. A special comb-like structure on the hind tibiae rakes up the oil droplets which accumulate in the abdominal pads and the oil is mixed with pollen in the scopae.

The most bizarre oil bees live in southern Africa and provide some of the best examples of co-evolution between bees and flowering plants. The bees are species of *Rediviva*, which, like *Macropis*, are members of the Melittidae. Also like *Macropis*, the bees collect floral oils using velvety pads on the undersides of the foretarsi, but here the resemblance ends. The forelegs are tremendously elongated. In *Rediviva emdeorum*, the forelegs are longer than the bee's body. The females collect oils produced in a pair of long spurs in flowers of *Diascia*, spp., members of the figwort and foxglove family Scrophulariaceae. The bee settles on the lower petal of the flower and puts a front leg in each of the spurs of the flower to gather the oil. In so doing, the bee's head is dusted with pollen; when it visits another flower, some of the pollen brushes against the stigma and the flower is pollinated.

BEES AND CROP POLLINATION

About 15 per cent of our diet consists of crops which are pollinated by bees. The meat and other animal products we consume are ultimately derived from bee-pollinated forage crops and account for another 15 per cent. It follows that around one third of our food is directly or indirectly dependent on the pollinating services of bees.

On a world basis, the annual value of agricultural crops dependent on the pollination services of bees is estimated at £1000 million ($1590 million). Much of this pollination is due to honeybees and in monetary terms it exceeds the value of the annual honey crop by a factor of fifty.

But the honeybee is not always the best pollinator. Red clover, *Trifolium pratense*, is an important hay crop for cattle. With its corolla tube of 9–10 mm, it is not well-pollinated by honeybees, which have tongues of only 6 mm. Nevertheless, the production of clover seed requires cross-pollination and here, bumblebees come into their own, with their much longer tongues.

Early settlers in New Zealand learned this the hard way. They found themselves in a land ideal for cattle and sheep ranching, but the meagre native bee fauna could not pollinate red clover effectively. New Zealand therefore had to import clover seed from abroad. Then, in the late 1800s, four species of bumblebee were introduced from England and became well-established. Within a very few years, New Zealand became not only self-sufficient in clover seed but also an exporter. It is no exaggeration to say that the cheap meat and dairy produce from New Zealand, enjoyed by the British for so many years, was made possible by those bumblebee immigrants of the last century.

In North America, farmers manage two species of wild bee to ensure efficient pollination of alfalfa, *Medicago sativa*. Alfalfa, known in Britain as lucerne, originates from the steppes of central Asia. It is a member of the pea family, Papilionaceae, and is an important forage crop for cattle. The pollination mechanism involves the explosive release or 'tripping' of a mass of stamens, which strikes the underside of the visiting bee with some force. Honeybees dislike both the pollen of alfalfa and the explosive 'tripping'. They visit the flowers for nectar only and soon learn to avoid tripping the flower by stealing nectar via a natural slit. Only one in twenty honeybee visits results in tripping and so honeybees are very poor pollinators.

By contrast, two wild bees, the alkali bee, *Nomia melanderi* and the Alfalfa leaf-cutter bee, *Megachile rotundata*, relish the pollen of alfalfa and are not discouraged by the tripping mechanism. *Nomia melanderi* is a solitary, ground-nesting halictid. It prefers to nest in alkali beds with little or no vegetation, at densities of up to 500 nests per square metre. Farmers create and maintain artificial beds alongside alfalfa fields for *N. melanderi*, with just the right soil texture and moisture. In this way, nesting densities can reach 2000–3000 per square metre and seed-set is much greater than that achieved with honeybees.

Unlike *N. melanderi*, *Megachile rotundata* is not native to North America. It was accidentally introduced there from the Old World, and soon made its presence felt as a highly efficient pollinator of alfalfa. It originated in the steppes of Eastern Europe and Central and Southwest Asia, where it has a similar distribution to that of alfalfa. The females are typical opportunists nesting in existing cavities such as beetle borings in dead wood. Farmers build up huge populations by providing vast numbers of nesting cavities in grooved wooden boards. These are dotted about the fields on trailers, forming bee houses. In winter, these are towed indoors, where the overwintering pupal cocoons can be screened for disease and parasites. *Megachile rotundata* is just as efficient as *Nomia melanderi* in pollinating alfalfa; it is largely replacing that species because it is easier to rear and maintain in artificial nests.

THE POLLINATION MARKET PLACE

The apparently harmonious relationship between bees and plants conceals a conflict of interests. Although flowers need bees and vice versa, it pays each partner in the contract to minimize its costs and maximize its profits. This may sound like anthropomorphism taken to extremes, but using the market place and the principles of double-entry book-keeping as metaphors may give us some insights into what is really going on between bees and flowering plants.

In this chapter we have discussed the pollination mechanisms of individual species of plants and their relationships with particular bees. But in the real world, both flower and bee operate in a competitive market place. A community of retailers, the flowers, seeks to attract more or less discriminating consumers, the bees. Each flower has to juggle the costs and benefits of investing in advertising, by colour and scent, and providing rewards, nectar and pollen. Clearly, a species which depends on cross-pollination is on a knife edge; it must provide sufficient nectar to attract the interest of a bee, but not enough to satisfy all of its needs in one visit. A satiated bee would return to its nest rather than visit another flower. A bee, on the other hand, is out to get the maximum amount of pollen and nectar; it must assess the quality and quantity of rewards which are on offer and juggle its energy costs so that it makes a calorific profit on each foraging trip.

The apparent harmony between plants and bees is therefore not all that it seems. Instead, it is an equilibrium based on compromises between the competing interests of the protagonists. This sounds remarkably like the ideas of the 18th-century economist Adam Smith. In his book, *The Wealth of Nations*, he postulated that in human society every 'economic unit' seeks to maximize its own financial well-being independently of others. The competitive interactions of this behaviour result in an equilibrium or an 'harmonious' society.

One might predict, therefore, that economists would find the relationships between bees and plants of some interest. This is precisely what is happening in Israel, where a long-term study of the pollination biology of the native flora is under way. Botanists, entomologists and economists are collaborating in an attempt to understand the dynamics of bee–plant relationships at the community level.

This sort of study is of more than passing, academic interest. It is important that we understand the dynamic relationships between plants and their pollinators. This is especially true when, say, devising conservation policies for tracts of tropical rain forest.

A good example comes from the forests of tropical South America. Here, as in all rain forests, there is a very high diversity of tree species. There may be more than 120 species per acre, but in a given acre there may only be one or two individuals of a species. These trees are pollinated by large, fast-flying bees. There is evidence that species of *Xylocopa* and *Eufriesea* learn the distribution of these scattered trees and forage regularly along the same routes. This is called trap-lining and the bees forage for up to 23 km from their nests. The bees are therefore acting as long-distance pollinators. It is likely that other large bees such as species of *Centris*, *Epicharis*, and *Eulaema* do likewise.

An issue of current concern in tropical forest conservation is that of trying to estimate the minimum sustainable size of 'islands' of forest reserve in areas where large-scale felling is taking place. There is much discussion on seed dispersal distances. But this is only one half of the equation so far as the reproduction of trees is concerned. There is another question that must be addressed: 'Is the proposed forest reserve close enough to the nearest large tract of forest to be within the flight range of long-distance foragers?' We need to know much more about the biology of the bees and their relationships with plants before this question can be answered.

Bees, then, are vital to our survival. Much of the visual impact of human environments derives from vegetation. And most vegetation is dependent on bees for pollination. Thus, as pollinators of crops and natural vegetation, bees occupy key positions in the web of relationships which sustain the living architecture of our planet.

Chapter 12

Unlikely Partners: Bees and Orchids

There is something indefinably special about orchids. We associate the more colourful and fleshy species with opulence and grand passion: many a lovelorn gentleman has sought to win a fair lady by giving an orchid as an extravagant token of adoration.

The majority of orchids, however, produce small, unshowy flowers which no one would consider wearing as a corsage. With 20,000 known species, orchids comprise the largest family of flowering plants and have an almost limitless variety of flower form and a host of bizarre pollination mechanisms. Many of them are pollinated by bees, while others are adapted to attract moths, beetles, flies, wasps and even birds.

In general, flowers offer bees nectar and pollen in return for their unwitting participation in the sex life of the plant. For orchids, sex is still the name of the game, but they have bent the rules in their own favour. They present their pollen in a form that is useless to the foraging bee and perhaps more than half of them produce no nectar at all. Paradoxically, nectarless species have evolved some of the closest and most specialized relationships with bees. In this chapter, we explain how and suggest why some bees have developed close relationships with these apparently unrewarding plants.

Bees are attracted to orchids, as they are to other plants, by scent and colour. The orchid flower provides the bee with a landing platform with nectar guides. In orchids, the landing platform is a modified petal called the labellum or lip (Fig. 33b). Here, the resemblance of other flowers ends, because when a bee enters an orchid flower, it encounters a structure quite unlike that of an 'ordinary' flower. If we cut in half a simple, bee-pollinated orchid, like the flamboyant South American *Cattleya maxima*, which is often cultivated in greenhouses, or the European early purple orchid, *Orchis mascula*, the most striking feature is the apparent absence of both stamens and a central pistil. These structures have become fused so that the male and female parts of the flower are born on a single organ, the column. The single anther is at the apex of the column and is separated from the stigma by a projection called the rostellum. The stigma is usually in the form of a shallow, sticky depression in which the pollen is deposited. The pollen is bound together by sticky threads into a pair of compact masses called pollinia.

Cross-pollination is the rule in orchids. With a few exceptions, self-pollination is physically impossible because the rostellum is a barrier between anther and stigma. The precise positioning of pollen on the bee's body is one of the more obvious adaptations for cross-pollination in orchids. When the bee visits another flower of the same species, the pollen cannot fail to contact the stigma. To ensure that this occurs, the orchid presents pollen as pollinia in the form of discrete packages. Here, the normal flower–bee relationship breaks down: pollinia are useless to the bee because their pollen-collecting and transport structures are only effective with free pollen. While orchids may satisfy some of their nectar requirements, the bees must seek pollen from other sources. Thus, orchids are free-loaders in the plant community, depending on bees, but relying on other flowers to provide pollen for them and to subsidize them with nectar.

The orchid is a gambler. When a bee visits an ordinary flower, it does not greatly affect the reproductive success of the plant if that individual bee never visits another flower of the same species. Normal flowers produce copious quantities of pollen and the plant can be sure of further visitors. But when a bee visits an orchid flower and unwittingly carries away the pollinia, it carries off all of the male genetic investment of that flower. The bee may die, be eaten by a predator before it visits another orchid, or it may simply never visit an orchid again in its short life. After all, it has gained little from the first visit. In the wild, few of the many flowers of an orchid plant ever get pollinated. Nevertheless, the gamble obviously pays off. The ovary of a single orchid flower produces thousands, perhaps hundreds of thousands, of light, easily dispersed seeds, so if only one flower on the orchid is pollinated, or if only one set of pollinia are delivered to another plant, there is still the potential for many offspring. Clearly, the rewards in terms of seed production are so high that it is worth the risk of wasting some pollinia.

Many orchids have a pollination mechanism like that of *Cattleya maxima*. This fine species is pollinated by species of the neotropical euglossine bee genus *Eulaema*. Other species of *Cattleya* are pollinated by large carpenter bees, *Xylocopa* spp. When a *Eulaema*, such as *E. polychroma*, alights on the labellum of *Cattleya maxima*, it crawls into the flower, forcing the labellum down and away from the column, and probes into the nectary with its long tongue. Like many orchids, the nectary of *Cattleya* is very deep, so that the pollinator has to crawl deep into the flower until it is in a position to receive the pollinia. As the *Eulaema* backs out, it pushes the flap-like rostellum backwards with the back of its thorax and sticky stigmatic fluid is smeared on to the bee. Immediately afterwards, the back of the thorax brushes against the anther cap and the base of the pollinia is cemented to the bee by the stigmatic fluid already on the bee's back. The bee flies off bearing the pollinia and when it next visits a flower of *Cattleya maxima* the pollinia are wrenched from the bee as it backs out of the flower and adhere to the stigma: the flower is thus pollinated.

In a single visit to a *Cattleya* flower, a bee may deposit one pollinia and collect another, thus enabling the flower to set seed through its female parts and also giving it a reasonable chance of having offspring through its male parts. In most orchids, however, two visits by pollinating insects are necessary because the flowers are dichogamous, that is the male and female parts mature at different times.

In some orchids, the labellum plays a more important role than it does in *Cattleya* and is directly involved in the mechanism of pollination. The European orchid called Autumn Lady's Tresses, *Spiranthes spiralis*, derives its name from the spiral arrangement of its attractive little white flowers around the stem, which is said to resemble a girl's plaited hair. The flowers smell of hyacinths and secrete nectar at the base of the labellum. The labellum is reduced and the space between it and the column is only wide enough for the bee's tongue to enter. A close North American relative, *Spiranthes gracilis*, has an identical pollination mechanism, involving solitary bees such as *Calliopsis andreniformis* and *Megachile brevis*, and a bumblebee, *Bombus americanum*.

The pollination mechanism of *Spiranthes spiralis* was first described by Charles Darwin in his classic book, *The Various Contrivances by which British and Foreign Orchids are Fertilized*. The flat, delicate rostellum projects horizontally from the end of the column, with the anther above and the stigma below (Fig. 34). The tips of the pollinia are attached to a central area of the rostellum. When a bee inserts its tongue between the column and labellum, it touches the rostellum, which immediately splits on either side to expose the disc bearing the pollinia. These become cemented firmly to the upper side of the bee's tongue.

These flowers are well-adapted to cross-pollination. A flower cannot be pollinated by a visiting bee until its own pollinia have been removed. Shortly after this event, the remains of the rostellum shrivel and the column bends upward, exposing the stigma. When a bee carrying pollinia visits the flower, these adhere to the stigma when the bee inserts its tongue.

Darwin wrote that he had seen Autumn Lady's Tresses pollinated by bumblebees but no subsequent author had observed it. Photographer-naturalist K.G. Preston-Mafham has succeeded in photographing a worker bumblebee, *Bombus lapidarius*, visiting flowers of Autumn Lady's Tresses in Gloucestershire. The pollinia are clearly visible on the bee's tongue.

So far, we have seen the orchids in the role of free-loaders. Many species also play the role of deceiver.

Deception is a recurrent theme in orchid–bee relations. In North America, species of the bee genera *Augochlora* and *Xylocopa* are fooled into visiting the nectarless flowers of *Calopogon* by tufts of yellow hairs on the labellum which resemble the massed, pollen-bearing stamens of some ordinary flowers.

In South America, there are at least fifty nectarless species of *Maxillaria*

Fig. 34   The flower of Autumn Lady's Tresses, *Spiranthes spiralis*: (a) side view of single flower; (b) side view of column, labellum and sepal removed; (c) rostellum, from above; (d) 'boat-formed disc' with attached pollinia. (After Darwin, C., 1862, *The Various Contrivances by which Orchids are Fertilised*, J. Murray, London.)

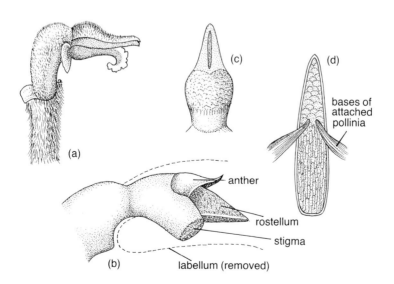

A worker bumblebee, *Bombus lapidarius*, visits tiny flowers of the orchid Autumn Lady's Tresses, *Spiranthes spiralis*. Orchid pollen is presented in discrete packages or pollinia, which in this case adhere to the bee's tongue (Family: Apidae).

which attract bees by means of 'pseudopollen' on the labellum. This consists of powdery, starch-filled hairs which visiting bees collect as though they were real pollen. Presumably it has some nutritive value for the bee and her larvae. *Maxillaria* has boxed itself into an evolutionary corner. It cannot 'de-evolve' pollinia, so has to resort to the production of a pollen-substitute to attract bees.

A common deceiver in Europe is the Early Purple orchid, *Orchis mascula*. The flowers are borne on a single stem, which may reach 30 cm (1 ft) in height. This species qualifies as a deceiver because the long spur of the flower contains no nectar. It exploits the natural urge of bumblebees to explore with their tongues the long, nectar-yielding spurs of flowers like columbines and nasturtiums. When a bumblebee lands on the labellum, it inserts its tongue into the spur and cannot avoid touching the rostellum with its head. The rostellum ruptures in front and the movements of the bee expose the pollinia with their sticky pads, which adhere to the bee's head. At first, the pollinia on the bee stand upright, but do not remain in that position or they would strike the anther of the next flower instead of the stigma. While the bee flies to another flower, the sticky pads dry out and the pollinia swing forward so that they point forward at an angle which guarantees contact with the stigma.

Among many bees, the females emit scents, called sex pheromones, which are characteristic of each species. These attract and sexually arouse the males. Orchids of the Old World genus *Ophrys* take advantage of the scent-based sexual communication systems of solitary bees by producing their own chemical attractants. The males, which are thus attracted by the flower, attempt copulation with it. For a very obvious reason, *Ophrys* species are sometimes called 'fetish orchids' and the males' behaviour at the flower is called pseudo-copulation. The thrusting, copulatory movements bring the bee into contact with the pollinia, which stick to the insect's body. Pollination is completed when the male tries to mate with another orchid and, in so doing, deposits the pollinia on its stigma. *Ophrys* flowers produce no nectar and female insects never visit them.

Most of the thirty or so species of *Ophrys* live in the Mediterranean region. Ten of them have been studied in detail and are pollinated by male bees. The labellum bears a superficial resemblance to a female bee and this was once thought to be the main attraction for the males. However, scent plays a major role. The labellum of the orchid secretes a blend of scents, some of which are identical to those produced by female bees. Each species of *Ophrys* emits its own specific scent so it attracts the males of only one or, at most, two or three closely related species of bees.

By removing the labellum from the flowers, the Swedish biologist, Dr B. Kullenberg, showed that it was the source of the scent. Male bees were attracted to an isolated labellum but not to the rest of the flower. They also showed that males were attracted to a labellum hidden from view, demonstrating that scent rather than visual cues are the initial attractants.

The scent is a long-distance attractant, alerting the male to the possibility of a mating encounter in the vicinity. When the male arrives to within a few centimetres of the labellum, its visual resemblance to a female bee reinforces the impression that he has found a mate. Moreover, the disposition and density of the velvety pile on the labellum are like those of the female of his own species. These final tactile cues induce the male to take up the mating posture.

The Bee Orchid, *Ophrys apifera*, attracts males of the long-horn bees, *Eucera longicornis* and *E. tuberculata*. The male rests head upwards, nearest the column and rostellum, so that when he attempts copulation, pollinia are deposited between his eyes. With *Ophrys lutea*, which is pollinated by males of *Andrena nigro-olivacea* and *A. senecionis*, the male rests the opposite way round, so that when he copulates with the flower, the pollinia are attached to the tip of the abdomen; tactile cues given by the disposition of the hairs on the labellum are responsible for the final positioning of the bee for pseudocopulation. The labellum of *Ophrys lutea* is bright yellow, with a velvety, dark reddish-brown, raised area in the centre. The dark area resembles a female *Andrena* sitting on a yellow flower. This is appropriate, because *A. nigro-olivacea* and *A. senecionis* belong to the subgenus *Chlorandrena*, the females of which are oligolectic on yellow flowers of the daisy family, Asteraceae.

The role of the disposition of the hairs on the labellum was demonstrated in a simple, but ingenious, experiment by Dr Bertil Kullenberg in Sweden. He removed the labellum from a flower and replaced it with the apex glued to where the base would normally be. The *Andrena* males which later visited this modified flower attempted copulation with the head nearest the column instead of the tail, and pollinia were deposited on the head instead of on the tip of the abdomen. In other words, the bees aligned themselves according to tactile cues given by the hairs, irrespective of the overall position of the labellum.

The pollination mechanism of *Ophrys* is remarkable because it is based on the detailed mimicry of a chain of signals, chemical, visual and tactile, emitted by female bees. Presumably, the relationship between the orchids and their pollinators continues because the females have no part in the relationship and are under no competitive pressure to change the signals they present to their mates.

The most specialized relationships between bees and orchids have evolved amid the biological exuberance of the New World tropics. In the humid forests of Central and South America, we find the bees of the subfamily Euglossinae. There are about 200 species in the genera *Eulaema*, *Euglossa* and *Eufriesea*, six in *Exaerete* and one in *Aglae*. The first three genera are most strongly associated with orchids, the two latter less so.

Euglossine bees range in size from species which are smaller than a honey-bee worker, to those as large as the queens of bumblebees. They all have very long tongues. Many of these bees are brilliantly coloured, the commonest hues being metallic greens and blues, bronze and burnished gold. It is appropriate that these, the most spectacular of bees, should pollinate some of the most bizarre orchids.

Two subfamilies of orchids, the Catasetinae and the Stanhopeinae, are specialized for pollination by euglossine bees. Nectar is not provided and it is the male bees, attracted by scents, that play the all-important role in the sex life of the plant.

Fig. 35 A male orchid bee, *Euglossa cordata* (Apidae), showing the enormously long tongue and the greatly expanded tibia of the hind leg: (a) section through the tibia showing the spongy tissue in which the bee stores orchid fragrances; (b) side view of *E. cordata* male, showing the pollinia of a bucket orchid, *Coryanthes* sp., attached to the base of the abdomen.

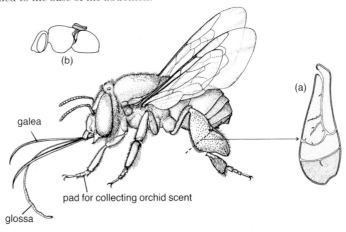

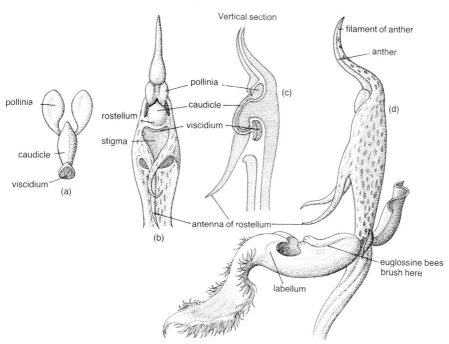

Vertical section

filament of anther

anther

pollinia

caudicle

(c)

pollinia

(d)

rostellum

viscidium

pollinia

stigma

caudicle

viscidium

(a)

antenna of rostellum

(b)

euglossine bees
brush here

labellum

Fig. 36   A male flower of the South American orchid, *Catasetum saccatum*;
(a) pollinia and associated structures; (b) front view of column; (c) vertical section
through column; (d) side view of whole flower, dorsal petal and sepals removed.
(After Darwin, 1862, *The Various Contrivances by which Orchids are Fertilised*, J. Murray,
London.)

The specific relationship between an orchid and its euglossine bee is not
one-sided. The very scent which attracts the bee is its reward. The males
collect droplets of the orchid fragrance by brushing on the surface of the
labellum with special pads on their front feet (Fig. 35). At intervals, the bee
takes to the air and hovers close by the flowers while it passes scent droplets
back to the hind tibiae. The latter are greatly enlarged, with a small slit on the
upper surface. The slit, guarded by velvety hairs, leads by branching tubes
into a spongy storage tissue (Fig. 35a). The bee deposits droplets of the orchid
fragrance on to the slit and the oily liquid passes into the spongy storage tissue
by capillary action.

The exact use to which the bees put these collected fragrances is still unclear.
The chemicals involved have been identified and include methyl salicylate,
which is the smell of oil of wintergreen, eucalyptol, cineole and skatole. Some
researchers have suggested that the bees use the scents to attract other males of
the same species in order to set up a special kind of all-male assemblage called a
'lek' although there is no clear evidence of this. Females are said to be attracted
to the conspicuous group of brightly coloured males and select a mate from
among them. One thing is certain: female euglossines never visit the orchids.
And if isolated hind legs of male bees are pinned out on pieces of card in the
field, only males of the same species are attracted to them. The same occurs if
blotting paper impregnated with synthetic orchid scents is placed in the field.

Whatever attracts the females to a lek, orchid scents seem to play no role. We discuss the behaviour of male euglossines further in Chapter 13.

Once a male euglossine has been attracted to an orchid and has spent some time brushing for scent droplets, he is likely to be subjected to some rough treatment. In *Catasetum* (Fig. 36), the rostellum is extended on each side into a long filament which Darwin called the antenna. The rostellum stretches between the bases of the pair of antennae, restraining the highly elastic parts of the pollinia under tension. When a euglossine male brushes the sac-like labellum for fragrance droplets, he cannot help but touch an antenna. This transmits the slightest vibration to the rostellum which ruptures, releasing its stored tension and flinging out the pollinia violently. These adhere to the bee's

Fig. 37   Pollination of the South American Orchid, *Stanhopea grandiflora*, by a male of the orchid bee, *Eulaema meriana*: (a) the bee enters from the side and brushes the sac-like base of the labellum; (b) the surface of the labellum is very smooth and the bee may slip and fall when it withdraws from the flower, hooking the viscidium of the pollinia under its scutellum or depositing pollinia in the stigma; (c) dorsal view of the bee with the pollinia attached; (d) outline of bee showing placement of pollinia, from the side; (e) longitudinal section of column with pollinia in place, showing the projecting rostellum with the viscidium; (f) same, with the pollinia removed, showing how the pollinia are inserted into the stigma. (Redrawn after Dressler, R.L., 1967, *Evolution*, **22**, 202–10.)

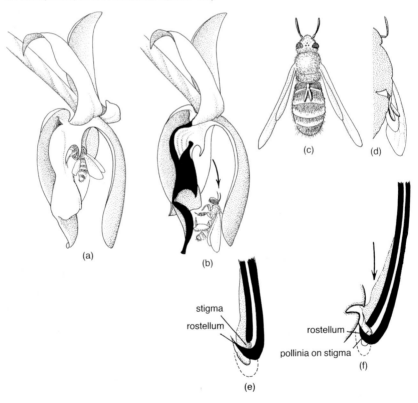

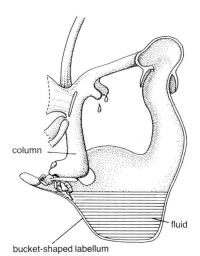

Fig. 38   Section through a flower of the South American bucket orchid, *Coryanthes speciosa*, which has temporarily trapped a male orchid bee, *Euglossa* sp. (Apidae), as part of the pollination process. (See text for explanation.)

head by means of the sticky viscidium. Darwin reported that, while examining a greenhouse specimen of *C. callosum*, he touched the antennae and the pollinia were flung about a metre, where they stuck fast to a pane of glass. He also mentioned that pollinia of *Catasetum* often stick to the faces of unwary orchid growers.

Euglossine bees are very wary insects, with a rapid, darting flight. The violent flinging out of *Catasetum* pollinia is an adaptation for hitting these fugitive targets.

There are about eighty species of *Catasetum*, ten of which have bisexual flowers, which is normal for orchids. The remaining seventy species have unisexual flowers. The flower of *C. saccatum* illustrated in Figure 36 is male. The female parts are non-functional. Pollination takes place when the euglossine male transports pollinia to the smaller female flowers. *Catasetum* therefore ensures cross-pollination by separating the sexes in space.

A brilliantly metallic male *Euglossa* sp. approaches a bucket orchid, *Coryanthes* sp., in a South American rain forest. He will collect scent droplets from the orchid (Family: Apidae).

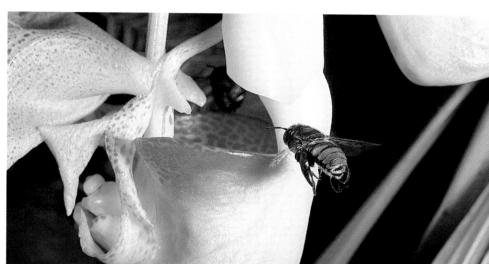

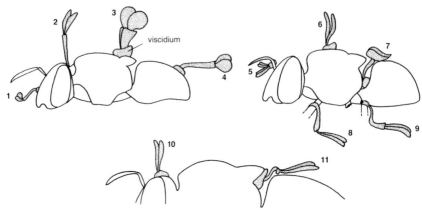

Fig. 39 Outlines of male euglossine bees, showing how the pollinia of various orchid genera are placed: 1. *Notylia*; 2. *Lacaena*, between head and prothorax; 3. *Mormodes*; 4. *Cycnoches*; 5. *Kefersteinia*, on the base of the antenna; 6. *Peristeria*, sp.; 7. *Coryanthes*; 8. *Cirhaea*, on the base of the foreleg; 9. *Sievekingia*, on the base of the hind (or mid) leg; 10. *Peristeria elata*; 11. *Acineta*. (Redrawn after Dressler, R.L., 1967, *Evolution*, **22**: 202–10.)

Orchids of the genus *Stanhopea* lure the euglossine male to the base of the labellum, where it collects droplets of scent. As it moves deeper into the flower, it reaches an area of slippery cells and loses its foothold. The bee falls backward, brushing against the rostellum and picking up the pollinia. *S. grandiflora* is pollinated by males of *Eulaema meriana* and the mechanism is explained in Figure 37.

Bucket orchids of the genus *Coryanthes* have the most bizarre pollination mechanism of all South American orchids. A male of *Eulaema* or *Euglossa* is lured to a point on the labellum where it loses its foothold. The labellum of *Coryanthes* is a vessel containing fluid secreted by a pair of glands on the column (Fig. 38). The bee falls into the fluid and the only exit is via the spout-like aperture between the column and the labellum. Just before the bee escapes, it is trapped by the finger-like rostellum, which catches the bee tightly between its thorax and abdomen. The bee struggles for about forty minutes in *Coryanthes speciosa*, which is pollinated by *Euglossa cordata*. Other species of *Coryanthes* detain the bee for shorter periods than this. The bee finally emerges with the pollinia firmly attached to the base of its abdomen (Fig. 39, no. 7). When the bee is subjected to the same procedure in another flower, the pollinia catch onto the stigma, pollinating the flower.

Within minutes of the pollinia being removed, the flower of *Coryanthes* ceases to emit scent. This ensures that it is unlikely to be visited and self-pollinated by the bee which just removed the pollinia. Within a day or so, the flower resumes the emission of scent and attracts bees once more, though now the stigma is receptive and the flower is female.

Each orchid species produces a combination of fragrances, characteristic of the species. There may be up to forty orchid-pollinating species of euglossine bee in any given locality, but often only one species is attracted to a particular orchid. The specific fragrance of an orchid screens the pollinators, because each bee species is adapted to respond only to a limited range of fragrances.

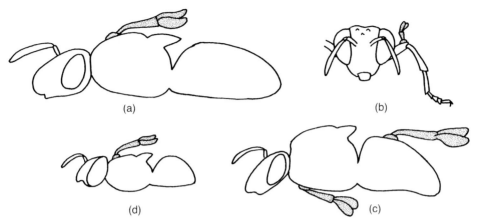

Fig. 40   Outlines of male euglossine bees showing how pollinia of five species of
Catasetum are placed: (a) *Eulaema meriana* with pollinia of *Catasetum macrocarpum*;
(b) face view of *Eulaema meriana* with pollinia of *Catasetum warczewitzii* on 'elbow';
(c) *Eulaema cingulata* with pollinia of *Catasetum saccatum* on dorsal surface and pollinia
of *C. discolor* beneath thorax; (d) *Euglossa cordata* with pollinia of *Catasetum barbatum*.
These species of *Catasetum* occur in the same areas in various combinations, but no
hybrids between them are known. (Redrawn after Dressler, R.L., 1967, *Evolution*,
22: 202–10.)

By attracting a specific pollinator, an orchid flower ensures that it receives
pollinia only of the same species and that its own pollinia are transported to
other conspecific plants. This is important, because orchids are notorious for
their ability to hybridize with other species or even genera. Herein lies the
attraction for orchid growers and enthusiasts: there is plenty of scope for the
development of gaudy hybrids of commercial value. Hybrids are either infer-
tile or have a reduced fertility and are, as a rule, less well-adapted than either
parent species to local conditions.

However, hybridization in the wild is relatively rare among euglossine-
pollinated orchids and the orchid–bee relationship is, from the plant's point of
view, an excellent adaptation to avoid hybridization.

Another adaptation for maintaining reproductive isolation between orchid
species is based on the precise positioning of pollinia on the body of the pollinating bee. In five species of *Catasetum* which grow side-by-side in South
America, and which may be visited by the same species of bee, the pollinia are
deposited in a position on the bee that is characteristic for each species of
orchid (Fig. 40). The stigma of each species is positioned in a unique way, so
that when a bee bearing pollinia enters a given flower, only pollinia from other
flowers of its own species contact the stigma. Thus, while the five species of
Catasetum are interfertile, hybrids never occur in the wild because each species
is mechanically isolated from its fellows. Hybrids between different genera are
avoided in the same way.

Bees play an essential role in the pollination of orchids because they are
directly involved in the two dominant adaptations of the orchid flower, which
are for sexual reproduction by cross-pollination and reproductive isolation
from other species.

Chapter 13

The Male of the Species

Male bees have always had a bad press. The idea of the male honeybee as the lazy, feckless drone, relying on workers to feed him, has permeated our culture.

Even though the males of most bee species provide no parental care, they nevertheless serve a vital function. Bees are in business to make more bees. And the only way a male bee can do this is to find and mate with as many females as he can. In this way he ensures that his genes pass into the next generation and this fulfils his sole purpose in life.

Just how male bees act out their destinies is a fascinating and sometimes complicated story, and there is much we do not yet understand. Until recently, almost all attention was paid to the behaviour of female bees, either at the nest or at flowers. Nevertheless, it is already apparent that male bees have evolved a wide range of different strategies, all geared to solving the same problem: finding a mate.

The males of some bee species have arrived at solutions which we normally associate with the birds and mammals: some defend territories, others may set up eye-catching displays or leks.

But why is it that the males do all the searching? The answer is to do with the relative cost of sperm and eggs. We have seen how the eggs of bees are among the largest of all insect eggs. Moreover, with the exception of the highly social species, female bees lay rather few eggs. Solitary mining or leaf-cutter bees lay as few as 15–35 eggs in their entire lives, while the giant carpenter bees, *Xylocopa* spp., may lay no more than 8. By contrast, a male bee may ejaculate 2-11 million sperm in a single mating. An egg is many millions of times larger than the single sperm which will fertilize it. In terms of energy and nutrients, a sperm is very cheap to make, but an egg represents a much larger investment by the female.

In addition to producing the egg, the female also spends time and energy in searching for a nest site, building or excavating the nest, fashioning the brood cells and providing food for her offspring. Although the male bee spends time and energy in finding a female and mating with her, the investments made by the female are incalculably greater than those made by the male. It is not surprising that, with a few exceptions, female bees are not the mate-seeking sex. A female simply has to devote her energies elsewhere, whereas males have nothing else to do.

The differential in investments results in a conflict of interests. The females of most species mate only once (monandry), while male bees can mate many times. A single mating provides a female with more sperm than she can ever use. She stores it in a special sac called the spermatheca.

Monandry frees a female from the time and energy costs she would incur if she mated with every male which made the attempt. After mating, such females become either unattractive to males, or are able physically to repel unwelcome advances. Females may signal unreceptivity by simply ceasing to emit a male-attracting scent. The females of many species indicate that they are unreceptive by raising their hind legs along the sides of the abdomen and, at the same time, bending the abdomen down and forwards. There is also the possibility that the males of some bee species deposit a scent on their mates during copulation, which renders them unattractive to other males. This certainly happens in some butterflies and mosquitoes.

Whatever subtle factors are involved, it pays a mated female to signal that she is unreceptive: the number of offspring a female has depends largely on the amount of food she is able to collect and any disturbance while she is foraging could reduce this. Male bees are not noted for their finesse and a nesting female, returning from a foraging trip, is likely to lose much of her pollen load in the rough and tumble of mating attempts by one or more males.

The males of monandrous species have a problem. The number of virgin females in the population declines very quickly. With time, there is increased competition and encounters between males increase as they are faced with a rapidly diminishing resource; each male is under pressure to be the first one to mate with a receptive female.

One way in which male solitary bees have adapted to monandry is to emerge before the females, often *en masse*. Emergence may be spread over several days, but the peak is always in advance of that of female emergence, sometimes by as much as a week. This is called protandry. By emerging before the females, the males can find the local food sources, learn the geography of the area and the location of nest sites. Protandrous males are therefore in a good position to mate as soon as the females appear.

The females of a few species, such as the carder bee, *Anthidium manicatum*, mate more than once (polyandry). This creates another kind of problem for the males: here there is pressure on each male to be the last one to mate with any female. This is especially true if semen from several matings are not mixed in the spermatheca. This means that the last semen to be deposited inside a female is the first to be released when she fertilizes an egg just before it is laid. This 'last-in-first-out' principle is called 'sperm precedence' and, although it has not been demonstrated in bees, it is common in other insects and dictates much of male behaviour.

Indeed, much of the behaviour of male bees has evolved as a result of pressure to adapt to aspects of female behaviour, such as monandry, which are themselves adaptive, but which create problems for the males. In other words, the various mating strategies adopted by bees are a compromise, an attempt to attain an equilibrium between the conflicting needs of the sexes.

FINDING A MATE

We can identify at least three mate-seeking strategies among male bees: general searches, flight trails and circuits, territories and leks. To complicate matters, the males of some species may be split into two subpopulations, each with a different mate-seeking behaviour.

Whichever ploys the males use, both sexes must be sure that they belong to the same species before going on to mate. Correct species recognition is vital, especially in areas where there may be many species active at the same time.

A combination of visual, scent and, ultimately, tactile cues are important in probably all species. Scent is probably dominant. This is reflected in the fact that males not only have 13 antennal segments to the females' 12, but, in nearly all cases, each segment is much longer than in the females. Male antennae are therefore often twice as long as those of females of the same species.

The importance of scent is demonstrated by the fact that the males of protandrous species often detect females before the latter have emerged and while they are still digging their way to the soil surface. This is a common occurrence in species of *Colletes, Andrena, Centris* and *Epicharis*. Males of the mason bee, *Osmia rufa*, are attracted to caged females which they cannot see.

The identification of a female as being of the correct species is the last thing a male bee has to do before mating. For the female, though, there is one further step. She has to assess the quality of her suitor before accepting him. We indicate below just how some female bees are thought to make this discrimination.

The duration of mating depends on the species. In some *Centris* and in *Epicharis analis*, it lasts only a few seconds. In *Osmia rufa*, it lasts about a minute, in *Colletes cunicularius* it takes 9–11 minutes, while in *Epicharis dorsata*, it lasts for up to 43 minutes.

GENERAL SEARCHES

The males of many species concentrate their mate-seeking activities in areas where females are most numerous. Thus, in species with scattered nests, males search and patrol patches of flowers in the females' foraging area. In species where the females nest in dense aggregations, males search for females at the nest site. In either case, a male has to have just as good a sense of the local geography as do nesting females.

Males which patrol flowers in search of mates are common among species of *Hylaeus, Megachile, Dianthidium, Exomalopsis*, many Eucerini and in several species of *Centris*, including *C. fasciata* and *C. tarsata*.

The males of a species can adjust their searching behaviour to variations in local circumstances. Thus, in the Botanic Gardens of the University of Oxford, females of *Colletes daviesanus*, nest sparsely each June and July and the males search among flowers for females. A few kilometres west of Oxford, the same bee nests very densely in the vertical cliff faces of an old sandpit. Here, the males maximise their encounters with females by patrolling the nest site. Whether searching at flowers or at the nest site, the males fly about in dense, frenzied swarms, pouncing not only on females, but also on other males and on flies.

When males patrol dense nesting aggregations in the ground, their activities are often very conspicuous. Such is the case with the Eurasian *Andrena armata* and the North American *A. erythronii*. Hundreds or even thousands of males fly rapidly over the ground in wide, looping patterns, pouncing on females and other males.

Males of the Eurasian mining bee, *Colletes cunicularius*, also patrol dense nesting aggregations in large numbers in spring. The males emerge a few days before the females. A dense aggregation can be heard from some distance, with the vast numbers of bees looking and sounding like a hive of honeybees about to swarm.

When a female appears at the sand surface, one or more males pounce on her and attempt to mate. Often, a group of between 8 and 10 males digs frantically at a particular spot. Eventually, they meet a female which was digging her way to the surface. Sometimes, she emerges with a male already attached to her by his genitalia. Alternatively, the several males which have

Frenzied males of the solitary mining bee, *Colletes cunicularius celticus*, cluster around a mating pair, forming a 'mating ball'. Up to fifty males may cluster around a mating pair or a newly emerged female, forming a fist-sized mating ball. After four or five minutes, the males scatter, suggesting that the mating pair have suddenly become unattractive, perhaps because of a scent emitted by the female. Alone at last, the mating pair of *Colletes cunicularius* remain together, male uppermost, for another four or five minutes (Family: Colletidae).

The males of many solitary bees patrol nest sites in search of mates. Here, two males of *Tetralonia malvae* fight over a newly emerged female (Family: Anthophoridae).

dug down to meet her will tug and pull her to the surface, grasping her with their jaws, after which there is a scramble to be the first to mate with her. The male mounts the female from behind and mating lasts 9–11 minutes. A mating pair is attractive to other males and up to 50 may congregate in a fist-sized, jostling mass around it, each one trying to dislodge the male and claim the female for his own.

The females of *C. cunicularius* mate only once. With time, the number of virgin females declines in the local population and the males, faced with a diminishing resource, become more frenzied, pouncing on each other with greater frequency. Eventually, after about 10–14 days, they are worn out, with tattered and frayed wings and they quickly die, leaving the females to carry on nesting and foraging.

Many other species of *Colletes* have males which patrol the nest site in search of mates. In Israel, males of the large, ground-nesting 'carpenter' bees, *Proxylocopa olivieri*, and *P. rufa* also patrol the nest site and often dig females out of the ground.

TRAILS AND CIRCUITS
The males of many bee species patrol up and down a regular beat or circuit. Where this is a more or less linear feature of the environment, such as wood-

Male bees fuel their mate-seeking behaviour with nectar from flowers. Although they do not actively collect pollen, they become dusted with it during feeding and they are, therefore, important pollinators. Here, a male bumblebee, *Bombus lapidarius*, feeds at bramble, *Rubus fruticosus*, (Family: Apidae).

A male and a freshly emerged female of a bumblebee, *Bombus pratorum*, feed side by side at a thistle flower in England. This situation never leads to mating because the context is wrong: mating occurs only close to scent-marked sites on the males' special flight circuits (Family: Apidae).

A male carpenter bee, *Xylocopa* sp., hovers in his territory at the tip of a flowering branch in Kenya. By chasing away other males, he can monopolize any nubile female which enters his patch (Family: Anthophoridae).

land edge, a stream bank, or a gully, we call this a trail. Males with this kind of mate-seeking behaviour often adopt man-made features such as hedgerows and fences. Usually, trail and circuit routes do not include resources such as food plants or nest sites which would be of interest to females. If these resources are present, then they are too sparsely distributed to make it worthwhile for males to concentrate their searches in their immediate vicinity.

A male patrolling a circuit generally pounces on any other that has alighted at a flower, mistaking it for a female. Both fly off again immediately. Encounters of this type are greatly reduced if all the males fly in the same direction around the circuit; any male which flies against the stream is likely to meet other males and quickly learns to change direction.

Males of many *Andrena* species fly up and down trails or around circuits, the routes of which they mark with mandibular gland scents. They chase after any receptive females which enter the area of the circuit.

In the Atlantic coastal forest of Brazil, males of the anthophorid bee, *Rathymus fulvus* also patrol circuits. This bee is a cuckoo in the nests of another large anthophorid, *Epicharis analis*. The circuit of each individual may be 200–300 m (approx. 650–1,000 ft) long and it usually includes some forest edge. Certain sections of an individual's circuit may be shared with those of other males, so that an interlocking network of circuits may cover a vast area.

Such a network is created by the males of many bumblebee species, for they, too, seek mates by patrolling circuits. This was noticed by Charles Darwin, who observed that several male bumblebees flew along well-defined routes in his son's garden. He enlisted the help of his grandchildren in following them and it transpired that the bees flew along circuitous routes.

Darwin's notebooks show that he speculated correctly as to the nature of these circuit flights. He noted how several males of *Bombus hortorum* patrolled the same circuit and landed repeatedly at the same spots, which he suspected were scented by the bees. He wondered of the bees, at their landing places, 'is it like dogs at corner-stones?' Darwin also suspected that females sought mates at the scented points along the circuit.

In recent years, the behaviour of male bumblebees has been studied in some detail and it is true that they deposit secreted scents at specific points along their circuitous trails. The males produce a sweet scent in the labial glands of the head.

In Britain and Europe, a circuit is usually between 100 and 300 m (approx. 300–1,000 ft) long, with no more than 30 males flying along it. Things are very different in tropical South America. The American entomologist, Dr E.W. Stiles, estimated that in his study area between 460 and 720 males of *B. pullatus* patrolled a circuit 2.5 km (approx. 1½ miles) long.

At any one locality, there may be mating circuits of several species of bumblebee. The males make species recognition easier for themselves and their prospective mates in two ways. First, the labial gland scent of each species is unique, comprising a specific blend of scents. Second, the males locate their trails at different heights above the ground and use them at different times of the day. Circuits of *B. hortorum* and *B. terrestris* are less than 1 m from the ground, while those of *B. lucorum* are between 5 and 10 m high and those of *B. lapidarius* are up to 17 m high.

The scent spots on a circuit have an arrestant effect on any virgin queen which flies close by. While she is stationary at this 'pheromone trap', the next male to arrive along the circuit mates with her. A male rarely detects a queen if she is more than 40 cm (15 in) from a scented spot. Although several males may share a circuit, they are spread out along its length and competition between them is low.

A bumblebee mating circuit rarely contains many flowers. Males therefore fuel their mate-seeking flights by drinking nectar at flowers elsewhere. It is a common sight in summer to see males and young females of several *Bombus* species feeding together at thistle flowers, but with no sexual activity whatsoever. This is because the context is wrong: mating takes place on circuits, flowers are exclusively for feeding.

Dr P.H. Williams studied mating behaviour among several *Bombus* species in Kashmir. He noted that here circuit patrols of *B. pyrosoma* are especially effective in coniferous forests, where floral density is low and where the dense trees would obscure long range cues which might bring the sexes together: the web of 'pheromone traps' formed by a network of patrolled routes is likely to be the best way of securing mates where females are at low densities and do not aggregate in predictable areas. The same argument probably applies to open habitats such as arctic tundra.

The males of some species of *Bombus* are territorial (See below).

TERRITORIES AND LEKS

Territoriality involves a male defending an area against other competing males so as to monopolize receptive females which enter the area. The essence of true territoriality is that territory holders may be challenged and usurped, sometimes with physical clashes, which may result in injury or even death.

Typically, a territory is a few square meters in area. Its size and shape depend partly on the size of the male and his visual acuity. The males of some bees, such as *Centris* and *Xylocopa* species, mark the boundaries or the central area of their territories with mandibular gland scent. A male may hold a territory for many days. Individual territories may be widely or closely spaced, or even contiguous.

A territorial male patrols his territory with a rapid, darting flight, often interrupted with periods of hovering. He may also, depending on species, spend more or less time sitting perched on some prominent vantage point. Stationary males are particularly sensitive to the slightest movement and will dart out to investigate any flying insect which enters his domain. Indeed, a simple way to find out if a male is in residence is to lob a small stone into his territory; he generally dashes out to inspect it. A male cannot gauge size or distance easily until he approaches an object and he may even fly towards a bird that enters his field of view.

A territory holder flies at any other male which approaches. The pair may hover face to face, often only a centimetre or two apart, for a second or two. This confrontation is usually sufficient to chase off the intruder, but sometimes there is a violent fight. They fall to the ground, biting and grappling. Fights may be so vicious that one or other of the males loses part of an antenna, wing or leg.

We can divide the territories into two kinds, one which contains a resource of value to females and one which is not resource-based. The resources may be the nests and/or flowers.

A male carder bee, *Anthidium manicatum*, rests in his territory, a metre-square patch of Lamb's Ears, *Stachys lanata*, in England. This is the most aggressive territorial bee known. Males often kill or maim worker honeybees which enter their territories. By deterring other males and chasing away other insects, he enhances the attractiveness of his territory to females by maintaining a protected food resource (Family: Megachilidae).

A mating pair of the carder bee, *Anthidium manicatum*, at a flower of Lamb's Ear, *Stachys lanata*, in England. As in many territorial bee species, the male is larger than the female. The females collect the downy hairs of Lamb's Ear to line their nests (Family: Megachilidae).

Territories at nests   Males of *Osmia rufa* may be territorial at the nest site, say, a log pile with many beetle holes or the crumbling mortar of an old wall. At one locality in southern England, about one male in twelve held a territory, the rest were rove males, which patrolled nest sites and flowers.

There is a dominance hierarchy among territorial males of *O. rufa*. A male must occasionally leave the nest site to feed at flowers. During his absence, his territory is invariably usurped by another male, but he usually has no difficulty in chasing the intruder away when he returns. Sometimes, the intruder holds a nearby territory and he, in turn, must chase intruders away.

The dominance hierarchy was demonstrated by removing males temporarily from a popular territory. The dominant male won all 112 fights with other males; a second male won 15, beating all but the dominant one; the third male won five fights, beating all but the top two males, and a fourth male beat only two lower males. When the males were released, the original hierarchy was quickly restored.

Males of the snail-nesting mason bee, *O. aurulenta*, set up small territories which contain a clean, dry, snail shell. The male spends his time making short flights around the shell, frequently perching on top of it or sitting in its entrance. Often, he spends time in the shell, possibly inspecting its interior. He attempts to mate with any nest-seeking female which approaches. Mating usually occurs at the nest entrance, after the male and female have been inside it. Males chase other males away from the vicinity of the shell, though they seem not to make physical contact.

Presumably, a female *O. aurulenta* assesses the quality of her would-be mate by the quality of the snail shell he has defended against rivals.

Male orchid bees are so-called because they collect orchid scents for sexual purposes. Males sometimes collect exudates from tree wounds instead, like this *Eulaema bombiformis*, investigating bark in Atlantic coastal rain forest, Brazil (Family: Apidae).

Males of a primitively social species of mining bee, *Lasioglossum calceatum*, cluster on a dead knapweed flower in what may be a mating assembly or lek, to which females are attracted (Family: Halictidae).

Territories at flowers The males of many bee species maintain territories at flowers. The carder bee, *Anthidium manicatum*, is a good example and is the most aggressive species known.

A male establishes and defends a territory which consists of a clump of flowers frequented by females. In Britain, these are usually labiates such as *Stachys lanata*, *S. sylvatica*, sages, *Salvia* spp. or horehound, *Marrubium vulgare*. In

North America, where it was accidentally introduced, the species is known only from flowers of *Caryopteris clandonensis*. There is no evidence that males of *Anthidium manicatum* scent mark their territories; the areas they defend are small, their vision is acute and they constantly patrol the boundaries.

A male approaches and drives off any flower-visiting insects which enter his territory. He is well-equipped to do so. The end of his abdomen is armed with a series of stout spines. In grappling with an intruder, he curls his abdomen so as to crunch the spines into his opponent. This is sufficient to kill or maim relatively soft-bodied insects such as worker honeybees; the soil beneath a territory is often littered with dead or dying insects. The male's aggressive approach is enough to see off insects larger than himself, such as bumblebees.

Encounters between males of *A. manicatum* rarely result in injury. They hover face-to-face, both then dart about after one another. Almost always, the territory holder chases the other male away. During face-to-face hovering, the males probably assess the other's size and/or state of aggression.

Anthidium manicatum is unusual for solitary bees in two ways. First, a proportion of the males are distinctly larger than the females. This is connected with their aggressive territoriality. Second, the females mate many times rather than just once. In Oxford, one large male successfully defended his territory for four consecutive days. The territory was a patch of *Stachys sylvatica* in full bloom, occupying an area of 2.5 sq m. He mated up to 16 times a day. The most frequent of the female visitors mated with him three times in one afternoon.

In an American study of this species, the number of females entering a territory was roughly proportional to the number of flowers it contained. Moreover, the male with the 'best' territory, that is with the most flowers, enjoyed the most frequent copulations.

A territory is attractive to females not only because it has more flowers than others, but also because it is likely to have more reward per flower because the male is so efficient at deterring other flower-visiting insects. It is likely, therefore, that the time and energy costs of multiple matings is the price a female *Anthidium* is prepared to pay in return for a protected food resource.

Territories without female resources   Some species of bumblebees provide good examples of non-resource-based territories. In Kashmir, males of *Bombus rufofasciatus* occupy perches which they defend against other males, often violently enough to cause injury. The males of this species have enlarged eyes, as do those of the North American *B. nevadensis*, which is territorial in much the same way. In both species, the males leave their vantage points to chase rapidly after females or any other flying insects.

The carpenter bee, *Xylocopa varipuncta* lives in the deserts of the south-western United States and Mexico. The males occupy sites with no resources attractive to females. These are usually the crowns of non-flowering trees in dry water courses in the desert, where a male hovers for up to two hours at a time. A male will repel rivals of the same species. Females are apparently attracted to a scent emitted by a male. *Xylocopa varipuncta* has been studied by Dr J. Alcock of the Arizona State University and his associates. They speculate that this kind of territorial behaviour evolved because in the desert food plants are dispersed and nest sites are scattered and difficult to find. The best way for a male to demonstrate his quality as a potential mate is to dominate a superior and prominent landmark territory. This almost certainly applies to *X. pubescens* in Israel, another desert species with males that occupy territories devoid of resources.

Alcock called this mating system a dispersed lek. The term 'lek' normally refers to a special kind of display staged by certain male birds such as the sage grouse of North America and mammals such as the Uganda kob. A lek is an assembly of displaying males which congregates at a site that contains no resources of interest to females except a number of males ready and willing to mate. Females are attracted to this and have the opportunity to assess the quality of a range of potential mates before making a choice.

In Chapter 12 we alluded to the suggestion that males of the orchid bees (Euglossini) in some way use scent collected from orchids and other sources to attract other males of the same species so as to set up leks. Although males of *Eulaema meriana* and *Euglossa imperialis* form leks on rare occasions, there is no convincing evidence that they use orchid scents to do so. These species normally have individual territories in forest glades and display from perches. They defend territories against other males. Occasionally, a particularly favoured glade may have a large number of territories and this may have given rise to reports of lekking behaviour. Large aggregations of males at scent sources may also have given rise to this view. The males may modify the orchid scents to make pheromones which are attractive to males.

While lek behaviour has yet to be demonstrated unequivocally in euglossines, it may occur in males of the primitively social halictid, *Lasioglossum*

Males of a species of solitary mining bee, *Amegilla*, sleep, hanging on to twigs with their jaws. While the females of nearly all solitary bees spend the night in their nests, the males of many species sleep in communal roosts, often in the open, as here in the Buffalo Springs Game Reserve, Kenya (Family: Anthophoridae).

Eleven males of an as yet undescribed species of *Eucera* settle down for the night in a communal roost on a flower of *Chrysanthemum coronarium*, in Israel (Family: Anthophoridae).

A sleeping male cuckoo bee, *Nomada flavoguttata*, hangs by his jaws from a spurge flower, in England. Males of some *Nomada* spp. spray their mates with a mandibular gland scent which mimics that of the Dufour's gland of the host female, generally *Andrena* sp., making it easier for the *Nomada* female to gain access to the hosts' nests (Families: Anthophoridae and Andrenidae).

calceatum. Males of this species often congregate in large numbers on dead flower heads of knapweeds, *Centaurea* spp. The males seem constantly to jostle for position at the top of the dry flower, with antennae erect and alert. Occasionally, a female is attracted to the aggregation and flies around it slowly, with antennae extended. She then enters the mêlée of males, often disappearing in the throng, only to reappear and drop to the ground, paired with a male. This situation satisfies all the requirements of a lek, as defined above.

MULTIPLE STRATEGIES

The males of some bee species have more than one mating strategy. In species such as *Anthophora plumipes*, studied in Oxford by Dr Graham Stone, males may initially be territorial at the nest site, then set up territories at foodplants and later establish circuit patrols rather like those of male bumblebees.

The males of the anthophorid mining bee, *Centris pallida*, have two kinds of mating behaviour but these are not time-related as in *Anthophora plumipes*. Instead, they are related to the size of the bee. This desert bee was studied by Dr J. Alcock in Arizona. He found that the male populations comprise small bees, which hover either over the nest site from which virgin females emerge or close to flowering trees visited by females, and larger males that patrol the nest site and defend small territories containing virgin females in the process of digging their way to the surface. The territories are short-lived and males often fight over emergent females, which they dig out of the sand. The small, hovering males rely on obtaining females which managed to emerge without being mated by patrolling males.

Two kinds of mate-seeking behaviour are found among males of *Andrena vetula*. The females of this unusual mining bee nest in the twilight zone in caves in Israel. There are two kinds of males 'walkers' and 'flyers'.

Walkers remain in the cave and patrol the nest site on foot. Although their wings are fully formed, they never fly in the cave. If one takes a walker out of the cave and allows him to warm up in the sun, he soon takes to the air. Walkers often dig down to emergent females and re-emerge in copulation. They are active throughout the night, although their movements then are much slower.

Flyers congregate at the cave entrance in a large, dense swarm. They often settle for short periods on nearby vegetation, which they seem to scent mark. Although matings are more rarely seen among flyers, the inference is that they mate with any females which have successfully run the gauntlet of walking males.

The factors which determine whether a male *A. vetula* becomes a walker or a flyer are unknown. If flyers are brought into the cave and confined in a net until they have cooled down to the same temperature as the walkers, on release they walk up a rock and then fly to the cave entrance. During the day, walkers operate, on average, at 10°C lower than flyers and at a relative humidity 10 per cent higher.

MATING BEHAVIOUR IN HIGHLY SOCIAL BEES

Virgin queens of stingless and honeybees leave the nest on mating flights. The males of stingless bees, *Melipona* and *Trigona* species, form dense swarms near nests or close to nests under construction. The swarms contain hundreds or even thousands of bees. A virgin female is mated very soon after entering such a swarm.

A colony of the honeybee, *Apis mellifera*, rears a batch of males or drones in summer. The males and virgin queens leave the nest on mating flights. Males leave the nest shortly after noon, about an hour before the queens. They fly to and assemble at special sites called congregation areas. Each area is 10–20 m (32–65 ft) above the ground and has remarkably distinct boundaries. The area is 50–200 m (164–656 ft) in diameter and contains thousands of drones from many colonies, some from as far as 7–12 km (4.3–7 miles) away.

An unsolved mystery is how and why males assemble each year at precisely the same spots. No males survive the winter, so there is no way they can communicate to males of the next generation where the best places are. In a long-term study in Austria, Professor F. Ruttner found that males used the same congregation area for 12 consecutive years. It is clear, though, that males and queens must be programmed in a highly tuned fashion so that both react in the same, positive way to whatever cues in the environment determine the location of a congregation area.

A queen flies to a congregation area about 2–3 km (1.2–1.8 miles) from her nest. As she flies through the assembly of males, the pheromone, queen substance (see Chapter 10), acts as an attractant to them. She leaves behind her a plume of scent 30 m (approx. 100 ft) long and this attracts up to 100 males, which jostle for the opportunity to mount her. It takes the successful male only 2–4 seconds to complete the act and inseminate the queen.

The males of both stingless bees and honeybees are unusual because they can mate only once. This is because they leave their genitalia behind in the vagina of the queen. The genitalia of the male honeybee detach explosively from his body, with an audible 'pop'. These are clearly visible at the tip of a queen's abdomen when she returns from a mating flight and are called, appropriately, the 'mating sign'. The number of mating signs indicates how many males she has mated with on a particular flight. She may mate as many as 10 times. On return to the nest, the workers remove the mating signs from the queen. A drone ejaculates 11 million sperm on mating and, on average, a queen returning after a mating flight has 87 million sperm in her reproductive tract. However, her spermatheca can store only 5 million sperm. It seems that the sperm are thoroughly mixed before being sucked into the spermatheca. The excess is expelled from the vagina and removed by workers.

With males mating only once and females mating many times, the honeybee reverses the situation normally found in solitary and primitively social bees.

OTHER KINDS OF MALE BEHAVIOUR

SLEEPING AGGREGATIONS

Male bees often spend the night in dense aggregations, hanging by their jaws from plant stems or leaves. Surprisingly, many such aggregations contain the males of several species. Others seek shelter in flowers, especially those, such as poppies, which close up for the night.

The males of some mining bees excavate temporary bivouacs in sandy soil. Males of *Colletes cunicularius* are unusual because, after a day spent in intense competition for mates, groups of males, up to 25 at a time, cooperate in the late afternoon in excavating communal sleeping chambers in the sand. Likewise, eight males of *Osmia rufa*, which fought each other during the day, regularly slept together at night in a crack in a window frame.

PATERNAL CARE

Although it is true that the males of almost all bee species contribute nothing to the rearing of offspring, there are exceptions. Dr S.A. Cameron found that males of the North American bumblebees, *Bombus griseocollis*, *B. pennsylvanicus*, *B. affinis* and *B. bimaculatus*, incubate broods just like queens and workers. It is possible that this behaviour is more widespread in bumblebees.

In South America, the males of some stingless bees, *Melipona* and *Trigona* spp., not only receive nectar from incoming workers and place it into storage pots, they also secrete wax and use it to help build brood cells and storage pots. Dr D.W. Roubik has seen males of *Melipona marginata* help to ripen the honey.

Chapter 14
Enemies and Associates

Bees are surrounded by enemies. Adult and larval bees are prone to attack by a wide range of predators and specialized parasites. Birds, lizards, toads, hornets, hunting wasps, robberflies, assassin bugs, spiders and mites all take their toll.

Birds such as wagtails and flycatchers often eat solitary bees and bumblebees. Woodpeckers can be a pest among beehives, pecking holes in the wooden sides to get at the larvae. They can be a particular problem in winter, when the damage they cause may result in the bees becoming chilled, with the loss of overwintering colonies.

Specializing in surprise tactics, a crab spider, *Misumenops* sp., has caught a male cuckoo bee, *Coelioxys* sp. in Trinidad (Family: Megachilidae).

Some birds, such as the bee-eaters, *Merops* spp., specialize in catching and eating worker honeybees in Africa, the Mediterranean region and India. There are 14 species in the African savannas and honeybees account for up to 30 per cent of their diets. The diet of some individual birds may consist of 96 per cent honeybees. Bee-eaters can be serious pests. Flocks of up to 250 may migrate from apiary to apiary, staying long enough in one locality to wreak havoc before moving on. A bee-eater catches prey on the wing and flies to a perch. Here, it rubs the bee's abdomen against the perch so as to disable the sting.

Nests of the highly social stingless bees, with their stored honey and thousands of larvae, offer rich pickings to many predators. Some animals brave the massed defensive response of honeybees and tolerate being stung in order to gain access to honey and grubs. In Africa, chimpanzees and baboons often raid the nests of stingless bees and honeybees; in Sumatra and Borneo, the orang-utan does the same.

Among mammals, though, the honey badger or ratel of Africa and India, *Mellivora capensis*, is a much more serious threat both to wild nests of honeybees and hives in apiaries. This fierce little predator has a tough, leathery skin and is apparently impervious to stings. It uses its powerful claws to break into nests and hives, from which it removes a piece of comb which it carries off to eat elsewhere. It feeds on larvae as well as the stored honey and pollen.

The honey badger is often led to a nest by one of the most specialized of predators. These are birds called honeyguides, comprising the appropriately named family Indicatoridae, with 11 species, which feed on beeswax.

Two African species, *Indicator indicator* and *I. variegatus*, are the only members of the family which have actually been seen to guide honey badgers to bees' nests. They feed almost exclusively on beeswax, which they prefer to honey or larvae. However, they have no means of breaking into the nest and rely on the services of the honey badger to do this. Having found a nest, the bird attracts the attention of a honey badger, or perhaps a baboon or even a person, and makes repetitive churring notes. It comes to within 15 to 50 feet of the honey badger and then fans out its tail to expose white feathers, in an eye-catching display. The bird continues with its churring call and flies off and perches in a tree or bush, sometimes out of sight of the following badger or person. The bird's call maintains the attention of the honey badger and when it is within sight of the bird and near to it, the honeyguide leads it on again until, eventually, bird and badger arrive at the nest of the honeybees.

At this point, the bird shows remarkable patience. It perches quietly for up to an hour and a half until the honey badger has broken into the nest and eaten its fill. The bird then swoops down and picks at the scraps of wax comb lying around. This is a remarkable example of symbiosis, for it involves the honeyguide in cooperative relationship with three different animal species, the honey badger, baboons and people.

Hornets are voracious predators of honeybees. In Israel, apiaries can be severely damaged or even wiped out by marauding workers of the oriental hornet, *Vespa orientalis*. In 1949, the hornet destroyed 3,000 out of 28,000 hives belonging to members of the Israel Beekeepers Association. It is not surprising that Israeli beekeepers try to prevent this problem by offering a bounty in spring for hornet queens. At this time of the year, the queens are commonly seen searching for nest sites and killing them reduces the number of colonies which are established.

Vespa orientalis uses its powerful jaws rather than its sting to kill honeybees. The same is true for the world's largest hornet, *V. mandarinia*, which can cause havoc among apiaries in India, China and Japan. Over several hours, as few as 20–30 worker hornets can kill 5,000–20,000 honeybees. The hornets eventually take over the hive and transport larvae, pupae and adults to their own nest, where they feed the booty to their own larvae.

Many insects make a more specialized living at the expense of bees. Female bee-flies, *Bombylius* spp., scatter their eggs near the nest entrances of mining bees such as *Colletes*, *Andrena* and *Halictus*. The eggs hatch almost immediately into small, active larvae, which enter the nest. Here, they develop as ecto-parasites, feeding on the bee larvae and the stored food.

Females of another fly, *Miltogramma punctatum*, follow solitary mining bees, especially species of *Colletes*, back to their nests. Here, they loiter near the nest entrance until the bee leaves again on a foraging trip. The fly enters the nest and lays a larva rather than an egg in the cell currently being provisioned. The fly larva eats the pollen and nectar stored by the bee and the bee larva starves to death.

Mason bees such as *Osmia rufa* attract the attention of small greyish flies called *Cacoxenus indagator*. This fly belongs to the family of fruit flies, Drosophil-idae which also includes the many species of *Drosophila*, the fruit flies of genetics fame. The female *Cacoxenus* waits near the entrances to the *Osmia* nests until a female bee leaves. The fly then enters and lays several eggs in the cell being provisioned. These hatch and the larvae feed on the stored pollen. Usually, the bee larva is starved out, but in cells with only a few fly larvae the bee larva may survive to produce a small individual.

Cone-head flies of the family Conopidae develop as internal parasites of adult bees. The female fly shadows a bee and pounces on it, inserting an egg between two of the abdominal segments. The larva eats the internal organs of the bee, eventually killing it. The fly pupates inside the hollowed out husk of the bee's body. Species of *Myopa* attack *Andrena*, while some species of *Physoce-phala* attack bumblebees. In one Oxfordshire population of *Andrena bucephala*, 13 per cent of the bees were infested with larvae of the host-specific conopid, *Myopa bucephalae*.

Related to the beetles, the strange insect order Strepsiptera contains many species which develop as internal parasites of wasps and bees. Species of *Andrena* are frequently infested with *Stylops* spp. The adult male strepsipteran is free-living, but the female remains as an internal parasite of the bee. The female's body is largely a membranous sac full of eggs and larvae. Only her fused head and thorax have a thickened cuticle and stick out between two of the bee's abdominal segments. The pupa of the male also protrudes in the same way. On emergence, the male seeks out females in other hosts and mates with them.

The female eventually produces up to two thousand tiny 'triungulin' larvae, which exit via her genital opening. The larvae climb up stems on to flowers, where they wait for a visiting bee. Then, according to species, they either hitch a lift by grabbing on to the bee's body hairs, or, in the case of the American *Stylops pacifica*, the larva gets drawn into the bee's crop with nectar and is regurgitated on to the pollen store back at the nest. The bee larva eventually eats the *Stylops* larva, which develops inside, absorbing nutrients across its thin, membranous body wall. Fig. 41 shows the life-cycle of *Stylops pacifica*.

The brilliantly metallic ruby-tailed wasps, *Chrysis* and *Chrysura* spp., can

173

This bee-fly from Israel, *Bombylius punctatus*, mimics the colour pattern of a species of *Thyreus*. By so doing, the stingless fly gains protection against attacks by insectivorous birds, which associate such 'warning' patterns with a painful sting. Like the cuckoo bee, *Thyreus*, this bee-fly is a parasite of species of *Amegilla*, a genus of solitary mining bees (Families: Bombyliidae and Anthophoridae).

A female parasitic fly, *Miltogramma* sp., waits patiently at the nest entrance of a solitary mining bee, *Tetralonia malvae*. When the bee leaves to forage, the fly enters the nest and lays an active larva in the cell currently being provisioned by the bee. The fly larva feeds on the food store of the bee larva (Families: Sarcophagidae and Anthophoridae).

A flightless, lumbering oil beetle, *Meloe* sp., crawls about the nest site of a solitary mining bee scattering her eggs. These hatch into minute, active larvae which enter the nest burrow and feed on the stored pollen in the cells (Family: Meloidae).

often be seen sitting near the nests of mason bees. These wasps lay a single egg in the cell of the bee. The wasp larva does not normally eat the pollen store. Instead, it waits until the bee larva is fully grown, then feeds on it.

Honeybees are sometimes infested with the mite, *Acarapis woodi*. Mites are arachnids, eight-legged relatives of the spiders. *A. woodi* lives and breeds in the tracheae or breathing tubes of the bee's thorax. Here, they pierce the thin walls of the tracheae and suck body fluids. Unless the bee is very heavily infested, it behaves normally, but has a reduced life-span. Badly infested colonies die out in spring, especially if they are stressed for other reasons.

Another mite is a growing threat to beekeeping in western Europe. This is *Varroa jacobsoni*, which originated in Asia, where it is endemic on *Apis cerana*. It has spread to the Western honeybee, *A. mellifera*, but has not yet reached Britain. Female mites lay eggs in the brood comb. The eggs hatch to produce nymphs which attach to the bee larvae and suck their blood. Not all infected brood is killed. The adult mites cling to the thorax of adult bees and are visible with the naked eye.

CUCKOO AND ROBBER BEES

Some bees have given up the nesting habit and become cuckoos or cleptoparasites: they lay eggs in the nests of other bees. The cuckoo habit has arisen at

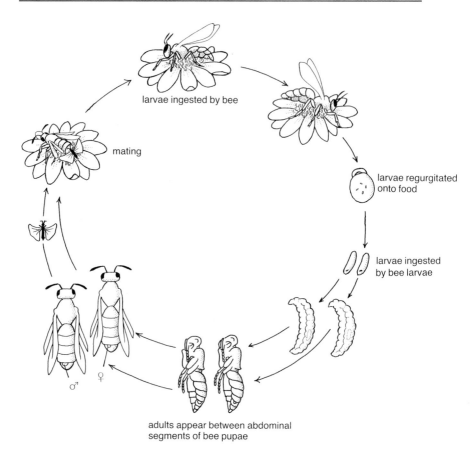

Fig. 41   An outline of the life cycle of a North American strepsipteran, *Stylops pacifica*, parasitizing *Andrena* (Andrenidae). (Redrawn after Linsley, E.G. & McSwain, J. W., 1957, *Univ. Calif. Publ. Ent.*, **11**: 395–480.)

least 15 times in the bees. Indeed, about 3,700 bee species are cuckoos, that is roughly 19 per cent of all bees. It has been estimated that 20 per cent of all bees in North America are cuckoos.

The cuckoo habit is found in the bee families Colletidae, Halictidae, Megachilidae, Anthophoridae and Apidae. All cuckoos have several characteristics in common. They do not forage and therefore lack pollen scopae or corbiculae. They usually have a thick cuticle to withstand attack from their hosts and many of them are brightly coloured, some with wasp-like liveries of black and yellow.

Female cuckoo bees produce many more eggs than their hosts and have more mature eggs in their ovaries at any one time. This is an adaptation which allows them to exploit a host population to the full once it has been located.

Cuckoos find their hosts by smell. We have often found a nest site of, say, an *Andrena* species by following a female of its cuckoo, a *Nomada* species. The males of *Nomada* spp. mimic the specific odours of the females of their host, *Andrena* spp. They patrol the host nest site and by emitting the same scent as the host,

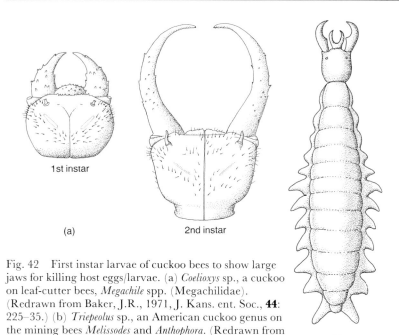

1st instar

(a)

2nd instar

Fig. 42   First instar larvae of cuckoo bees to show large
jaws for killing host eggs/larvae. (a) *Coelioxys* sp., a cuckoo
on leaf-cutter bees, *Megachile* spp. (Megachilidae).
(Redrawn from Baker, J.R., 1971, J. Kans. ent. Soc., **44**:
225–35.) (b) *Triepeolus* sp., an American cuckoo genus on
the mining bees *Melissodes* and *Anthophora*. (Redrawn from
Stephen, W.P., Bohart, G.E. & Torchio, P.F., 1969.)

(b)

presumably make it easier for the female *Nomada* to find the area. In this way,
the males increase the likelihood of mating success. It is also possible that the
male *Nomada* transfers some of the scent to a female during mating and that she
uses it in a 'Trojan horse' strategy to gain access to the host nest without being
detected.

The first instar larvae of many cuckoo bees have large, sickle-shaped jaws,
which they use to destroy the host egg or young larva (Fig. 42). At the first
moult, the cuckoo larva loses these jaws and thereafter has the small jaws,
usual for bee larvae.

The best-known cleptoparasitic bees are the cuckoo bumblebees in the
genus *Psithyrus*. Like many cuckoo bees, *Psithyrus* is closely related to and
clearly derived from its host, in this instance species of *Bombus*.

The females of some *Psithyrus* species enter the host nest stealthily and lie
'doggo' for a day or so among the nest debris or moss lining. During this
period, the female absorbs the nest odour and when she emerges into the body
of the nest she excites no suspicion on the part of the *Bombus* workers. She then
sets about her task of laying eggs in cells which will be provisioned by the host
workers. She eats the eggs of the host queen whenever she finds them.

Other species of *Psithyrus* are more aggressive. A female enters the *Bombus*
nest and kills any workers which attempt to block her entry. She has a powerful venom and her thick cuticle protects her from the workers' stings. She then
seeks out the host queen and kills her, thereby taking over the nest. She relies
on the host workers to provide food for her and her offspring.

Among the stingless bees, species of *Lestrimelitta* in South America and *Cleptotrigona* in Africa make a living by raiding the colonies of other species. They
steal stored food and nest materials.

A female cuckoo bee, *Nomada flava*, feeds at a dandelion flower, *Taraxacum officinale*, in England. This bee lays its eggs in the nests of the solitary mining bee *Andrena scotica* (Families: Anthophoridae and Andrenidae).

A female cuckoo bee, *Melecta armata*, loiters near the nest entrance of her host, *Anthophora plumipes*, in Oxford. When the host female leaves to forage, the cuckoo enters the nest and lays an egg (Family: Anthophoridae).

A female cuckoo bumblebee, *Psithyrus bohemicus*, feeds at a thistle. This species lays its eggs in the nests of *Bombus lucorum* and relies on the host workers to rear the offspring (Family: Apidae).

A female parasitic wasp, *Gasteruption assectator*, uses its long ovipositor to lay an egg in the cell of a solitary mining bee, *Hylaeus signatus*, which has nested in a sandy cliff in southern England (Families: Gasteruptiidae and Colletidae).

This fly, *Fallenia fasciata*, mimics species of the mining bee genus *Amegilla* (Families: Nemestrinidae and Anthophoridae).

DEFENCE

Anyone who has been stung by honeybees knows, from the sudden searing pain, that this species has mastered the art of colony defence. The sting is barbed (Fig. 1c), catches in the skin and remains behind as the bee struggles to get away. The bee dies, but the venom gland continues to pump poison into the wound. A gland at the base of the sting emits a highly volatile alarm pheromone that recruits yet more workers, which attack any moving object in the vicinity. The beekeeper is well aware of this reaction and does his best to dissuade any bee from stinging by moving slowly when tending his hives.

This rapid response is usually more than enough to see off any potential enemy. But, more often than not, it is used in defence against any workers from other colonies which try to gain access to the nest in order to steal honey. Guard bees recognize an alien worker by her smell. All of the bees in the same colony have much the same scent, which is recognizably different from that of another colony. Hence the passport to enter the hive is to possess the accepted body scent. The guard, somewhat like a customs officer, also responds to the behaviour of the arriving bees, for this may also reveal an unwelcome visitor. A robber from another colony flies faster and is far more wary in her approach, taking flight as the guard comes nearer. The guards have little difficulty in distinguishing this behaviour from the confident arrival of a nest mate.

The evolution of a strong defence reflects the fact that a colony of bees may have several kilograms of honey and several thousands of young brood in the nest, all worth defending. Apart from the obvious question of survival, the bees have a great deal of time and energy invested in the nest contents.

By contrast, solitary bees have very small food stores and hence not much to defend. They never attack an intruder, and to be stung one has to handle the bee roughly. Their stings range from a mere pin-prick to one that is quite painful. None is as painful, however, as a honeybee sting and both the degree and duration of the reaction are far less.

The 'stingless bees' (Meliponinae) do have microscopic stings but the bees have lost the ability to use them. Nevertheless, they are well able to defend the nest without them. In the New World tropics, where both the stingless bees and social wasps are most diverse, the bees are generally much better able to defend their nests than are the wasps which have very powerful stings. The bees' ability stems from the sum of several factors. They select a nest site deep within a tree trunk or underground, which is difficult for an intruder to reach. Their defence is aimed principally at smaller intruders such as beetles and ants: it is threefold. First, the bees construct several layers of tough batumen that are not easy to perforate. Second, the nest entrance is in the form of a narrow, often trumpet-shaped tube and the bees ensure that this is constantly covered in a sticky coating of wax and resin. Small insects adhere to the coating and have great difficulty in escaping. Third, the bees daub any intruder with a sticky secretion.

It is difficult to see how the bees avoid being daubed with their own glue, but somehow they manage to clean their legs and even their wings of the secretion, whereas ants and beetles cannot prevent their feet from becoming entangled in the sticky threads. The self-defence of stingless bees is so efficient that they are able to maintain nests for several years without suffering the invasions of ants that are the bane of wasp colonies.

The bees' response to larger intruders, including man, is, like that of *Apis*, to attack *en masse*. The workers of many species of stingless bees have sharp mandibles. They leave the nest in large numbers and bite the intruder, often with such force that their mandibular muscles lock and a bee that is brushed off is decapitated, leaving the mandibles sunk into the skin of the victim. Some species also secrete irritating fluids in their head glands which they spill into the wound. In a few species of the genus *Trigona*, subgenus *Oxytrigona*, the intensely burning liquid has earned them the name of firebees. The bites of these bees cause painful blisters, so bad that the American entomologist, W.M. Wheeler, said his encounter was one of the worst experiences of his life. He happened to venture too close to a nest and his face was attacked, leaving large areas of burnt skin. Even some of the milder species have little difficulty in putting intruders to flight because they attack in such large numbers, getting into hair and biting into scalps so that they rapidly become intolerable. However, not all of them are so aggressive; some of the tiniest species are so timid that they retreat into the nest if it is approached.

Females of some solitary bees use various decoy methods to prevent parasitic flies and cuckoo bees from harming their offspring. Females of the solitary Eurasian mining bee, *Panurgus banksianus*, have two nest entrances. The first nest entrance is always obscured by a tumulus and is never used. It has been suggested that the tumulus, situated several centimetres away from the functional entrance, may act as a decoy in diverting the attention of cuckoo bees and parasitic flies, which may be attracted, in the first instance, to the tumulus, which is normally found at the nest entrances of mining bees.

Females of *Colletes succinctus* and *C. halophilus* in Britain regularly make unusually small cells, which they provide with a small amount of pollen and nectar. There is evidence that these act as a decoy for the parasitic fly *Miltogramma punctatum*. Perhaps one cell in five is a decoy cell and sometimes contains a

Feeding at a bramble flower in England, this hoverfly, *Criorrhina berberina*, mimics the appearance of ginger-haired bumblebees, *Bombus pascuorum* and *B. muscorum*. When attacked, they even mimic the bees' defensive posture, with middle legs raised in threat, and accompanied by a loud buzzing (Families: Syrphidae and Apidae).

This assassin bug, *Notocyrtus* species, is a remarkably close mimic of some worker stingless bees, *Trigona* species. The bug takes advantage of its superb mimicry to prey on *Trigona* bees at flowers and even at the bees' nest entrance (Families: Reduviidae and Apidae).

Workers of the stingless bee, *Trigona* (subgenus *Oxytrigona*) *tataira*, take pollen from the male flowers of a dwarf palm in *cerrado* country (savanna) of Brazil. Known as the 'fire bee', this aggressive species defends itself with a caustic secretion from glands in the head, which causes painful and long-lasting swellings (Family: Apidae).

Fig. 43   Section through the body of a female African carpenter bee, *Xylocopa flavorufa* (Anthophoridae), showing: (a) mite pouch or acinarium in first abdominal segment, which houses symbiotic mites, *Dinogamasus vollosior*, and; (b) the entrance to the mite pouch seen from in front; (c) the symbiotic mite, *Dinogamasus vollosior* known only from the bodies and nests of carpenter bees. (Redrawn, after Madel, G., 1975, *Entomol. Ger.*, **1**: 144–50.)

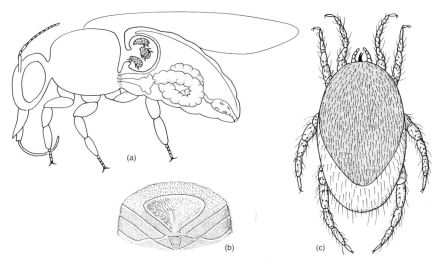

small, stunted, fly larva. We speculate that it pays the female *Colletes* to invest some time and energy in making and provisioning a small cell: it has enough food to dupe a female fly into laying an egg, but usually not enough for the fly larva to complete its development. We did rear one *Miltogramma* from such a cell, but it was dwarf, with stunted wings.

NEST ASSOCIATES: MITES

Not all mites are detrimental to bees. Some, such as *Parasitus bomborum*, apparently serve a useful purpose in the nests of bumblebees by scavenging on debris in the nest. They walk all over the cells, the queen and workers. At the end of the colony's life, hundreds of mites climb on to the newly mated queens, which leave the nest to find a place in which to hibernate. In the following spring, most freshly emerged queens have mites attached to them and in this way, the mites become established in the nests of the new season.

In some African and Indian subgenera of the carpenter bee *Xylocopa* (*Mesotrichia*, *Koptortosoma*, *Platynopoda* and *Cyaneoderes*), the females have special pouches at the front of the abdomen for mites of the genus *Dinogamasus* (Fig. 43). The mites lay eggs on the bee pupae, where the nymphs feed on exudates from the skin and are believed to prevent fungal infections.

Glossary

Aculeate Hymenoptera Hymenoptera armed with stings: the wasps, ants and bees, including the so-called stingless bees.

Bee milk *See* Royal jelly.

Caste One of several different functional types of individual living in the colony of a social insect species. The queen, drones and workers are all different castes.

Communal Of a colony of females of the same generation which share a nest. Each individual makes, provisions and lays eggs in her own group of cells, with no cooperation.

Compound eye The typical insect eye, made up of thousands of facets, each with its own lens and nerve connection to the brain.

Corbicula The pollen basket on the hind tibiae of female Apidae (orchid bees, bumblebees, stingless bees and honeybees). It is formed by the smooth, slightly concave outer surface of the tibia, fringed by long, stiff hairs and is used to transport pollen and building materials, such as resin, to the nest.

Eusocial Of a colony of adults of two or more generations, comprising mother(s) and daughters, the former being egg-laying queen (or queens), the latter being non-reproductive workers.

Exoskeleton The horny, outer shell of an insect which encloses and protects the body and to which the muscles are attached.

Hamuli The tiny hooks which form a row on the leading edge of the hindwings in bees and wasps and which, in flight, engage a fold on the trailing edge of the forewings, uniting the wings to make a functional whole.

Hive An artificial nest for honeybees provided by beekeepers.

Honey Nectar which has been collected by bees, partially digested and ripened by the evaporation of water.

Honeycomb The double-sided array of thousands of hexagonal wax cells, in which honeybees store honey, pollen and rear their brood.

Hymenoptera The order of insects which includes the sawflies, wasps, ants and bees.

Mass provisioning The habit, practised by all solitary bees, some bumblebees and stingless bees, of providing all the food required for a larva's development in a sealed cell in which an egg is laid.

Nasanov gland A gland which opens between two of the dorsal (upper) segments of the abdomen of a worker honeybee. It emits a scent, which recruits workers to a source of water or to scentless flowers. The scent is also emitted by scout bees which have found a new nest site attracting the rest of the swarm.

Nectar A liquid mixture of sugars secreted by the nectaries of plants, which all bees collect for their own and larval food and which worker honeybees ripen into honey.

Ocellus (plural: ocelli) Simple eyes arranged in a triangle on the top of a bee's head, each with a single, thick lens and which detect changes in light intensity.

Oligolectic Of a bee species which specializes in collecting pollen from only a few closely related species or genera of plants.

Ovipositor The egg-laying tube in female insects, modified in aculeate wasps and bees as a sting.

Parasocial A colony in which all the nest-sharing females are of the same generation, a collective term for communal, quasisocial and semisocial colonies.

Pheromone A volatile chemical messenger or scent produced by one animal which affects the behaviour of other individuals of the same species.

Polylectic   Of bee species which collect pollen from a wide range of plant species.

Progressive feeding   The habit, in highly social bees, of feeding larvae at intervals during their development, usually in open cells.

Quasisocial   Of a colony of females of the same generation, in which members cooperate in constructing and provisioning cells. All females are mated, have enlarged ovaries and lay eggs.

Queen   The principle or only egg-laying female in a social colony, which does little or no foraging.

Queen substance   A complex pheromone released from the mandibular glands of queen honeybees, which inhibits ovarian development in workers, prevents them from constructing queen cells and may encourage foraging behaviour.

Royal jelly   A food secreted from glands in the head by worker honeybees, which they feed to larvae. The food comprises two liquids, a colourless one from the hypopharyngeal glands and a thicker, whiter one from the mandibular glands. Sometimes called bee milk.

Scopa   A brush of specialized hairs with which bees transport pollen to the nest. In most families it is situated on the hind legs, sometimes also on the sides of the thorax or, in the Fideliidae and Megachilidae, on the underside of the abdomen.

Semisocial   Of a colony of females of the same generation, with some kind of division of labour, i.e., with some females tending to lay most of the eggs and functioning as queens and with some females tending to lay few or no eggs and behaving as workers.

Solitary   Of a female bee or wasp which lives alone in a nest of her own construction and which she provisions with no cooperation from any other females.

Spermatheca   A reservoir for sperm cells in the female, from which sperm are released to fertilize eggs just before they are laid.

Subsocial   Of a colony comprising an adult female bee and her immature offspring, which she feeds progressively.

Trophallaxis   In social bees, the mouth-to-mouth exchange of food and, incidentally, pheromones, between colony members.

Worker   A member of a social colony which lays few or no eggs but is very active in nest construction, foraging and brood care.

Guide to Further Reading

Askew, R.R. (1971) *Parasitic Insects*, Heinemann Educational Books, London.

Barash, D. (1979) *Sociobiology: the Whisperings Within*, Harper & Row, New York.

Barth, F.G. (1985) *Insects and Flowers: The Biology of a Partnership* (trans M.A. Biederman-Thorson), George Allen & Unwin, London.

Bell, W.J. & Cardé, R.T. (Eds) (1983) *The Chemical Ecology of Insects*, Chapman & Hall, London & New York.

Birch, M.C. & Haynes, K.F. (1982) *Insect Pheromones*, Studies in Biology no. 147, Edward Arnold, London.

Blum, M.S. & Blum, N.A. (Eds) (1979) *Sexual Selection and Reproductive Competition in Insects*, Academic Press, New York & London.

Breed, M.D., Michener, C.D. & Evans, H.E. (Eds) (1982) *The Biology of Social Insects*, Proceedings of the 9th Congress of the International Union for the Study of Social Insects, Westview Press, Boulder, Colorado.

Brian, M.V. (1983) *Social Insects, Ecology and Behavioural Biology*, Chapman & Hall, London & New York.

Butler, C.G. (1954) *The World of the Honeybee*, New Naturalist Series, Collins, London.

Crane, E. (Ed) (1975) *Honey: A Comprehensive Survey*, Heinemann, London.

Crane, E. (1983) *The Archaeology of Beekeeping*, Duckworth, London.

Darwin, C. (1859) *The Origin of Species*, John Murray, London.

Dawkins, R. (1976) *The Selfish Gene*, Oxford University Press, Oxford.

Fabre, J.H. (1914) *The Mason Bees* (trans A. Teixeira de Mattos), Hodder & Stoughton, London.

Free, J.B. (1970) *Insect Pollination of Crops*, Academic Press, London & New York.

Free, J.B. & Butler, C.G. (1957) *Bumblebees*, New Naturalist Series, Collins, London.

Frisch, K. von (1967) *The Dance Language and Orientation of Bees* (trans L.E. Chadwick), Belknap Press of Harvard University Press, Cambridge, Massachusetts.

Gilbert, L.E. & Raven, P.H. (Eds) (1975) *Coevolution of Animals and Plants*, University of Texas Press, Austin.

Gould, J.L. & Gould, C.G. (1988) *The Honeybee*, Scientific American Library, New York.

Heinrich, B. (1979) *Bumblebee Economics*, Harvard University Press, Cambridge, Massachusetts & London.

Hermann, H.R. (Ed) (1979–82) *Social Insects* (4 vols), Academic Press, New York & London.

Iwata, K. (1971) *Evolution of Instinct: Comparative Ethology of Hymenoptera*, Amerind Publishing Co. New Delhi, for Smithsonian Institution, Washington, DC and National Science Foundation.

Krombein, K.V. (1967) *Trap-nesting wasps and Bees: Life Histories, Nests and Associates*, Smithsonian Press, Washington, DC.

McGregor, S.E. (1976) *Insect Pollination of Cultivated Crop Plants*, Agriculture Handbook No. 496, Agricultural Research Service, US Dept. of Agriculture, Washington, DC.

Meeuse, B. (1961) *The Story of Pollination*, The Ronald Press Company, New York.

Meeuse, B. & Morris, S. (1984) *The Sex Life of Flowers*, Faber & Faber, London.

Michener, C.D. (1974) *The Social Behaviour of the Bees, a Comparative Study*, Belknap Press of Harvard University Press, Cambridge, Massachusetts.

Morse, R.A. (Ed) (1978) *Honeybee Pests, Predators and Diseases*, Comstock Publishing Associates of Cornell University Press, Ithaca & London.

Oster, G.F. & Wilson, E.O. (1978) *Caste and Ecology in the Social Insects*, Monographs in Population Biology 12, Princeton University Press, New Jersey.

O'Toole, C. (1985) *Discovering Bees and Wasps*, Wayland, Hove.

O'Toole, C. (1990) *The Honeybee over the Meadow*, Methuen, London.

O'Toole, C. & Preston-Mafham, K.G. (1985) *Insects in Camera: A Photographic Essay on Behaviour*, Oxford University Press, Oxford.

Pijl, L. van der & Dodson, C.H. (1966) *Orchid Flowers: Their Pollination and Evolution*, University of Miami Press, Coral Gables.

Pijl, L. van der & Faegri, K. (1980) *The Principles of Pollination Ecology*, Pergamon Press, Oxford.

Proctor, M. & Yeo, P. (1973) *The Pollination of Flowers*, New Naturalist Series, Collins, London.

Ransome, H.R. (1937) *The Sacred Bee, in Ancient Times and Folklore*, George Allen & Unwin, London.

Roubik, D.W. (1989) *Ecology and Natural History of Tropical Bees*, Cambridge University Press, Cambridge.

Seeley, T.D. (1985) *Honeybee Ecology. A Study of Adaptation in Social Life*, Monographs in Behaviour and Ecology, Princeton University Press, Princeton.

Stephen, W.P., Bohart, G.E. & Torchio, P.F. (1969) *The Biology and External Morphology of Bees, with a Synopsis of the Genera of Northwestern America*, Oregon University Press, Corvallis, Oregon.

Thornhill, R. & Alcock, J. (1983) *The Evolution of Insect Mating Systems*, Harvard University Press, Cambridge, Massachusetts.

Wickler, W. (1968) *Mimicry in Animals and Plants* (trans R.D. Martin), Weidenfeld & Nicolson, London.

Wilson, E.O. (1971) *The Insect Societies*, Belknap Press of Harvard University Press, Cambridge, Massachusetts.

Wilson, E.O. (1975) *Sociobiology, the New Synthesis*, Belknap Press of Harvard University Press, Cambridge, Massachusetts.

Winston, M.L. (1987) *The Biology of the Honeybee*, Harvard University Press, Cambridge, Massachusetts & London.

Index

Numbers in *italic* refer to black and white illustrations.
Numbers in **bold** refer to colour plates.